THE NEW HISTORICISM
AND OTHER OLD-FASHIONED TOPICS

THE NEW HISTORICISM

AND OTHER OLD-FASHIONED TOPICS

Brook Thomas

PRINCETON UNIVERSITY PRESS   PRINCETON, NEW JERSEY

Copyright © 1991 by Princeton University Press
Published by Princeton University Press, 41 William Street,
Princeton, New Jersey 08540
In the United Kingdom: Princeton University Press, Oxford
All Rights Reserved

Library of Congress Cataloging-in-Publication Data
Thomas, Brook
The new historicism and other old-fashioned topics / Brook Thomas.
p.   cm.
Includes index.
ISBN 0-691-06893-3. — 0-691-01507-4 (pbk.)
1. American literature—History and criticism—Theory, etc.
2. English literature—History and criticism—Theory, etc.
3. Literature and history.   4. Historicism.   I. Title.
PS25.T49   1991
801'.95—dc20   91-7487

This book has been composed in Linotron Caledonia

Princeton University Press books are printed
on acid-free paper, and meet the guidelines
for permanence and durability of the Committee
on Production Guidelines for Book Longevity
of the Council on Library Resources

Printed in the United States of America

3   5   7   9   10   8   6   4   2

Contents

Preface

THE END of the cold war continues to raise hopes for a new global order, a new sense of history. In the United States, however, even before the anticipated peace dividend began disappearing into the oil fields of the Persian Gulf, cold war rhetoric had been mobilized to deal with two domestic concerns: drugs and education. There is no simple cause and effect relationship between the end of the cold war and the rise of the cultural and drug wars. Nonetheless, the displacement of cold war rhetoric onto the other two is a convenient way to highlight what is at stake in the rise of a new historicism in the academic study of literature. George Bush provided an economic way to link the newly declared domestic wars when he appointed as his "Drug Czar" William Bennett, the former head of the National Endowment for the Humanities and secretary of education. For Bennett and some other cultural conservatives the nation's massive drug problem is related to the failure of our educational system to pass on values embodied in the Western cultural heritage, values that are the foundation of American political and social institutions. For them one of the worst manifestations of the closing of the American mind has been the wasting of many American minds through drugs. This decay in cultural values, we are told, is directly related to permissive policies espoused by liberal educators.

But the escalation of the cultural wars indicates that more is at stake than liberalism. As if liberal ideas were not bad enough, liberals' lack of vigilance in protecting and preserving our cultural heritage has allowed the infiltration of ideology into the sacred realm of culture. Just as the cold war worked to preserve democracy by containing communism and the War on Drugs hopes to shut off the import of drugs across the border, so the cultural wars will be won and the American mind reopened by closing off the subversive influence of disgruntled academics who threaten the purity of the body of great works representing our cultural heritage. The marxist military threat may have waned, but a threat persists in the cultural wars.

For cultural conservatives the new historicism is not the only subversive movement afoot, but it is a part of a general threat. Allan Bloom indicates why. Aware of the paradox of blaming liberal openness for the closing of the American mind, Bloom offers a historical summary: "Civic education turned away from concentrating on the Founding to concentrating on openness based on history and social science. There was even a general tendency to debunk the Founding to prove the beginnings were flawed in order to license a greater openness to the new. What began in Charles Beard's Marxism and Carl Becker's historicism became routine. We are used to hearing the Founders charged with being racists, murderers of Indians, representatives of class interest."[1] For Bloom an older historicism led to a relativistic celebration of the new at the expense of time-honored values. A historicism that self-consciously flaunts its newness would seem to be even more reprehensible, especially one with marxist associations.

It would be as much of a mistake to identify, as some have, the new historicism with marxism as it is to call Beard a marxist.[2] In fact, marxists have accused prominent new historicists with defeatism or complicity with capitalism. Nonetheless, in targeting the twin evils of marxism and historicism Bloom does more than evoke a term whose very mention in this country can close off rational discussion. Like Beard, new historicists have engaged marxist thought. For instance, even new historicists attacked by marxists admit their debt to marxism, albeit a particular brand of it. Catherine Gallagher acknowledges that marxism, especially its "own edgiest, uneasiest voices,"[3] has anticipated many new historicist concerns. Stephen Greenblatt admits a preference for "those Marxist figures who were troubled in relation to Marxism."[4] The very seriousness of this engagement with marxism by a movement gaining increasing popularity in humanistic study is noteworthy, because it indicates that, unlike a previous generation of critics, this generation does not feel comfortable with dismissing marxism merely by ignoring it. Any discussion of the rise of the new historicism needs to address this phenomenon.

The renewed attention to marxism just when it has seemed to reach an impasse with continental intellectuals has been interpreted as proof of how divorced left-wing intellectuals in the United States are from the real world, especially as the Soviet empire faces its biggest crisis. While global commentators announce the end of an era of ideology and a move toward political pragmatism, United States intellectuals seem to have—belatedly—rediscovered it. But the fact that ideological criticism finds new vitality in the United States, the Western democracy where it has had the least impact, is not surprising. The very paucity of a marxist presence in cultural debates since the 1930s gives added force to the questions that its tradition raises. This is even more the case because much of the most sophisticated rethinking of marxism in Western Europe has occurred since the 1930s. To engage the many continental thinkers so fashionable in today's theoretical debates requires an understanding of the neo-marxist tradition because, even though many have distanced themselves from marxism, their thought has been shaped within its horizon.

Even so, within the United States, an engagement with the marxist tradition in humanistic study is not so much usable in developing a positive political program as in helping to raise neglected questions about structures of domination and their links to modes of cultural production. The new historicism arose in the context of this situation. New historicists may not agree with marxist answers to these questions, but they agree that such questions should be raised. These questions are especially pertinent because it is in the United States that the failings of capitalism to confront major social problems like poverty and drugs are most apparent. If some cultural conservatives read the need for a war on drugs as a symptom of decaying American values, those on the cultural left can interpret it as a symptom of the failure of capitalist values to confront the causes of pressing social problems. It may be too symmetrical to conclude that capitalism has difficulty solving social problems whereas socialism has difficulty solving problems of capital. Nonetheless, if Western capitalistic democracies seem to make the promise of a better life accessible to all, they also seem to rule out deliverance of that promise to many members of particular groups within various societies. To be sure, the mixed social welfare economies of most Western European countries at least have a better record on poverty than the purer capitalist form in the United States. But a global perspective suggests that even their success is partially at the expense of massive poverty in the Third World. It is no accident that the battle over cultural politics in the United States today often pits those celebrating Western civilization as the birthplace of the democratic tradition against those insisting on its repressive and exclusionary practices. Just because such oppositions are too simple does not mean that the issues such debates raise are not important.

I need to stress their importance from the start because, although my book does not directly participate in the cultural wars, it presupposes them. Its focus is the new historicism itself and, as its title indicates, I am skeptical about the trendiness accompanying the recent turn to political and historical criticism. All too often liberal scholars set themselves up for attacks cultural conservatives are all too willing to deliver. The close scrutiny to which I submit problems raised by the new historicism might make me seem a hostile critic. But my skeptical and critical attitude should not be mistaken. If what is at stake in today's cultural debates is whether or not it is appropriate to raise questions of power, domination, exclusion, *and* emancipation in conjunction with the study of literature my position is clear. Raising such questions is to enhance literature's value as a form of discourse able to speak to central and important questions about the destiny of humanity. The purpose of my criticism is not to deny the importance of such questions, but to generate more satisfactory answers to them.

Thus my criticism of the new historicism is quite different from people like Frederick Crews, Ihab Hassan, and Richard Poirier, who share with me the concern that simplistic ideological criticism avoids wrestling with the complex problems raised by complicated works of literature. Rather than turn to literature as a way to enhance debates about complicated and important questions, however, these three have reacted to the polemical thrust of much recent political criticism with fierce, sometimes simplistic, polemics of their own.[5] That two of these have used their institutional power to conduct their polemics in widely circulated reviews has, no doubt, created a fairly reductive view of the new historicism in the minds of many. These three, of course, are not Bennett-like conservatives, and their positions demonstrate the need to complicate a residual cold war rhetoric that would see current cultural debates in terms of simple opposi- tions. The intensity of their resistance and the appeals they make to a certain version of the American literary tradition reveal the investment many *liberal* intellectuals have in a sense of American exceptionalism. It is, to be sure, an exceptionalism quite different from Bloom's political one, but it is a version of exceptionalism nonetheless. Before I turn to a critical stance toward the new historicism, I want to use the persistence of these various versions of exceptionalism to explain why I agree when new historicists stress the importance of a historical approach in confronting the types of questions they find so pressing.

Underlying the exceptionalist position is an assumption about the United States as the *end* of history, with "end" implying both goal and completion. Recently, the most highly publicized speculation of this sort has come from Francis Fukuyama. Using liberal in the classical sense, Fukuyama announces the "victory of liberalism," a victory "as yet in- complete in the real or material world" but one virtually assured in the "realm of ideas or consciousness." This victory means that we may be watching "the end of history as such; that is, the endpoint of mankind's ideological evolution and the universalization of Western liberal democ- racy as the final form of human government."[6] Fukuyama's argument adds a new twist to celebrations of American exceptionalism. For him, as for David W. Noble, who wrote a book announcing *The End of American History*, the United States's difference with the rest of the world is over. But whereas for Noble exceptionalism has ended because its ideological assumptions are no longer tenable, for Fukuyama American values have triumphed around the globe. With that triumph we need to turn to discus- sions about how we will conduct their reign. As Bloom puts it, "Fuku- yama's bold and brilliant article, which he surely does not present as the last word, is the first word in a discussion imperative for us, we faithful defenders of the Western Alliance. Now that it appears that we have won, what are we and what do we do?"[7]

Crews, Hassan, and Poirier would challenge this sort of political chau- vinism as much as they challenge political interventions by those on the left. But it is precisely in their claim to stand above such petty political squabbles that they betray *their* exceptionalist thought. For them the glory of the American literary tradition is its ability to transcend the political. This is most clearly seen in the recent return to Emerson in response to the import of continental "theory." Faced with this massive trade debt in terms of ideas, Poirier especially has tried to balance accounts by re-instituting Emerson as the most important of representative men. Indeed, as far as Poirier is concerned one of the major flaws of Bloom's argument is his failure to list Emerson as an American classic.[8] At a time when an engagement with continental thinkers has helped a generation of critics raise questions not easily raised within an American context (such as questions concerning the ideological implications of the term America itself), Poirier creates an American thinker who has always already contained it all. "It can aptly be said that a good scholar will find Emerson full of de Man, Derrida, and Barthes, just as, with many differences, he is full of Frost and Burke."[9] Poirier does not need to announce the end of history, because in the realm that concerns him—reading—history already stopped with Emerson. But despite obvious differences from Fukuyama's political argument, Poirier's Emersonian one shares an important similarity. American exceptionalism is no longer defined by its difference from the rest of the world. Instead, American ideas and institutions turn out to be everywhere one looks.

In the context of such thought a new historicism's stress on the historical and cultural specificity of ideas serves an important function. On the one hand, as the vehemence of Crews's, Hassan's, and Poirier's responses indicate, it challenges the latest versions of American cultural exceptionalism. On the other, it disrupts teleological accounts of the past as a triumphant march culminating in the present. Indeed, the uncertainty with which we face the outcome of political events in 1989 would seem to support arguments about history's contingency, not its end. Those events might produce simple imitations of Western liberal democracies. They also might produce positive alternatives, revivals of repressive nationalisms, or unforeseen political disasters.

But a new historicism can challenge more than the latest versions of American exceptionalism. Its distrust of historical ends also explains its difference from marxism, for marxism too has a tendency toward teleological thinking. Furthermore, even marxists who challenge its teleological tendency must wrestle with the problem of a radical historicism. As Steven B. Smith notes, "Taken to its extreme, the [historicist] approach would make it impossible for us to use words like *Marxism* at all, since they require a certain abstraction from the flux and multiplicity of particular ideas and events." Someone like Althusser, Smith argues, asserts "not only that it makes sense to distinguish certain concepts and ideas from the totality of Marx's writings as specifically 'Marxist,' but that to do so it is necessary to employ a theory of reading that allows us to reconstruct the 'object' of Marx's scientific discourse."[10] That way of reading cannot ultimately be historical, because such a reading would stress the historical contingency of those concepts and ideas, not their structural unity.

This historicist insistence on the contingency of ideas forces me to complicate my previous observation about the new historicism's relationship to ideological analysis. Just as it is too simple to identify those defending selected aspects of the Western tradition with cultural conservatism, so it is too simple to say that new historicists necessarily return us to ideological analysis just at the moment that global politics take a pragmatic swing. To be sure, much new historicist analysis involves ideological unmasking that exposes the historical constructedness of ideas and beliefs. But staying consistent with a rigorous historicism causes problems for those who would offer an alternative set of ideas and beliefs. These problems suggest that of the two threats evoked by Bloom—marxism and historicism—historicism may be potentially more subversive for those attempting to establish foundational values. Bloom, of course, abhors the values professed by marxism, but it at least does not make it so difficult to abstract a *positive* ideology from the flux of history. In contrast, a rigorous historicism has to acknowledge the contingency of its own ideas and beliefs. As a result, the seeming subversive potential of historicism is often subverted by its own capacity for subversion. And it is on this point that I can start to focus on problems raised by the new historicism, for it leaves those insisting on the return to history as a mode of ideological analysis in a difficult position.

Historicists who do attempt to replace unmasked ideologies with ideological positions of their own find themselves contradicting their own historicist premises, sometimes going as far as to reemploy teleological narratives, even if told from different points of view. Those remaining consistent with a rigorous historicism find their ideological analysis accompanied by a pragmatic distrust of the attempts to abstract a coherent ideology—even a theory—from the flux of historical events, a distrust that returns some to the Emersonian tradition celebrated by Poirier. If the former face the embarrassment of inconsistency, the latter face the possibility that their analysis lacks definable political consequences. For some, this sense of inconsequentiality becomes a new ideology, as they argue that in a historically contingent world the lack of political consequences for historical analysis is quite simply the way things are. Others, sounding curiously like Fukuyama, celebrate the advent of a post-political era.

These various responses are related to a noticeable feature of current leftist academic arguments in the United States: a failure to connect with existing political programs. If leftist academics share responsibility for that failure, so do political regulars, who have generally failed to offer anything more than New Deal or populist solutions to problems. The situation in Western Europe is not all that much better, but, at worst, there is a Social Democratic alternative, as well as the remains of a Communist party and the problematic beginnings of a Green party.[11] In the United States, in contrast, the only alternative to Reaganite conservatism in the last presidential election was a Democrat, who explicitly stated that the issue in the campaign was not ideology but competence and who then proceeded to show how incompetent he was. The failure of progressives to come up with a viable political alternative to a New Deal vision helps to account for some bizarre circumstances that can produce endless amusement for cultural conservatives.

For instance, at the height of the cold war many leftist literary critics worked as hard as they could to avoid charges that they were subversives. Today some feel insulted when told that they are not. This insult does not, however, come from conservatives, who at least pay the cultural left the compliment of taking it seriously enough to decry its subversion of values. Instead, more often than not, it comes from those within the cultural left itself, which has found that one way to justify its frustration is to come up with more and more sophisticated explanations as to why it continues to fail. To take one example, on the dust jacket of Walter Benn Michaels's *The Gold Standard and the Logic of Naturalism*, Philip Fisher writes of an "exhausted oppositional criticism."[12]

One symptom of this exhaustion is the sense of betrayal that critics feel upon discovering that their progressive past is no longer usable. In the 1930s and 1940s Van Wyck Brooks and F. O. Matthiessen turned to the literary tradition of the United States for an alternative in a time of international crisis. In the 1980s that very tradition has been linked with a cultural logic that is at least partially responsible for a new form of global domination. For some the shock has been too much. Once students of the myth and symbol school, today they busy themselves with demystification. They, after all, know what needs to be demystified.

Justifiably Poirier has responded with scorn to those disillusioned by literature's fall into a corrupt world. Nonetheless, his effort to distance himself from their fall from innocence reveals an equally disturbing response to a progressive tradition that has lost its usefulness. Once associated with the old *Partisan Review*, which provided a public forum for progressive cultural politics, today Poirier celebrates the private act of reading as a "lonely discipline that makes no great claims for itself."[13] Poirier's remark is aimed not only against those disillusioned with their previous faith in the progressive function of literature but also against those who would turn an apolitical mode of rigorous reading into an act of political subversion. Reading as Poirier was taught it and as he would teach it "can be subversive only to the extent that it encourages us to get under and turn over not systems and institutions, but only words." Poirier could never be "*dis*illusioned about literature" because he claims never to have had any illusions about it.[14]

It is hard to call the passion with which Poirier defends an activity that makes no great claims for itself a sign of exhaustion, and we might wonder why he feels such an activity should be required training for all students. Nonetheless, his argument is a sign of a particular tradition of criticism turned back upon itself, just as John Barth once described a type of literature turned back upon itself as a "literature of exhaustion."[15] The power of the progressive literary tradition was deeply implicated in the old historicist faith that literature expressed the spirit of a nation, in this case the democratic values of the United States. The assertion that literature represents nothing more than itself, that its words represent nothing more than words, is one response to the failure of that faith. Its demise is connected with a crisis in representation faced by United States society at large.

In December 1933 when Judge Woolsey cleared James Joyce's *Ulysses* of obscenity charges, Morris Ernst, Random House's attorney, explicitly linked the decision with progressive politics. "The new deal in the law of letters is here."[16] Accompanying his belief that "the victory of *Ulysses* is a fitting climax to the salutary forward march of our courts"[17] was his belief that even if "people as a mass are inarticulate," public opinion is "definitely ascertainable." Just as the "body politic registers its will through representatives chosen at the polls," so professionally trained experts, including literary critics, can "speak for the body social."[18]

The progressive vision assumed not only that the body politic spoke through representative elected officials but also that the body social generated representative works and critics who could articulate its spirit. Today the class, race, and gender biases of both forms of representation are under intense scrutiny. Elected officials are accused of representing special interests and their own desires for reelection, while literary works and critics no longer represent universal or even national values, but instead much more local and historically contingent ones. Indeed, even before we can ask whether the American mind is open or closed, we need to ask whether we can speak of an American mind at all.

One of the conditions giving rise to the new historicism, and also a major challenge facing it, is this crisis in representation. Given this crisis, it is appropriate that the journal considered most representative of new historicist work is called *Representations*. The new historicism in literary studies is concerned with representation in many ways. For one, it is concerned with the question raised by the canon wars as to whether a select group of texts can speak for a culture as a whole. For some that question goes hand in hand with a demand for new works to represent cultural diversity. An even more basic question concerns the representative status of literature itself. To use literature to represent a culture or even segments of a culture may be to privilege it over other forms of discourse. Nonetheless, at the very moment that critics question literature's representative status they have become increasingly fascinated with it as a representational activity, one that calls attention to the representational modes of other forms of discourse.

Finally, the question of representation turns back on the new historicism itself. How representative is the evidence employed in its analysis? And if it is representative, what does it represent? One of the claims of the new historicism is that literary history cannot be seen in isolation from other historical forces. But moving from the concrete analysis of particular texts, events, and concepts to claims about shifts in, for example, global power or the construction of subjectivity is extremely tricky. There is an ever-present risk of letting evidence speak for more than it should. For me it is better to take that risk than to adopt the far safer strategy of letting the evidence we employ, the texts we analyze, or the language we read represent nothing more than themselves. Nonetheless, the new historicism's ambition to have its analysis speak for culture(s) as a whole carries with it many problems, some of which I will be exploring in this book.[19]

Those problems do not, however, negate the political importance of considering modes of representation. Events in the German Democratic Republic in the fall of 1989 dramatize this importance. In a marvelous, almost utopian, moment protestors in Leipzig seemed to merge sign and signifier as they wore inscriptions on their bodies declaring, "Wir sind das Volk." For years having heard the party claim to speak for the body politic, people put their bodies on the line, making it clear who should represent them. Within a week, however, the signs transformed into "we are *one* people," a slogan rightfully evoking painful memories throughout the world, including Germany itself.[20] This transformation indicates potential dangers in any mode of representation that assumes the independent, preexistence of that to be represented. Even in its seemingly utopian moment of "we are the people," the phrase worked by exclusion, as it defined "the people" *against* another entity. "*We* are the people; the party isn't." In its nationalistic version, its exclusionary function is even more obvious, as a preexistent German people is defined against all others.

Granted, the phrases were not purely imitative. In the best tradition of Aristotelian mimesis, they helped to produce the very thing they claimed to represent. Nonetheless, it is instructive to compare this mimetic mode of representation with the much more explicitly performative mode at work in the United States Constitution. Rather than identifying an already existing people, the preamble works rhetorically to bring into existence a people by having "we, the people" perform its own constitution. Working by inclusion, not exclusion, the Constitution creates the possibility for anyone wanting to speak it to become part of the people it represents. More than a set of timeless values held by the founding fathers, this performative mode of representation helps to account for the power of the United States Constitution to assimilate so many diverse people into a national identity. To recognize its power is not necessarily to celebrate it uncritically or to reinstitute a new form of exceptionalism. Indeed, in what follows I explore the dangers of pluralistic modes of assimilation. Nonetheless, to compare these two ways of representing "the people" points to the importance of considering the politics of modes of representation.

Although I make no claim to speak for the body politic, I do face my own problem of representation in this book. How should I represent the new historicism? What figures will I choose to speak for it? Are there various assumptions and ideas that we can abstract from a body of work to define it as a distinct mode of thought? Or does the historicist enterprise rule out such attempts at definition? But if it does, is not that enterprise itself identifiable? These questions help to explain why so far I have avoided posing the most obvious question for a preface to a book on the new historicism. The answer to the question—What is the new historicism?—is not an easy one. The difficulty in answering it helps to account for a preface that has tried to explain the context in which people ask it in the first place. In my first chapter I will start to answer this question that so far I have avoided. But be warned. As much as describing an already existing field, I will make an effort to constitute one. Indeed, rather than start with a direct answer, I will begin with that favorite new historicist ploy—the anecdote, one that should help place me in relation to my subject matter.

Acknowledgments

THE ALEXANDER von Humboldt-Stiftung of the Federal Republic of Germany supported this project when similar institutions in the United States did not. The University of California, Irvine, made it possible for me to accept that support. Once again the University of Constance proved a stimulating environment for writing. Audiences at Stanford University, University of Massachusetts, Amherst, Stuttgart University, Frankfurt University, Munich University, and the John F. Kennedy Center for North American Studies in Berlin gave me a chance to test out ideas. I am indebted to conversations and exchanges with many individuals. Jerry Graff deserves special mention for suggesting (wisely or unwisely) that I expand arguments made in essays and conversations into a book. Routledge, *Annals of Scholarship*, and *boundary 2* gave permission to reprint previously published material. Without the help of Madeline Jaroch, an author illiterate in the language of computers might never have prepared a final manuscript. Finally, I want to thank my colleagues and students in Humanities Core Course, "Confronting Cultural Difference," a course in which we tried to put into practice some of the ideas discussed in this book.

THE NEW HISTORICISM
AND OTHER OLD-FASHIONED TOPICS

CHAPTER 1

Fair Warning

AT THE 1982 Modern Language Association convention in Los Angeles I was on a panel hosted by the Nathaniel Hawthorne Society. After the talk a graduate student approached me with, "So you must be one of the new historicists?" I felt like Huckleberry Finn when late in the book he arrives at Phelps's farm and is identified by Aunt Sally. I was so glad to find out who I was. But, as I remembered, Aunt Sally calls Huck "Tom Sawyer," and like Huck I was not sure if I was what I was taken to be. My suspicions were especially aroused because the respondent to the panel was Roy Harvey Pearce, who in 1969 published a collection of essays entitled *Historicism Once More*. Pearce himself was the subject of a chapter in Wesley Morris's *Toward a New Historicism* published in 1972. Since Morris ends by using Murray Krieger's work as an example of his version of a new historicism and because the interdisciplinary work on law and literature that I was doing did not seem to resemble Krieger's work, I remained puzzled. Thus, when I got home I was glad to find a special issue of *Genre* waiting for me in which Stephen Greenblatt's introduction announced the rise of a new historicism, or what he also called a poetics of culture. Greenblatt's description of such work seemed closer to what I thought I was doing, so I was reassured. After all, it's always prudent to be on the cutting edge of the profession.[1]

Nonetheless, a nagging doubt remained. Morris had taken some time to outline the confused use of "historicism" in English, distinguishing four different uses, ranging from Karl Popper's in *The Poverty of Historicism* to J. Hillis Miller's in his introduction to *The Disappearance of God*. In contrast, Greenblatt made no concerted effort to define the term's historical uses. This caused me problems. Even though I was struck by Greenblatt's description of what the new historicism tried to do, I could not help but remember my own exposure to historicism in my freshmen Western Civilization course, which for all of its Eurocentric bias had taught me to be very suspicious of any movement calling itself a "historicism." This suspicion resulted from the uses put to historicism by Europeans, especially Germans, in the nineteenth and early twentieth centuries. If, as I had learned, historicism had experienced a crisis, at least partially because of its political conservatism, why would a group of scholars in the United States intent on establishing a critical stance toward society want a *new* historicism?

Some of my difficulty resulted from the confused history of the term "historicism" in English that Morris addresses. To simplify, "historicism" can refer generally to any sort of historical method. But it can also refer to a specific brand of historiography that flourished in the nineteenth century, especially in Germany, where it was known as *Historismus*. Trying to guarantee precision, some translators evoke "historism" to refer to *Historismus*. Nonetheless, "historism" never took. Even if it had, precision would not be assured, since exactly what *Historismus* meant in Germany is not completely clear. For instance, Herbert Schaedelbach distinguishes between three sorts of *Historismus*.[2]

Such complications have caused Herbert Lindenberger to avoid the term "historicism" altogether.[3] But not all are as restrained as Lindenberger, and it remains a historical fact that the label "new historicism" has caught on. Its popularity is somewhat embarrassing for Greenblatt, who admits that he first used it very casually and who prefers the descriptive label "cultural poetics."[4] The result is that the new historicism has general and specific meanings. The general meaning can best be described by evoking Fredric Jameson's claim that historicism refers to "our relationship to the past, and of our possibility of understanding the latter's monuments, artifacts, and traces."[5] A new historicism in literary studies, therefore, promises a new relationship to the literary past. Specifically, the label refers to a particular brand of cultural poetics associated with work of the sort appearing in *Representations*, which Greenblatt helped to found. Thus the essays in a recent collection entitled *The New Historicism* could be divided in different ways depending upon one's perspective. For some, all of the essays included would be examples of a "new historicism" that tries to establish new connections between literature and history. For others, only the first essays by Greenblatt, Louis A. Montrose, Catherine Gallagher, and perhaps Joel Fineman would be examples of the "new historicism" as represented by some of its well-known practitioners.[6] Even more confusion results because Greenblatt himself is quite generous about what he includes under the label, more generous than those who would want to identify the new historicism with a particular method. In his latest book he explicitly states that "there can be no single method, no overall picture, no exhaustive and definitive cultural poetics."[7] There can be, in short, no representative work of the movement.

Greenblatt's disclaimer is a cautionary response to those who would establish a set of methodological rules to govern the practice of historical criticism and those who consider the new historicism a particular practice that can be mechanically imitated. At the same time, we should not read Greenblatt's statement too inclusively. He still implies that the goal of historical criticism is to produce a cultural poetics. It is on this point that my own complicated relationship to the new historicism becomes somewhat clearer. In the general sense, I am a new historicist. I do, none-theless, have specific disagreements with various practices of cultural poetics.

In accepting a label that I admit causes confusion, I could be accused of a lack of precision. Indeed, my original strategy was to introduce a new term that would avoid the confusion caused by the new historicism. But that strategy would have had the opposite effect because it would ignore an insight that practitioners of cultural poetics (among others) have stressed: the power of rhetoric partially to shape history. Discontent with the label's confusion or not, I am confronted with its power. There are both historical and linguistic reasons for that power. The very sound of the label the "new historicism" serves rhetorically to displace the most influential brand of criticism that preceded it: the New Criticism. At the same time, the "new" in the label helps to distinguish it from an older historicism. Faced with the rhetorical power produced by the economy of the label, I decided that a better strategy than trying to displace it would be to appropriate it by taking more seriously than most the adjective "new."

The starting point of my intervention into debates about the new historicism is, then, the question of newness. One consequence of that starting point is that my study will be as prescriptive as it is descriptive. Whereas the purpose of many recent books on theory has been to explain and describe a particular school of thought—a sort of professional version of Cliff Notes—my assumption is that, if the new historicism is to live up to the adjective in its label, it must always be made new. Thus, rather than assume that the new historicism consists of a given, definable body of work that we can dissect, I hope to define directions in which a new historicism will project itself.

To call attention to the prescriptive element of my study is not to deny the need to describe existing historical situations. My appropriation of the "new historicism" signals a desire to participate in its redefinition, but that redefinition would be ineffective if it did not pay attention to the ways in which the label is currently used. In the descriptive component of what follows I will use "new historicism" to refer generally to work claiming to "return to history." Within that general field I will identify two strains: a reconstructive strain—the effort to reconstruct more inclusive literary histories—and what we could call the new historicism proper—work resembling Greenblatt's version of a cultural poetics. The former is more explicitly concerned with how the writing of new literary histories can be put to present uses, how writing a new history can help bring about a new future. Its ways of doing so, however, rarely offer new modes of historical analysis. The latter comes much closer to presenting a new mode of analysis but seems less concerned with actively intervening into the making of a new history. My concern will be to bring the two types of newness together. In doing so I will reserve my most detailed analysis for two whose work has become representative of the latter strain—Walter Benn Michaels and Greenblatt. Their representative status is, to my mind, well-earned. Their work is important. But it is also symptomatic of problems raised by the project of a cultural poetics.

If choosing to devote detailed attention to two figures raises questions of representativeness, it should, at least partially, correct and complicate some of the generalizations that result from my too schematic—and yet enabling—division of the new historicism into two strains. The work of Greenblatt, with its own built-in self-correction and reexamination, is especially useful in pointing to moments when the boundaries that I draw between reconstructive histories and a cultural poetics need to be readjusted and renegotiated.[8]

Some new historicists would argue that, if, as I try to make it, the new historicism is a project to be pursued rather than merely an existing body of work to be identified, I should simply write a book exemplifying my practice. One reason for devoting an entire book to examining the practices of others, however, is that debates over what a label should mean (or represent) play a role in defining what directions a practice will take. To be sure, those directions will be determined by many more factors than intellectual debates. Nonetheless, when a movement promises something new, it is important to have some sense of what that newness is. Part of my contribution to the debate over the new historicism is to emphasize the importance of a historical understanding of past historicisms, an understanding surprisingly lacking in many of its advocates. I can give a sense of what I mean and also define a number of the challenges that I see facing a new historicism by responding to someone else's description of the new historicism proper.

Explaining the new historicism to an audience interested in the history of the book, Michael Warner summarizes the recent interest in the politics of interpretation. He goes on:

> The same theoretical arguments that have been associated with poststructuralism and deconstruction have also led to what is known as the New Historicism, and thus to a strong interest in the history of the book. New Historicism is a label that historians don't like very much because they understand something different by historicism. But nobody's asking historians; the people the New Historicists are reacting against are the New Critics, and historicism seems an important term for that purpose because it emphasizes that meaning is established in concrete historical situations, and ought not to be abstracted as though it didn't matter who was reading or when or where or why.
>
> So if the "Historicism" in the New Historicism is to distinguish it from the New Critics and their idea that a text means what it means regardless of what

your cultural situation is, the "New" in New Historicism is to distinguish it from the somewhat dreary and encyclopedic historical work that the philologists used to do. And this latter distinction is no less important than the first. Because while critics have realized on one hand that language and the symbolic are never essential and timeless but always contingent on cultural politics, on the other hand they have realized that cultural politics is always symbolic. New Historicism has a motto: "The text is historical; and history is textual." The first part means that meaning does not transcend context but is produced within it; the second part means that human actions and institutions and relations, while certainly hard facts, are not hard facts as distinguished from language. They are themselves symbolic representations, though this is not to say, as many old historicists might conclude, that they are not real.[9]

Warner is one of our best young critics and when I first read this description, I was struck with how useful it might be as a summary of new historicist assumptions. He touches on its debt to poststructuralism, its attempt to distinguish itself from the New Criticism and an older historicism, and finally its acceptance of Louis Montrose's chiasmatic formulation that the goal of the new historicism is to examine both the "historicity of texts and the textuality of history."[10]

Reading this passage just after struggling to describe the new historicism, I found myself almost wishing that I had written it. Almost. Almost, because the very polish of its presentation is achieved at the cost of simplifying the very history that we are supposed to be returning to. Part of the simplification comes from a rhetoric too prone to slide into pronouncements about what "always" and "never" are and have been the case. But there is more to the simplification than assumptions about the eternal existence of categories like cultural politics.

Were the New Critics quite as naive as Warner makes them out to be? Did they really believe that a "text means what it means regardless of your cultural situation?" If I remember correctly, it was precisely the New Critical belief that a text's meaning changes over time that caused E. D. Hirsch sleepless nights eventually resulting in his distinction between a text's meaning and its significance and his attempt to anchor meaning by appealing to a historically determined authorial intention. And what about the famous debate between historians and T. S. Eliot over the meaning of "vegetable love" in Marvel's "To His Coy Mistress?" Furthermore, did not many New Critics agree with Eliot's argument in "Tradition and the Individual Talent" that the production of a new classic changed the meaning of all works that came before it? New Critics might have had a different sense of what a "cultural situation" is, and they might have felt that great works of art transcended what Warner and I would consider a cultural situation. But their aesthetic was more complicated than Warner allows.

So was that of old-fashioned historicists. Should we lump the work of Erich Auerbach and Leo Spitzer under Warner's label of "the somewhat dreary and encyclopedic historical work that the philologists used to do?" If I could only be so dreary. Rather than hastily consign such work to the dustbin of history, we might use it to pose challenges to our present projects. Indeed, I can cite Spitzer and Auerbach to pose two specific challenges.

In a footnote to his 1948 essay, "Linguistics and Literary History," Spitzer speaks to the desire to expand the range of literary studies.

Under the noble pretext of introducing "history of ideas" into literary criticism, there have appeared in recent times, with the approval of the departments of literary history, academic theses with such titles as "Money in Seventeenth-Century French (English, Spanish etc.) Comedy," "Political Tendencies in Nineteenth-Century French (English, Spanish etc.) Literature." Thus we have come to disregard the philological character of the discipline of literary history, which is concerned with ideas couched in linguistic form, not with ideas in themselves (this is the field of history of philosophy) or with ideas as informing action (this is the field of history and the social sciences). Only in the linguistico-literary field are we philologians competent qua scholars. The type of dissertations cited above reveals an unwarranted extension of the (in itself commendable) tendency toward breaking down departmental barriers, to such a degree that literary history becomes the gay sporting ground of incompetence. Students of the department of literature come to treat the complex subjects of a philosophical, political, or economic nature with the same self-assurance that once characterized those Positivists who wrote on "The Horse in Medieval Literature."[11]

Fledgling new historicists should read this note with the care that Michel Foucault clearly did when he translated the essay into French. It does more than remind us that many new historicist-sounding titles are not all that new, that the New Criticism did not have quite the hegemony in 1948 that is often attributed to it. It also forces those of us encouraging the "(in itself commendable)" move toward interdisciplinarity in literary studies to face the difficulties involved in that project by reminding us just how ambitious a cultural poetics is. Within the field of literary studies there is increasing agreement that it is impossible to "cover" all of the important works. Nevertheless, at the same time, we are being asked to expand our range of expertise to produce cultural, rather than purely literary, studies. As one encouraging such a move, I ultimately disagree with Spitzer's desire to contain us within existing disciplinary boundaries. Nonetheless, the danger that cultural studies will become the "gay sporting ground of incompetence" is great. Having struggled in my own work to gain a minimum competency in two disciplines—or more accurately, in two subfields of two disciplines (antebellum law and literature in the United States)—I marvel at the ease with which some of my colleagues can range across the entire spectrum of social practices in a particular era.

But there is more at stake than a question of competency. On the one hand, new historicists, indebted to both Clifford Geertz and the same Foucault who translated Spitzer's essay, have stressed the importance of "local knowledge," knowledge that is culturally and historically specific.[12] On the other, the goal of producing a cultural poetics encourages use of bits and pieces of local knowledge to represent a culture at large. In doing so, the new historicism resembles work like Spitzer's more than it would like to acknowledge. For an example I can cite another Spitzer essay, one that with some updated terminology might well belong in the pages of *Representations*. I refer to his "American Advertising Explained as Popular Art," in which he produces a dazzling reading of a Sunkist orange juice ad, one that gave him, an immigrant, the "grand avenue (a 'philological avenue') leading toward the understanding of the unwritten text of the American way of life."[13]

If Spitzer's essay reminds us that thinking of a culture textually is not a poststructuralist invention, in its brilliance it also indicates why we need a *new* historicism that draws on the interdisciplinarity that he so suspected. Spitzer's analysis was enabled by his faith in an organic model in which one could read the whole in the part. The rhetorical figure dominating organic studies of culture is synecdoche. Through synecdoche Spitzer could move from one advertisement to statements about the American way of life. Combined with his faith in an organic model was a faith in literature as "the best document of the soul of a nation."[14] Thus, despite an early book on slang and essays like the one on advertising, Spitzer could produce cultural analysis through a concentrated focus on literature. A major challenge to the new historicism is how to respond to the breakdown of the organic model and especially literature's relation to it. This challenge is especially important because of the political implications of synecdoche as a mode of representation. To allow a part (such as one party or one ethnic group or one discipline) to speak for the whole seems extremely problematic.

One response has been to replace synecdoche with chiasmus as the favorite rhetorical figure for cultural analysis. To rely on chiasmus to extend literary analysis to cultural analysis is to imply a different relation of literature to a culture. It no longer speaks for—or represents—culture as a whole. Instead, chiasmus allows the critic to place literature in relation to another specific cultural practice. The result has been a proliferation of titles such as "The Literature of Psychology and the Psychology of Literature" or "The Law of Literature and the Literature of the Law." The possibilities seem endless, as literature seems capable of coupling with any other social practice. The use of chiasmus has become so widespread that when I tried to disrupt it by titling an MLA talk "History as Literature, not History is Literature," the title appeared in the program as "History as Literature, Literature as History."[15] My stress on the lack of identity between the two disciplines in my title is, however, one reason why many are attracted to chiasmus. Unlike synecdoche, chiasmus is supposed to stress the production of difference. For instance, even in the title thrust upon me, the second use of literature becomes different from the first. Rather than an organic model in which literature relates to a cultural whole, we have a model in which literature is placed in relation to other concrete disciplines, thus creating networks of relations that resist totalization. Even so, problems continue to surface.

For one, the organic model is not all that easy to dislodge. In his introduction to the essays collected in *The New Historicism* H. Aram Veeser writes, "Taking their cue from Geertz's method of 'thick description' they seize upon an event or anecdote—colonist John Rolfe's conversation with Pochahontas's father, a note found among Nietzsche's papers to the effect that 'I have lost my umbrella'—and re-read it in such a way as to reveal through the analysis of tiny particulars the behavioral codes, logics, and motive forces controlling a whole society."[16] Paraphrased on the back cover advertising the volume, this sentence implies the ability to read the whole in the part. Much of what follows is my attempt to keep the new historicism from lapsing back into this organic mode of reading. Merely to rely on chiasmus is not enough.

For instance, there is a tendency to transform the chiasmatic relationship from one of difference into one of identity. This tendency is neatly illustrated by Warner's transformation of Montrose's formulation, "the historicity of texts and the textuality of history," into the assertion that "the text is historical; and history is textual." This replacement of difference by identity leads to another tendency—that of disciplinary imperialism, masquerading as interdisciplinary work. The chiasmatic coupling of two disciplines has the appearance of interdisciplinarity. But, if, as in the case of Warner, the other discipline can be reduced to textuality, the most perceptive cultural critics turn out to be—lo and behold—readers of texts. Since everything is a text and since literary critics are trained to read texts, some feel quite comfortable moving to texts produced in disciplines outside their field and telling the naive (but professionally trained) practitioners of those fields how those texts should be read. Such disciplinary arrogance is neatly expressed by Warner's assertion that "nobody's asking the historians," a bizarre comment for someone claiming to help reconnect the disciplines of literature and history.

To be sure, many new historicists have asked historians, and anthropologists, philosophers, and psychologists, as well. But when we do, we need to avoid the bias of Melville's Captain Vere who found in his reading "confirmation of his own more reserved thoughts."[17] Too often those whom literary critics consult outside their discipline are people like Hayden White, Clifford Geertz, Jacques Derrida, or Jacques Lacan who can be read so as to confirm their desire to see the world in textual terms.

In emphasizing the need to ask the historians and others, I want to distance myself from those critics of the new historicism who argue that we are not being historical enough unless our work conforms to the rules laid down by the discipline of history as to what constitutes real history.[18] After all, an important part of a project entitled a new historicism is to place under scrutiny what is accepted as proper historical analysis. My cautions against disciplinary arrogance are not meant to deny the extremely important work done by those who have tried to shake up the discipline of history by emphasizing its textual component.[19] The institutional reasons for the rise of a new historicism are not limited to the narrowness of disciplinary practices within literature departments.

In the 1960s and 1970s history departments experienced the rise of a new social history. In an important respect the new historicism in literary studies is indebted to the social historians because their fascinating specialized studies challenged both the consensus histories produced by a previous generation and the broadsweeping intellectual histories that presented a portrait of an age, the life of a mind, or an epic account of *The Rise of American Civilization*. But the social historians' distrust of intellectual history, their reliance on quantification, and their narrow specialization has produced a counterresponse in recent years with some historians calling for a renewed attention to the role of ideas, narrative, and synthesis in the production of history.[20] Thus the rise of a new historicism within literature departments has been accompanied by the rise of a new cultural history within history departments, producing the common ground of cultural studies for both historians and literary critics discontent with particular constraints within their respective disciplines.[21] For example, Jean-Christophe Agnew faults recent historical accounts of consumer culture for their refusal to go beyond quantifiable evidence. That methodological preference, Agnew argues, dictates a certain narrative about the development of consumer culture. In contrast, he risks broaching "unwanted and unwieldy issues of subjectivity" through a "detailed account of those values, conventions, and expectations within which and against which industrial society was formed." The attention to such details threatens the "classic linear movement of historical narrative. Indeed, to demand a 'thick' rather than 'thin' description of the symbolic world of goods is to open up vistas of interpretation that are almost vertiginous in their potential complexity."[22] As Veeser's quotation indicates, the notion of thick description comes from the anthropologist Clifford Geertz (who borrowed it from the philosopher Gilbert Ryle).[23] For his thick description, however, Agnew turns not to anthropology, but to the works of Henry James.

Unfashionable with many social historians, literature has become fashionable once again with cultural historians. To be sure, Agnew teaches in an American Studies program, which is by nature interdisciplinary. Even so, his institutional affiliation is with history, and his work indicates trends within the cultural history movement. As similar as cultural history is to the new historicism, I will not subject it to the close scrutiny to which I subject the new historicism. I focus instead on literary critics who are moving toward history. This focus is more a reflection of my training as a literary critic than an implication that the work of the cultural historians is less important. Part of my argument is, however, that such differences among starting points are important in determining the types of questions a critic raises. Even so, for the disciplines of history and literature to profit from one another, the questions raised from one point of view need to be, not only of interest, but instructive, for both historians and literary critics. I certainly hope that my audience will include cultural historians. Indeed, Agnew himself has articulated one of the major problems arising from the attempt to abandon an organic model.

The essay in which Agnew turned to literature as a way of providing historical thick description was published in 1983. In 1990 he published one detailing problems raised by historians' use of thick description. Turned to as an alternative to the statistical method of social historians, thick description has not overcome the problem of increasingly specialized studies. On the contrary, that problem goes hand in hand with Geertz's stress on "local knowledge." Rather than offer a one dimensional, static view of a particular culture, it offers, as Agnew points out, a dynamic sense of cultural interaction, one that is "overdetermined" in its complexity. But the very overdetermination of these descriptions undercuts the effort to link them causally to one another. Rather than provide the synthesis that some historians have called for, the marriage of anthropology and history has, so far, produced only a montage of isolated scenes.[24]

The question of how to relate one scene of thick description to another brings us back to the question of how to relate parts to the whole. As we have seen, the new historicist use of chiasmus seems to offer an alternative to the organic strategy of letting the part speak for the whole. Chiasmus relates not part to whole, but one particular part to another. Nonetheless, insofar as the goal of a new historicism is to produce a cultural poetics, new historicists find it difficult to break with the Aristotelian desire to come up with significant details that serve as concrete universals. Very often the chiasmatic relation established is itself employed as a form of synecdoche.

This common practice of letting a particular chiasmatic relation speak for an entire culture is double-edged.

On the one hand, it reasserts the organic model and all of its problems of totalization that chiasmus seemed to guard against. Furthermore, the connections established seem to rest more on sleight of hand than empirical evidence. In this regard the new historicist effort to move from the particular to the general has not gotten us much beyond Spitzer whose similar efforts always involved, as a sympathetic critic put it, some "trickery."[25] As Spitzer himself admits, they relied on "speculation."[26] The connections produced by a cultural poetics are also based, to a large extent, on speculation.

On the other hand, perhaps this persistent effort to make our evidence speak for more than itself points to the need for such speculative accounts of a culture, a need especially strong as increased disciplinary specialization makes rigorous synthetic analysis more and more difficult. A culture limited to understanding itself by one isolated scene after another may not be the healthiest, especially when thick descriptions of those scenes invite us to recognize connections—even if overdetermined ones—between them. Of course, we need not jump directly from detailed, local knowledge to statements about how an entire culture works. Nor need we let the interrelations between two disciplines speak for the entire field of cultural practices. In my own work on law and literature, for instance, I made no claim to describe an all-embracing "logic" of antebellum culture in the United States. I merely claimed that in cross-examining the histories of two disciplines, which have often been kept apart, I could produce a story about that culture which otherwise would remain untold.[27] We can recognize the importance of speculating about connections between parts while still resisting the tendency to grant those speculations the power to speak for the whole. The importance of such resistance is heightened when the parts to be related are not separate social practices, but various ethnic and national cultures.

The importance and difficulty of relating various cultural traditions without reducing them to an undifferentiated homogeneous standard brings us to the challenge posed by Auerbach. Auerbach is most famous for *Mimesis*, perhaps the most ambitious effort to make parts of individual texts speak for a particular culture's sense of reality. The challenge I have in mind, however, is posed in a 1952 essay entitled "Philology and *Weltliteratur*." Whereas Foucault translated the Spitzer essay into French in 1970, Marie and Edward Said translated the Auerbach essay into English in 1969.[28] It responds to the obvious limits of a national-based philology by urging critics to move beyond national boundaries to a world literature. I will return to this challenge because of its importance for how a new historicism can distinguish itself from an old. At this time I merely want to emphasize that those attempting to establish individual traditions according to gender, ethnicity, or even class can profit from Auerbach's criticism, for too often such historians reoccupy the narrative structures employed by a nationally based historicism. I also want to emphasize how Auerbach's and Spitzer's ability to move back and forth between a variety of traditions can serve as a model for a new historicism that wants to cross the boundaries of our existing understandings of culture. To be sure, both remained Eurocentric, and the new historicism's demands to move the boundaries of *Weltliteratur* beyond Europe is exemplary. The work done on postcolonial literature, the efforts to do comparative work not only within Europe, but also so as to involve Asia, Africa, the Caribbean, and North and South America seem to me to be responding to Auerbach's challenge in ways that he could not yet imagine. Nonetheless, there is also a danger of a renewed provincialism.

In part that provincialism grows out of a move toward increased specialization that Auerbach notes in his 1952 essay. Too often period specialists have such a narrow sense of history that they are prone to make exaggerated claims about the changes occurring within their period. The risk of provincialism is especially strong within the specialty of American literature. Recently, the "cultural elite" that helped to constitute the canon of American masterpieces has been attacked for the ethnic and gender narrowness of their perspective. But we would be wise to remember that much of that work grew out of a decidedly comparativist perspective. Not only were people like F. O. Matthiessen and Van Wyck Brooks trained in non-American literature, some of their most important work was written while outside of the United States. Brook's influential and critical *America's Coming of Age* was composed mostly while he was in England, whereas Matthiessen drafted his *American Renaissance* chapters on Melville and Hawthorne while travelling through Germany and the Soviet Union in the troublesome summer and fall of 1938. It will be objected, with some justification, that their perspectives remained too Eurocentric. But would we say the same of Richard Wright and James Baldwin, who also profited from a perspective on their native culture while living in Europe? The first piece published by Baldwin after he moved to France was his influential, "Everybody's Protest Novel," with its harsh criticism of *Uncle Tom's Cabin*.[29] Like Auerbach, Baldwin ventured to the edge of European culture, writing some of his most important work while in Turkey. Critics who keep in mind Auerbach's challenge to produce a *Weltliteratur* can both better understand a writer like Baldwin and avoid the danger of unintentionally contributing to a new form of United States isolationism by confirming Allan Bloom's charge that to "open" the canon can actually close minds. Given the world political scene, it is increasingly important that our students—and the critics of United States culture—be exposed to cultures outside the boundaries of the fifty states. As Auerbach urged, "The more our earth grows closer together, the more must historicist synthesis balance the contraction by expanding its activity."[30] The danger of provincialism involves more than spatial isolation. It is no accident that the 1980s could produce a book entitled *The Past Is a Foreign Country*.[31] One of the preconditions for a new historicism is the sense of an increasing cultural amnesia. Thus it is extremely important that the new historicism's desire to be new does not result in an arrogance toward the past. An important part of my polemic is, at strategic moments, to intervene into current debates by introducing the voices of old-fashioned critics too easily dismissed by today's up-to-date and politically correct theorists. The most obvious examples are the literary critics, Spitzer, Auerbach, and Northrop Frye. But I also call on historians such as James Harvey Robinson, Charles A. Beard, and Carl Becker. Statements by these historians might surprise a few critics who think that an awareness of the constructed nature of the past is a metahistorical or poststructuralist discovery. Indeed, one of the most important aspects of this study is to link the new historicism, which is at the moment a decidedly North American phenomenon, to a homemade tradition of pragmatic historiography. In doing so I hope to warn it against assuming that it is adopting an international perspective when, with surprising frequency, what is appropriated from continental theory takes on a form similar to a new—and not always so new—version of American progressive historiography.

The relationship between the new historicism and poststructuralism is another one of my concerns. It is commonplace to assume, as Warner puts it, that the "same theoretical arguments that have been associated with poststructuralism and deconstruction" have led to the new historicism. Once again I want to question Warner's assumed relationship of identity. This is not to deny that poststructuralism has influenced the new historicism, but there is also a tension between certain poststructuralist arguments and the project implied by a new historicism. One of the best ways to anticipate how I will explore that tension is to turn to Schaedelbach's argument in *Geschichtsphilosophie nach Hegel: Die Probleme des Historismus*. Schaedelbach starts by noting how *Historismus* developed as a reaction against the philosophy of history, especially that of Hegel, in which the contingency of history is subordinated to a philosophic system. Tracing developments within *Historismus* that led to its so-called crisis in the twentieth century, he identifies three efforts to overcome it: the phenomenological-hermeneutical tradition initiated by Husserl and developed by Heidegger and Gadamer, a neo-marxist response initiated by Georg Lukács's *History and Class Consciousness* and refined by the Frankfurt School, and analytical philosophy. Schaedelbach's provocative thesis is that, despite these various efforts, the problems raised by *His-*

torismus have not been overcome. Writing in 1974 Schaedelbach does not engage poststructuralism, but it can clearly be seen as a fourth effort to overcome *Historismus*. The rise of a new historicism in the United States, where poststructuralism has been most widely institutionalized, can be read as a symptom that poststructuralism itself has not been completely successful in overcoming the problems raised by *Historismus*. Indeed, one of the best examples of the tension between the new historicism and poststructuralism are recent French poststructuralist and postmodern readings of America. Just at a time when the new historicism in this country tries to break with a tradition of American exceptionalism, which claims that the United States is unique in escaping the problems of history, Jean Baudrillard embraces an exceptionalist interpretation with a vengeance. His interpretation reveals not only his inability to escape a history of French interpretations of America launched by Alexis de Tocqueville but also crucial differences between poststructuralist and new historicist assumptions.[32]

I place so much emphasis on dangers that the new historicism needs to be aware of because I, no more than Greenblatt, want to identify one and only one proper form of historical criticism. Indeed, one of my arguments is that historical analysis is generated in part as a response to pressing questions in the present. Those questions are not the same for all critics, and different strategies need to be developed to respond to different questions. Nonetheless, if a history is to be effective it needs to convince others of the importance of the questions that generate it. More often than not the prescriptive aspect of my study makes a case for the importance of some questions over others. I especially emphasize the need to question the narrative strategies used to structure new histories. There is, however, no inevitably proper narrative strategy any more than there is a proper method, which is not to say that I will not warn against the dangers of various narratives in our time. Rather than advocate a particular form of narrative, I argue for a continual experimentation with various modes of presentation and points of view to respond to the complex questions that we face.

My emphasis on the importance of narrative carries with it a danger of its own that I should warn against. It is a commonplace of current criticism to argue that narrative constitutes knowledge. Indeed, the two are etymologically related. But we should not forget that their relationship works in both directions. There would be no narrative if there were nothing to narrate. In stressing the importance of narrative, I do not want to give the impression that if we would only get the narrative structure right we would solve the problem of writing histories. One reason that Spitzer, Auerbach, and Frye can still intervene into current debates is because they knew so much. One prerequisite for a good history—old or new—is learning, and one reason to admire Greenblatt's work is that it is so learned. He not only has innovative narrative strategies, he also has done his homework. As I have already indicated, however, my admiration for his work does not keep me from entering into debate with it in the spirit of dialogue that it promotes.

The amount of learning present in the chapters that follow is up to the reader to decide. But since I stress the importance of narrative, I should say a word about my own mode of presentation. I am offering neither an exhaustive history of the history of historicism (I do not have the competence or learning for such a task.), nor an exhaustive description of the various versions of the new historicism—a sort of survey of a field so common today. (Such an account would be premature at the moment.) Instead, I make an argument about particular tasks and questions that I would like to see a new historicism address, an argument conducted by focusing on selected issues, problems, and possibilities connected with its rise to prominence in North America (however long-or short-lived that may turn out to be). To make my argument I rely (perhaps with mixed results) on a mixture of discourses. Polemic is combined with brief, if oversimplified, historical narratives and fairly detailed analyses of representative figures whose work raises the issues, problems, and possibilities that I want to consider. This mixture is supplemented by strategic interventions that invoke voices from the past and present, some discredited or forgotten (like Robinson), some currently popular (like Benjamin) and some relatively neglected in North American debates (like Blumenberg). The major purpose of this mode of presentation is to interrogate the present by raising questions about the uses put to studies of the past, especially literary modes from the past.

The emphasis I share with many others on the present uses of past studies has raised two especially vocal objections: (1) that such an emphasis has no necessary political consequences, (2) that it encourages a dangerous form of presentism. The two are, I believe, related.

The argument against political consequences is double-edged. First of all, insofar as people do argue for what Howard Horwitz terms an "oppositional, nonexploitive politics" as the "inherent and necessary result of method or of a model of historicism," he is correct to dispute their claims.[33] Even the briefest history of historicism reveals the falsity of such claims. But Horwitz and others have gotten a lot of mileage out of assuming that all political arguments claim a *necessary* causality. A much more subtle argument for the present need of a historically oriented criticism can be made.

If, as many historical critics wager, our situation in the world is at least partly determined by historical forces, then it is possible that an accurate knowledge of that situation will give us a better chance to alter it—if we so wish—than lack of such knowledge. This is especially the case in our present historical situation, which is one that leftists and conservatives alike have described as that of widespread cultural amnesia. Generally, the difference between leftists and conservatives on this issue is a difference over what is meant by a sense of historicity. For conservatives it too often implies a somewhat pious attitude toward and knowledge of the past. For leftists it is not an attitude toward the past but toward the present, an awareness that the present itself is a moment of history, an awareness dependent upon a historical consciousness.[34] To be sure, this sense of the present as history does not necessarily mean that human beings can make the direction of history conform to their desires. As Greek tragedy demonstrates, recognition of forces controlling us does not necessarily lead to their disappearance. Nonetheless, the *probability* of overcoming particular historical forces that unnecessarily limit us is increased if we are aware of them.

Having said this, I want to make it clear that I am not arguing that a leftist sense of historicity will necessarily confirm particular leftist political positions. In a historically contingent world in which we lack a foundation of ahistorical values to anchor our judgments, the advantage of considering historicity an attitude toward the present rather than the past comes precisely from the way in which it allows us to use knowledge of the past to judge the very conditions of our judgments. That includes our political judgments. To my mind one judgment that needs judging today is the fairly simplistic argument that "everything," including our constructions of the past, "is political." I am certainly not one to deny political consequences or even motivations to our constructions of the past. But it is precisely the reduction of all investigations of the past to present political positions that ultimately leads to an extreme form of presentism that would deny the uses of the past. This is because, if our constructions are no more than political, we may as well give up the sham of talking about the past and debate current events. But, for some reason or other, what happened in the past still seems to matter to a number of people. So long as that is the case, present politics will continue to be shaped as much by our understanding of the past as our understandings of the past are shaped by present politics. For revisionist history not to risk revising its enabling political positions in light of what it discovers is to turn it into little more than visionary history.

To argue that studies of the past increase in their utility when we allow them to become more than allegories of the present is not to deny the influence of the present. In my preface I already noted some of the present conditions to which the new historicism has responded. It has become fashionable to assert that there is always already an overdetermination of such factors. Nonetheless, it will not hurt to list a few others that have an obvious claim to attention.

The felt need to reconstruct existing histories is in part a response to professional demographics. For one, more women and minorities are teachers of literature today than in the heyday of the New Criticism. There may be a class factor as well. A few years before literature departments experienced the canon wars, history departments battled over the need for a "bottoms up" perspective in historical studies. One effect of literary critics' rediscovery of history is that they are reading a different account of the past from one produced by consensus historians, one that encourages a rethinking of the existing canon's representativeness. A possible reason for historians anticipating literary critics in raising such questions is suggested in a report on the history department of Yale University filed by the chairman July 15, 1957. "Apparently," he laments, "the subject of English still draws to a degree from the cultivated, professional, and well-to-do classes, hence more young men and women from able backgrounds. By contrast, the subject of history seems to appeal on the whole to a lower social stratum. . . . One may be glad to see the lower occupations working upward. . . . It may be flattering to be regarded as an elevator. But even the strongest elevator will break down if asked to lift too much weight."[35] Written at a time when New Critics were still firmly entrenched at Yale, this report gives a sense of the type of students English departments attracted as well as the role of cultural guardians that they, more than history departments, most likely projected.

The 1980s, of course, were not the 1950s. Differences are not confined to a move from consensus to conflictual histories. There is also the difference between the Eisenhower and Reagan presidencies. Part of the fascination with how power is staged, or as Leonard Tennenhouse puts it, with *Power on Display*,[36] results from Ronald Reagan and his handlers' masterful use of political theatricality in the 1980s. Reagan's success also signalled a dramatic shift in the temper of the country. In the mid-1970s Fredric Jameson could confidently write, "In the past few years, we have witnessed the intellectual and political collapse of that liberal world-view which for so long served as an explanation as well as a justification of our economic development and of the aims of our foreign policy—I doubt if there are many people left today who still believe either in the promise of the older American liberalism or in the theoretical accounts it used to give of the organization of American life."[37] Whereas for some liberals the Reagan era was a conservative disaster, in a broader perspective it helped to salvage the classical liberal worldview that seemed so close to collapse, much as the New Deal had fifty years earlier. Exactly why this required the dismantling of various New Deal programs still needs to be explained.

Furthermore, it is very possible that the Reagan years will eventually lead to an even larger crisis, foreshadowed by the monumental deficit and the savings and loan disaster. Nonetheless, the dramatic turnabout in American confidence left a generation of intellectuals who loosely shared Jameson's sense of the bankruptcy of the liberal worldview in an awkward position.[38] The sometimes tiresome debate about subversion or containment that dominates so many new historicist polemics is at least partially a response to that situation. The debate has the potential to be especially acute in Berkeley, a community that in comparison with much of the country seems like a time capsule that preserves a simulated appearance of the 1960s, but also a community whose famous university benefitted greatly from having a Republican governor (not Reagan) who restored a budget and salaries depleted under the previous Democratic administration.

Mention of salaries raises the question of economics that is also so fascinating for new historicists. Perhaps the most important reason why studies linking literature and authorship to the market have proved so popular is the apparent newness of the topic for those trained in New Critical assumptions. The theme alone seems innovative. But certainly another factor to consider is literary critics' own experience of the professional marketplace when academic jobs were drastically reduced in the 1970s. For those peddling their academic wares in the job market, it became increasingly difficult to separate the study of literature from economic considerations. I was once tempted to offer a reading of "Bartleby, the Scrivener" as the story of an untenured assistant professor forced to live in his office (as some I knew were) because of high housing costs and the need to save for an uncertain economic future. In retrospect, Bartleby as a lecturer or graduate student would have been more appropriate. Indeed, to be an assistant professor at least meant that you had a position. As much as the job market reminded literary critics of their marginalized status in the United States of the 1970s, we should not forget that for the most part those who published on literature and the marketplace were professional success stories. They had procured jobs in a competitive market. In this narrow sense, at least, much of the work considered new historical should be seen as what Benjamin calls a history of the "victors." I do not point this out to cause those who "made it" to feel guilty; only to emphasize how a particular generation's very local historical situation made various complicated relationships between literary studies and economic and social conditions obvious avenues to explore. Those relationships might seem even more complicated to those who have friends who failed in the profession only to occupy nonacademic positions offering more economic success.

At this time I could add a brief professional biography that would establish my authority to represent such circumstances. But I will resist that temptation and note instead that it is fairly easy to point to present influences on our studies of the past (although impossible to come up with an exhaustive list of such influences). A more interesting and difficult question is how our studies of the past influence our understanding of the present and what role the reading of literary texts might play in such studies. It is those difficult questions that I will address in what follows.

Before addressing them I should warn the reader that the waters I enter are troubled ones. To make my way through them I sometimes go very fast (making far too simple generalizations) and sometimes slow down (almost to a halt) to scrutinize a figure or idea with what might seem an unscrupulous closeness.[39] Amidst calls for institutional and materialist studies of culture, mine is unapologetically a study of ideas and concepts about the relationship between history and literature. I fully acknowledge the importance of material forces in shaping these ideas and concepts, and I devote some attention to how they have been influenced by the institutions of literary and historical studies, at least in the United States. But I limit myself by focusing on the ideas and the concepts themselves. For readers wishing that my study were even more limited and defined, I will briefly trace the main currents of my argument. Such a summary presupposes that the navigating will not always be easy. I make no claim to part the waters that we are about to enter, delivering us to the promised land of a fully integrated relationship between literature and history. At the same time, I do not want to shipwreck or have too many readers jump overboard.

This chapter has tried to introduce, interweave, and orchestrate a number of the issues that I will explore and questions that I will raise. The second examines the tensions between the two strains of the new historicism that I have identified: its use of poststructuralism to deconstruct existing literary histories and its desire to reconstruct more representative ones. I explore that tension by asking what it means to announce the rise of a *new* historicism in a *post*modern age. Having emphasized tensions between two seemingly competing strains of the new historicism, I end by arguing that the two are united by a tendency to construct monolithic histories of modernity in the West.

The third chapter starts by showing how this tendency to simplify the complicated history of Western modernity limits the explanatory power of much important work concerned with the West's representation of cultural difference. Drawing on the debate generated by the collection entitled '*Race,' Writing, and Difference,* I identify the most difficult challenge facing those writing such histories as the appropriation of Western narratives of pluralistic inclusion rather than the somewhat easier one of appropriating narratives of monological exclusion. As a model for how this might be done I turn to the narrative strategy suggested by Auerbach's response to the dead end of nationally based literary histories. The chapter ends with a discussion of Blumenberg's complicated assessment of modernity. The importance of Blumenberg's work for a new historicism is twofold. On the one hand, he offers a persuasive defense of various modern concepts that no new historicism can afford to do without. On the other, he manages his defense by proposing a mode of temporality at odds with the modern sense of temporal continuity.

This modern sense of temporality is at the heart of the tradition of American pragmatic historiography, and in the fourth chapter, which stands at the heart of my book, I place the new historicism within this tradition. Indeed, many of the so-called poststructuralist assumptions of the new historicism can actually be traced to the pragmatic tradition's effort to produce studies of the past usable in the present. Marking a moment when pragmatism is used against itself, recent uses of pragmatism in literary studies that question the political consequences of re-writing the past indicate the limits of that tradition for the new historicism. At the same time, these neopragmatic responses are themselves limited because, relying on a particular reading of the definition of the truth, they remain lodged within a sense of temporal continuity, thus eliminating as inconsequential some of the most troubling problems of reconstructing the past. The power of the poststructuralist challenge to the pragmatic tradition is not the claim that histories are constructs; pragmatically influenced historians have made the same claim. Instead, it is to question the pragmatic sense of temporality. In turn, the pragmatic challenge to poststructuralist narratives is their usability, especially for previously underrepresented groups. For an alternative mode of historiography to the tradition of pragmatism and its recent poststructuralist appropriations, I end with a discussion of Benjamin.

The discussion of Benjamin raises the important question of the role of literary works in reconstructing the past. But before addressing that question, I turn to Walter Benn Michaels to illustrate the totalizing perils of a particular pragmatic appropriation of poststructuralism. Because Michaels and I work in the same historical period, I can examine his use of historical evidence in detail, showing how he constructs a narrative that fits into a preexisting structure, even if a structure of difference.

Michaels returns us to questions about the role of the literary because in his attempt to fit all within logical structures he denies literary works a relationship of difference with other cultural practices. I devote the last two chapters to exploring such differences and consequences they can have for our new histories. In the sixth I directly confront arguments that, on the one hand, want to abolish categories such as the literary and the aesthetic as ideologically discredited realms of recreation, and, on the other, try to assert the importance of literature by insisting on the "cultural work" that it accomplishes in fixing beliefs. On the contrary, I appeal to the notion of play associated with bourgeois aesthetics to argue that literature can serve an important, if limited, role in our construction of the past by unfixing present beliefs.

In the last chapter, I turn to the latest work of Greenblatt and examine closely, not his use of historical evidence, but his mimetic model for the literary text. Mimesis for Greenblatt is not a passive act. Instead, in the tradition of Aristotle, he asserts that it produces that which it imitates. Indeed, his work is one of the most sophisticated examples of what has come to be an enabling assumption for many new historicists: literature both produces and is produced by a period's ideology.[40] On the one hand, this chiasmatic formula admits literature's connection with ideology; on the other, it allows it to retain its representative status. Drawing on the work of Wolfgang Iser, I describe, not the bankruptcy, but the limits of Greenblatt's mimetic model for historical criticism. Most important is the way in which Iser's nonmimetic model can help us imagine fissures in what Greenblatt calls an "inescapable historical process."[41]

Narrative strategies, modes of temporality, models of literary texts, and their interrelations in the practice of writing literary history: These are my focus.

CHAPTER 2

The New Historicism in a Postmodern Age

· I ·

AN IMPRECISE LABEL, the new historicism is used with most precision in Renaissance studies where it is contrasted to feminism and British cultural materialism, as well as an older historicism and formalism. Its powerful impact on Renaissance studies has led, predictably, to numerous critiques, some hostile, but many sympathetic, conducted as they are by people who are themselves labelled new historicists.[1] One of the most important is Louis Montrose's comparison of the new historicism with cultural materialism. Recognizing important similarities between the two, Montrose goes on to argue that cultural materialism is more concerned with cultural politics than its American counterpart. For instance, Montrose distinguishes between the two by noting that, whereas both British and American scholars of the Renaissance offer new histories, in the United States "the emphasis has been almost exclusively upon a refiguring of the sociocultural field in which Renaissance texts were *originally* produced—although not without an awareness of the role of the present in (re)making the past. In Britain . . . there has been a relatively greater emphasis upon the uses to which the *present* has put its versions of the past."[2]

The question of how to put versions of the past to present uses is a central one for any movement calling itself a *new* historicism. This question, in turn, raises questions of narrative, most obviously point of view, for to worry about the uses of the past is to worry about the point of view from which we reconstruct the past. This observation is not meant to deny the complexity of the question. On the contrary, it increases its complexity, for, as any student of narrative knows, a narrative can at times more effectively show than tell. Thus various complaints that the new historicism is not up-front enough about its assumptions seem to forget that a point of view can be embodied in a narrative without explicitly acknowledging it.[3] One measure of a new historicism might be, then, the extent to which it risks experimenting with new forms of narrating the past.

To pose the question this way is to identify two strains of the new historicism. One tries to offer new narrative structures to present the past. The other retains traditional narrative structures but offers new voices from which to tell the past. Ironically, the one more self-conscious about offering the present new uses of the past is the one that retains more traditional forms. We can see this more clearly if we shift fields from the *English* Renaissance to the *American* Renaissance. Montrose may well be right that in the field of the English Renaissance British cultural material-ism is more self-conscious about present uses of the past, but if we look at studies of the American Renaissance we get a different story. It is no acci-dent that American critics are more concerned with uses the present puts to versions of their own Renaissance rather than England's. As the debate over the canon, the numerous efforts to reconstruct American literature, and the completed and proposed Columbia and Cambridge literary histo-ries demonstrate, there is a concerted effort to make American represen-tations of its literary past more usable to its present population. Often these efforts to rewrite American literary history adopt different narrative strategies from those employed in new historical analysis of the English Renaissance.

One way of ascertaining that difference is to look at the relationship that these various narratives maintain with poststructuralism, for, although it has become commonplace to distinguish the new historicism from the old because of its engagement with poststructuralism, poststructuralism and the new historicism have an uneasy relationship with one another. Post-structuralism is generally considered a phenomenon of a postmodern age. Merely to contrast the labels "postmodernism" and "new historicism" is to sense possible tensions. Within themselves the labels suggest contra-dictory relationships. New historicism suggests the newness of the past, whereas postmodernism suggests the pastness of the new. To place the two in relation to each other, therefore, calls attention to the contradic-tory nature of the present situation, in which the widespread use of the prefix "post" is matched only by the use of the adjective "new" to describe critical schools. In a world in which the modern is described as postmod-ern and that which is considered behind us is referred to as the modern age,[4] the new historicism and postmodernism could be considered com-plementary descriptions of the same condition.

But similarities should not disguise important differences. "Post" im-plies a belatedness, an age in which everything has always already oc-curred. Appropriately, poststructuralism and postmodernism question the assumptions of self-consciously modern ages, especially the Enlight-enment and its belief in progress and rationality. "New," in contrast, im-plies an impulse toward the very modern that poststructuralism is at pains to discredit. In conflict are different notions of temporality, which have implications for how histories are to be narrated and, thus, for how they are used in the present. I do not want to get caught in the mistake of identifying a particular mode of narration as inherently radical or conservative. This type of formalist thought plagues the work of even someone like Roland Barthes, who identifies the realist mode of narration with bourgeois ideology. But if no inherent political valence adheres to particular modes of narration, within particular historical and cultural contexts they can acquire relatively determinant political forces, even if that force is always subject to change through either cooptation or appropriation. Part of my task in this chapter is to analyze the political consequences in our time of traditional historicist modes of narration and poststructuralist challenges to them.

The label "poststructuralism" is as imprecise as that of the "new historicism," and in using it I will often neglect important differences between its various versions. Nonetheless, I risk such overgeneralizations because I am not only interested in describing what poststructuralism *is*, as if it had a set identity, but also in the historical power of the label itself. For many critics poststructuralism has had precise and determinant effects on studies of culture, especially those of literature. As I will argue, an insight attributed to poststructuralism is often one held by the most sophisticated practitioners of an old-fashioned historicism, so that there is a certain forgetfulness involved in attributing too much innovation to poststructuralism. Nonetheless, I do not want to deny an innovative force to it any more than I want to deny an innovative force to the new historicism. Furthermore, it remains important to examine how people think poststructuralism has affected them, whether what they attribute to poststructuralism originated with it or not.

One consequence that many critics see following from poststructuralism is a challenge to the canon. Listen, for instance, to Cathy N. Davidson's account of some of the influences on her extraordinarily productive revisionism in *Revolution and the Word: The Rise of the Novel in America*. Noting disciplinary changes within the study of both history and literature, she summarizes:

> Poststructuralist literary theory has challenged the notion, sacrosanct for several decades, that a critic's task is to explicate a predetermined syllabus of literary 'masterpieces.' Metahistorians have suggested that every work of history is essentially an imaginative work, a narrative little different from a novel. In both fields, women and minorities have challenged the canon by asking who we study, what we study, why, and how. In this book I have listened carefully to these diverse voices.[5]

Davidson offers a concise summary of three different forces helping to contribute to much of the revisionist work that I label the reconstructionist aspect of the new historicism. In the course of this study I will have something to say about metahistorical comparisons between histories and novels. For the moment, however, what interests me is the use to which revisionists put poststructuralism.

For many, as for Davidson, its most important consequence involves the canon. This use of poststructuralism has proved very productive, but along with much valuable work it has also produced some glaring contradictions. As a way of economically illustrating those contradictions I will turn to one of the most outspoken critics of the present constitution of canonical literature in the United States, Jane Tompkins. I do not single out Tompkins to make a personal attack on her. Quite the contrary, I have learned from her work. Nonetheless, as someone who identifies herself as a new historicist with a debt to poststructuralist thought, she brings into focus the tension between poststructuralism and the new historicism that I want to investigate.

· II ·

In her preface Tompkins claims that an engagement with structuralist and poststructuralist thought has helped her to produce a "new kind of historical criticism" that will challenge the canon of the American Renaissance as established by members of a "cultural elite," like F. O. Matthiessen.[6] The most obvious influence on her work is Stanley Fish's argument that texts are constituted by interpretive communities. Tompkins uses this argument to deny that aesthetic value resides within texts. Quite effectively she demonstrates that the criteria for aesthetic value change as the assumptions uniting interpretive communities change. If this is true, any argument for the intrinsic value of the canon seems seriously flawed.

Now clearly not all new historical challenges to the canon draw on the work of Fish, and it is even questionable whether Fish should be considered a poststructuralist. Nonetheless, poststructuralism has helped to deconstruct the canon. Most important is the poststructuralist critique of representation. Emphasizing the gap in any effort to re-present, poststructuralists remind us that the desire for full representation is linked to an impossible to achieve dream of presence. Constituted by both a temporal and spatial gap, representation is structurally dependent on misrepresentation. Since by definition representation can never be full, all acts of representation produce an "other" that is marginalized or excluded.

It is easy to see why such logic serves as a powerful weapon for those attacking existing histories and canons. The supposedly objective criteria used to establish a canon representing the interests of all humanity can be shown to be weighted in favor of a certain segment of the population. Indeed, the notion of objectivity itself is said to be a false one, since the inevitability of partial representation makes critical impartiality impossible. Deprived of a position outside society that allows a detached reflection upon it, all literature and criticism—like other social practices—are condemned to remain in the field of the power relations that produce them. In short, literature and criticism do not occupy a detached space free from political pressures but are inevitably subject to political constraints. All constructions of literary histories are political, and many new historians consider it their responsibility to redress past political inequities by giving representation to those previously excluded.

As important and valuable as these efforts are, one difficulty with them is obvious. If all acts of representation are structurally dependent on misrepresentation, these new histories inevitably create their own canons and exclusions. This difficulty is concisely illustrated by Tompkins's attempt to offer her version of "The Other American Renaissance," a version that emphasizes the importance of popular works of fiction like *Uncle Tom's Cabin*. These works, Tompkins argues, in making designs on a wide audience, produced important cultural work by effecting social change. In order to make a case for the importance of this popular tradition, Tompkins has to shift her interpretive assumptions from the view that interpretive communities produce texts, for now she is forced to describe a tradition with definable characteristics. Indeed, it is particular characteristics of popular fiction that have caused a "cultural elite" to exclude them. In other words, when the question she asks switches from "Is there a text in this classroom?" to "What text should we have in the classroom?" Tompkins abandons her up-to-date poststructuralist pose and returns to old-fashioned assumptions about literature and historical analysis. In terms of literature she adheres to the traditional notion that a text provides "men and women with a means of ordering the world they inhabit" (xiii). In terms of historical analysis she adheres to the traditional historicists' desire to "recreate, as sympathetically as possible, the context from which [these works] sprang and the specific problems to which they were addressed" (xiii). Reserving criticism of the social and political attitudes that motivated her writers, she "tried instead to inhabit and make available to a modern audience the viewpoint from which their politics made sense" (xiii).

That Tompkins identifies this old-fashioned method of historical analysis with the new historicism confirms how difficult it is to establish a truly "new" historicism. Indeed, she gets caught in a number of contradictions. For instance, her old-fashioned attempt to understand writers on their own historical terms seems in direct contradiction with her poststructuralist claim that her book is a product of her own interpretive assumptions, assumptions shaped by her place in history. Furthermore, in her emphasis on a book's popularity as a measure of its cultural work, Tompkins is not rigorous enough in asking that important new historicist question: works for whom? For instance, Tompkins places *Uncle Tom's Cabin* and Susan B. Warner's *The Wide Wide World* in a common sentimental tradition. To be sure, both were best sellers. But did they appeal to the same audience? *Uncle Tom's Cabin* was not popular in the South for obvious reasons. Most likely Warner's book was. If so, there is an important difference in how the sentimentalists tried to effect a "radical transformation" (145) of society in female terms. Before making sweeping generalizations about popular fiction, Tompkins needs to conduct much more careful, empirical research into the variety and specificity of literary markets.

The question of for whom a work works can be asked from a different angle, one emphasizing the question of present uses. Tompkins's criterion for the amount of cultural work done by a novel seems to be a fairly naive, positivistic one, measured by sales. But if so, could not defenders of the canon point to sales of canonical works, which in recent years have outstripped those of non-canonical works, as proof of the cultural work that they are performing in the present? Of course, Tompkins could argue that those sales are largely the result of a system of institutional forces that requires students to purchase selected works for classroom reading. But would she go on to argue that the marketplace that determines bestsellers is a system lacking constraints and thus a better measure of a work's "real" work? Indeed, in her appeal to a work's popularity, Tompkins unwittingly falls prey to the ideological notion of the "free play" of the marketplace.

Tompkins's stress on popularity highlights problems that plague her sort of cultural populism, which mistakes the values of a cultural elite for those of a culture's economic and political elite. As Spiro Agnew, Ronald Reagan, and other protectors of the culture's elite know quite well, attacks on cultural elites have a wide popular appeal. Certainly, a book's sales are no accurate measure of its political value. This is especially true in a country whose cultural critics (many of whom, like Matthiessen, were socialists) have often opposed the values of the country's economic and political elite. These critics may betray a greater complicity with the values that they oppose than we have traditionally granted. Nonetheless, it would be a terrible irony, if, in the name of oppositional criticism, we celebrate texts that, despite their challenge to the aesthetic values of custodians of culture, turn out to have effected a compromise with the political values of our culture's economic elite.

In fact, Tompkins's radical attack on the canon is not as radical as it promises to be. Tompkins ends her book with a jeremiadic cry steeped in revolutionary rhetoric. Her last paragraph begins by announcing that her "study and Matthiessen's are competing attempts to constitute American literature." It ends with the stirring call that "the literary canon, as codified by a cultural elite, has power to influence the way the country thinks across a broad range of issues. The struggle now being waged in the professoriate over which writers deserve canonical status is not just a struggle over the relative merits of literary geniuses; it is a struggle among contending factions for the right to be represented in the picture America draws of itself" (201).

Since Tompkins spends an entire chapter arguing that Hawthorne owes his literary reputation to "the influence of his friends and associates, and then on the influence of their successors" (4) and since Hawthorne is a writer canonized by Matthiessen, we might suspect that she is attacking the way reputations are made. But this is not the case. "The argument that follows is not critical of the way literary reputations come into being, or of Hawthorne's reputation in particular. Its object, rather, is to suggest that a literary reputation could never be anything but a political matter" (4). A book that announces itself as a radical attack on the canon turns out not to criticize the way literary reputations are made. Rather than advocate systemic change, it merely challenges those who have used the system's logic to get ahead. Furthermore, the only hope for those previously excluded seems to be to use that very logic to their advantage.

Indeed, to persist in maintaining Tompkins's version of poststructuralist assumptions would seem to guarantee marginality, for whereas they offer a lucid explanation of why exclusions always take place, they seem of little help in reconstructing new literary histories. Thus the very poststructuralist assumptions that help to attack past histories seem necessarily forgotten in efforts to create new ones. That forgetfulness is apparent in the narrative that Tompkins uses to structure the history of her "Other American Renaissance." Rather than challenge the narrative of progressive emergence employed by a supposedly discredited older historicism, she reoccupies it in order to tell her story about the tradition of popular literature that Matthiessen's narrative excluded. Similarly, in a recent talk she moved from celebrating an alternative tradition of popular literature to one of female literature. But as her ironic title—"Susan Rowsan, The Father of the American Novel"—indicates, Tompkins's way of challenging traditional histories about America's cultural past is merely to apply a new point of view to the narrative structures that they employ. A female rather than a male "fathers" the American novel, but the history proceeds according to familiar categories of development and influence.[7] And Tompkins is not an isolated case. Within the field of American literature alone we have histories of emergent female, black, Chicano traditions, and so on that challenge the established view of a monological tradition of American nationalism by creating their own unique traditions. At the same time, in the field of Third World literature, we are asked to take seriously the literature of "insurgent nationalism."[8] For some, at least, when excluded "others" become the primary object of representation, poststructuralist warnings about the exclusions inherent in such narratives no longer seem to apply.

Although their use by a previously discredited older historicism should invite extreme caution, these narrative structures are not inherently regressive. Furthermore, it would be a mistake of major proportion to claim that all feminist, ethnic, or postcolonial histories merely reoccupy old-fashioned narratives of emergence. Some of the most important revisionist work is being done by those working within and between these fields, who are fully aware of the problems involved with narrative structures inherited from an older historicism.[9] For instance, some postcolonial works of fiction may dramatize poststructuralist notions better than certain theorists themselves.[10] It is precisely those working with such texts who are most likely to face the tensions I describe. Especially important for all of them is the poststructuralist attack on identity. One of the attractions of narratives of emergence is their attempt to grant identity to specific groups. For those who "identify" with these groups and yet remain wary about the dangers of identity-politics, the question of how to find equally moving narrative forms is crucial.

My purpose, however, is not to offer a survey of existing studies in these fields. If I did not single out Tompkins to make a personal attack on her, neither do I mean to make her representative of feminism or any other field of study. Instead, I used her to highlight almost unavoidable tensions faced by a project calling itself a new historicism. Clearly, I am not the first to call attention to such tensions. Nonetheless, by emphasizing the importance of narrative structures, I have tried to show how they are related to the almost contradictory call for a new historicism in a postmodern world. After all, in his influential work Jean-Francois Lyotard has pointed to the demise of narrative as a way to define the "postmodern condition."[11] Rather than accept Lyotard's description, I would speak of a restructuring of narrative strategies. In the next chapter I will return to the question of narratives of emergence and propose how what we might call postmodern narratives can provide new historicists with productive ways to explore the tensions they face. In the remainder of this one I want to explore possible reasons for those tensions. A good place to start is to hazard a historical explanation.

My emphasis on the need for historical understanding may seem to align me with the practice of history rather than that of poststructuralist theory, which is often accused of being ahistorical. But if we are to understand why poststructuralist assumptions come into conflict with reconstructionists' efforts to create new traditions, we need to resist the temptation too hastily to call poststructuralism, even its deconstructive version, ahistorical. Indeed, whereas it is commonplace to see the new historicism as a response to poststructuralism, we need to extend our historical horizon to see poststructuralism as a historical response to historicism, especially *Historismus*. To do that requires a very brief history of historicism. For reconstructionist new historicists to proceed without an active memory of that history would make them, not poststructuralists, prone to charges of escaping history, a history that draws attention to the risks of merely reoccupying the old historicism's narratives of progressive emergence.

·   **III**   ·

The history of historicism reveals one obvious reason why it is so easy to dispute the new historicism's claims to newness: the coupling of "new" with "historicism" is redundant. This is because the historical imagination that gave rise to historicism is unthinkable without a change in the concept of reality that marks the beginning of the modern age. According to Hans Blumenberg, the ancient and medieval world assumed a closed cosmos in which nothing new or unfamiliar was allowed to become real. In contrast, the modern view "removes the dubiousness from what is new and so *terra incognita*, or the *mundas novas*, becomes possible and effective as a *stimulus* to human activity; if one might phrase the process as a paradox, surprise is something to be expected." The modern concept of reality, in which the *mundas novas* becomes possible, is related to the rise of historicism because it depends upon a changed notion of temporality. Opposed to belief in a closed cosmos, the modern view assumes an open context that "always looks forward to a future that might contain elements which could shatter previous consistency and so render previous 'realities' unreal."[12] Events, therefore, take place not only in history but through history, and temporality has become a component part of reality.

So long as temporality is a component part of reality, reality undergoes continual transformations, transformations necessitating continual rewritings of history. "That world history has to be rewritten from time to time," Goethe confidently announced, "is no longer doubted by anyone these days."[13] Put another way, historicism, a product of the modern imagination, assumes that history will always be made new. As a result, the history of historicism is marked by perpetual claims to newness.

For instance, if Goethe recognized the need to rewrite history, he continued to link history to moral philosophy by maintaining the enlightenment belief that universal laws governed its outcome. Historical events, for him, illustrated natural laws and the natural rights of man. Thus Goethe's notion of universal history was challenged by Herder's emphasis on the organic development of peoples and nations, developments that became the object of study for the new science of history. Determined finally to break history's subordination to moral philosophy, the great spokesman for scientific history, Leopold von Ranke, argued that the historian's task was not to judge the past or to instruct the present for the profit of future ages, but "to show only what actually happened (*wie es eigentlich gewesen*)."[14] To accomplish this goal, Ranke emphasized the difference between primary and secondary sources and stressed the need for historians to rely on the former. Reconstructing an era from the materials it produced, the historian could sympathetically reinhabit the past.

As opposed to the Enlightenment, which harshly judged the superstitions of past eras, Ranke's *Historismus* considered all ages equal in the eyes of God and demanded that they be understood on their own terms. In retrospect, however, we can see that its understanding of past eras never made quite the break with moral philosophy that it claimed. Indeed, a moral vision was smuggled in through the narratives that *Historismus* used to structure its stories of the past. Often that vision was linked to an existing or, especially in Germany, emerging national consciousness. Drawing on the model of art historians who felt that a country's spirit was expressed through its literary and cultural genius, *Historismus* produced numerous histories, not of Culture, but of individual national cultures. Different in their details, these histories were similar in yoking together the modern sense of linear temporality with the celebrated logocentrism of Western thought to produce narratives of progressive emergence. Ostensibly *Historismus'* narratives were not necessarily teleological, as its emphasis on empirical inquiry in part countered the teleological vision of the philosophy of history. Nonetheless, an implied teleology remained. If, unlike the Enlightenment, *Historismus* did not use present values to judge the past, its narratives of progressive emergence did, nevertheless, imply that God's will led inevitably to the present. As Walter Benjamin observes in one of the most severe criticisms of *Historismus*, the result was a history of the victors.[15]

Not all of *Historismus'* narratives were put to nationalistic uses, however. At times its narratives of progressive emergence were linked to remnants of the enlightenment ideal of universalism and efforts were made to tell the story of the world, rather than national, or even European, history. But just as the effort to understand past eras on their own terms turned out to justify the present, so efforts to understand non-European cultures turned out to justify a Eurocentric view of world history, thereby justifying European imperialism. World history, it seemed, confirmed God's will to have a higher state of civilization emerge in Europe.

Paradoxically, the very success of Western imperialism helped to bring about a questioning of the assumptions of *Historismus*, since as the West dominated other cultures it was forced to adjust its narratives about the unfolding of world history to include them. To be sure, these non-European cultures were absorbed into a Eurocentric narrative that denied them proper representation. Nonetheless, the presence of these repressed "others" made possible a decentering of the Eurocentric version of history. Registered most forcefully in the thought of Nietzsche, the questioning of *Historismus* led to a general crisis in historicism, a crisis intensified by the destruction wrought by World War I, a crisis that found many thinkers sharing Yeats's anxiety that the center would not hold. If the unfolding of history led, not to a unified European culture, but a shattered and chaotic Europe; not to a higher rationality, but an unleashing of irrational barbarism within European culture; not to an emergent truth, but "the bottomless pit of relativism" feared by German historian Friedrich Meinecke,[16] assumptions of *Historismus* needed to be questioned.

Granted, the fragments that intellectuals shored up against Europe's ruin more often than not were a defensive maneuver, an attempt to preserve the order of a culture that perhaps never existed other than in the promise. Few knew the dangers of clinging to this reactionary nostalgia for the lost presence of a center that never ever was than Paul de Man, who, as we now know, with reprehensible consequences faced the crisis in Western thought and politics by embracing the cause of a European culture unified through its literature. Knowing in an intensely personal way the blindness of Western logocentrism—as well as the need actively to forget—de Man developed an insight that made him highly skeptical of revolutionary promises to make history new, especially those depending on teleological narratives of emergence, such as those he found in marxism. But he also maintained a skepticism toward any vestiges of the enlightenment project to find a universal foundation for human self-criticism and self-reflection within philosophical rationalism.

For instance, in his essay "Criticism and Crisis," which along with Derrida's "Structure, Sign and Play in the Discourse of the Human Sciences," can be seen as a "foundational" essay for deconstruction, de Man cites Husserl's description of philosophy as "a universal critique of all life and all the goals of life, of all the man-created cultural systems and achievements and, consequently, 'a criticism of man himself' (*Kritik der Menschheit selbst*) and of the values by which he is consciously or pre-consciously being governed." Turning this description on itself, de Man points to the numerous sections in Husserl's own text "in which philosophy is said to be the historical privilege of European man. Husserl speaks repeatedly of non-European cultures as primitive, prescientific and pre-philosophical, myth-dominated and congenitally incapable of the disinterested distances without which there can be no philosophical mediation. This, although by his own definition philosophy, as unrestricted reflection upon the self, necessarily tends toward a universality that finds its concrete, geographic correlative in the formation of supratribal, supranational communities such as, for instance, Europe. Why this geographic expansion should have chosen to stop, once and forever, at the Atlantic Ocean and at the Caucasus, Husserl does not say." Noting that "we are speaking of a man of superior good will," de Man does not condemn Husserl for his blindness but instead points to "the pathos" of Husserl's Eurocentrism "at a moment when Europe was about to destroy itself as a center in the name of its unwarranted claim to be the center." Then, in a sentence that is difficult not to read personally, de Man writes, "The point, however, transcends the personal situation."[17] It does, according to de Man, because Husserl's blindness speaks for the blindness inherent in the Western project to found action on truth. It may be impossible not to read de Man's comments on Husserl personally, but a personal reading does not rule out the possibility that there is truth in his argument about an inevitable structure of blindness and insight, truth gained at the cost of much personal error.

To evoke de Man in the present situation may appear to appeal to sensationalism, but my point is to show to what extent poststructuralism, and especially deconstruction, is a historical response to a crisis in historicism from which Western thought has not yet recovered. Indeed, whereas it is fashionable today, as the subtitle of one essay puts it, to see "Historicism in a Deconstructed World," it is more accurate to see deconstruction as a response to a historicized world.[18] To do so does not refute the claim that deconstruction is ahistorical, and it is possible to read de Man's work as an attempt to escape his responsibility for a particular set of historical actions. Nonetheless, it is also possible to see it as an attempt to correct a mistaken view of history to which he once subscribed. Read this way, de Man's work is not an escape from history but an effort to make us rethink what we mean by "history." Most importantly, it challenges the notion that history is a chronological development through linear time, a notion of history assumed by narratives of progressive emergence. I do not, however, need to rely solely on poststructuralist and deconstructive theories to emphasize why skepticism about such historicist narratives is justified. A good old-fashioned American empirical historian, David Hackett Fischer, makes the point just as forcefully.

> Historicism was many things to many people, but in a general way its epistemology was idealist, its politics were antidemocratic, its aesthetics were romantic, and its ethics were organized around the nasty idea that whatever is becoming, is right.
>
> The classical expression of ethical historicism is Schiller's epigram "die Weltgeschichte ist das Weltgericht." This doctrine reduced ethics (and much else) to a province of historiography. And it was radically destructive, not merely of other ethical systems but of itself as well. Ethical historicism com-

monly took one of two untenable forms. Some historicists—Ranke is an eminent example—unwittingly smuggled an ethical system into history, and then discovered it as the objective teaching of history itself. Others later converted ethical historicism into an ethical relativism. Meinecke, for instance, asserted that "nothing can be immoral which comes from the innermost individual character of a being." This doctrine must necessarily become an ethical nihilism. It would prevent any moral judgment against the filth which flowed from "the innermost individual character" of many Nazi beings. Historicism, relativism, nihilism. There is *no* stopping place in this downward descent to nothingness.[19]

Fischer's description places in perspective the charge that poststructuralism is a nihilistic escape from history. Quite the opposite, at its best it is an unflinching historical response to the nihilism into which at least one version of historicism led. An important effort to rethink our relation to the cultural past without succumbing to errors in the recent past, it provides a powerful warning to those adopting narratives of progressive emergence. Those warnings are succinctly summed up by Werner Sollors's survey of the field of United States ethnic scholarship. Sollors is no more a poststructuralist than Fischer, but he remains acutely aware of the dangers of old-fashioned historicist narratives.

The problem with numerous ethnic histories that are based on a writer's descent, he argues, is that they "all but annihilate polyethnic art movements, movements of individual and cultural interaction, and the pervasiveness of cultural syncretism in America." Rather than increase our understanding of "the cultural interplay and contacts among writers of different backgrounds," individual narratives of emergence too often create new traditions of "insiders" and "outsiders." Furthermore, such histories legitimize a "static notion of eternal groups," much as nineteenth-century historicism's nationalistic narratives of emergence legitimized national and racial identities by positing the existence of boundaries between cultures.[20]

Viewed from this perspective such new histories can seem downright dangerous. Despite these dangers, however, they seem to speak to the needs of important segments of our population more than either traditional histories or those new histories that are more rigorously poststructural. To see why we can turn to the narrative structures employed in the early work of Stephen Greenblatt. Greenblatt's early work cannot stand for all poststructuralist efforts to rethink our relation to a cultural past any more than Tompkins's can stand for all efforts that occupy the fields of feminist, ethnic, and postcolonial criticism. It would even be a mistake to call his work poststructuralism proper, if such a thing exists. Nonetheless, his work, especially the early version, is symptomatic of the difficulties

that arise when new historicists draw more rigorously on poststructuralism in order to avoid the errors of the reconstructionists. The nature of
these difficulties helps to explain why reconstructionists find poststructuralist assumptions of limited use, even when combined with the militant
call to historicize put forth by proponents of the new historicism associated with the work of Greenblatt.

· IV ·

The most obvious poststructural influence on the early Greenblatt is the
work of Foucault. Foucault, however, never worried about constructing a
model for literary texts. In this regard, Greenblatt is equally indebted to
Bakhtin, as are many reconstructionists. Bakhtin's appeal to Greenblatt
indicates that, like reconstructionists, he hopes to combat official, monological histories by listening to voices that have been repressed or marginalized. But if reconstructionists operate by identifying emerging new
voices that must be reckoned with, Greenblatt, more often than not, con-
centrates on letting us hear various voices within canonical texts by returning them to the dynamic field of social conflict in which they were
originally produced.

If we want to understand why his histories are prone to attack from
those hoping to establish new traditions, Greenblatt's continued concern
with canonical texts is an obvious place to start. This is not to imply that he
is inattentive to questions of race, gender, and class. Quite the contrary,
he is very sensitive to issues of domination and power. But precisely because those issues get played out within the sphere of the "dominant"
literary tradition, Greenblatt is accused of containing the subversive force
of the conflictual voices that he lets us hear. Since Greenblatt's intent is
not to contain conflict, we need to ask why his early work evokes such
charges. Eventually that question will lead to his uses of Foucault. But
first we need to see what sort of history Foucault helped him to overcome.

If reconstructionists start with the desire to expand the official canon
and eventually find poststructuralism of limited use in doing so, it would
be more accurate to say that Greenblatt's call for a new historicism developed more directly out of poststructuralist criticism of traditional historical criticism. Taking very seriously charges, like de Man's, that critics too
often appealed to history in order to close off readings, Greenblatt works
to keep historical readings open. Thus Greenblatt contrasts the new historicism to an older one "concerned with discovering a single political
vision, usually identical to that said to be held by an entire literate class or
indeed the entire population." Once discovered, that vision served as a

"stable point of reference, beyond contingency, to which literary interpretation can securely refer."[21]

Although Greenblatt does not elaborate on this description, it is worth noting that there are both materialist and idealist versions of such histories. In the materialist version the political vision is determined by social and economic forces that have the status of independent variables. In contrast, literature as part of the superstructure is a dependent variable. Thus the task of the literary historian is to show how changes in literature react to a predetermined narrative about social and economic transformations. Although in this tradition literature is a dependent variable, it is often (but not always) granted a status of relatively greater independence from social and economic forces than an institution such as the law. This greater independence allows literature, or at least great literature, to occupy a position outside of social and economic forces, a position from which it offers us a privileged view of the complexities of a historical moment.

This privileged status granted to great works might recall formalism. But there is an important difference. In formalism great works transcend the contingency of history altogether in order to inhabit a different temporal order. In this older brand of historical criticism great works transcend their age only in the sense that they give us a privileged view of what their age was really like.

Literature's independence from social and economic forces can become so considerable that a reversal takes place and literature itself becomes the independent variable. In this idealist, as opposed to materialist, version of historical criticism great literature, or at least the spirit that it expresses, becomes the motor for social and economic transformations. It may be more accurate to argue that historically the idealist version preceded the materialist, which was, like Marx's inversion of Hegel, a response to an idealist tradition. Nonetheless, whether literature serves as the most complex reflection of historical transformations or as a cause of them, a study of great works of literature can provide the most accurate account of the development of human civilization.

Greenblatt's histories challenge both the idealist and materialist versions of this tradition by trying to restore the historical contingency that their stable visions repress. Most importantly, he challenges the very possibility of having an independent variable that could determine historical transformations. Historical change is not determinate but overdetermined. If all social practices are dependent variables, there can be no self-contained political vision that literature either reflects or expresses. Instead, a political vision is continually determining and being determined by a complex field of interrelated social practices. Or to put it in terms more familiar to literary critics, there is no predetermined context in which we can place a text in order to understand it historically. On the synchronic level, the text is itself part of the context that is supposed to help us understand it. As a result, no text can achieve a position outside of its context to reflect it. On the diachronic level, the context, including that of a historical period, is at least in part the construction of present critics.

In challenging the text/context opposition Greenblatt hopes to avoid the impulse to appeal to history only to close off readings of both text and context. To be sure, placing a text in a historical context can open up aspects previously ignored or misunderstood. Too often, however, this opening leads to a final resting point of stability. On the one hand, we can read through a stable, if highly complex, text in order to get a picture of an age. On the other, a stable historical context can anchor our reading of a text. One of the most important ways that Greenblatt tries to avoid such reductionism is by refusing to adopt the commonplace narrative strategy that begins with a discussion of historical background and then moves to an analysis of a text that is either revealed by or reveals that background. Greenblatt, in contrast, combats the metaphor of foreground and background by placing all social practices, including those of literature and the theatre, on the same plane. In doing so, he is strongly influenced by Geertz's method of "thick description" that I mentioned in the last chapter. But since his concern remains that of literary texts, he adds his own twist to thick descriptions designed to deal with the overdetermination of cultural formations. Starting with the analysis of a particular historical event, he then cuts to the analysis of a particular literary text. The point is not to show that the literary text reflects the historical event but to create a field of energy between the two so that we come to see the event as a social text and the literary text as a social event. Furthermore, in choosing the examples that he does, Greenblatt does not claim to represent the totality of Renaissance culture. Instead, he brings various representational practices into a relationship of identity and difference. Their similarities show how they fit into a common *episteme*. Their differences preserve the sense of conflict that monological historical narratives repress.

As far as the social institution of literature is concerned, Greenblatt demonstrates how the boundary between literary text or performance and other social practices is not a fixed and stable one but one in a constant process of negotiation and reconstitution. Indeed, one reason that the Renaissance is fascinating for the new historicists is that the boundaries around the institution of literature as we know it today are starting to be defined. As Montrose notes, "During the sixteenth and seventeenth centuries, the separation of Literature and Art from explicitly didactic and political discourses or from such disciplines as history or moral and natural philosophy was as yet incipient."[22] Institutionalized literary criticism created a boundary between such discursive practices and the one that today we call literary. New historical analysis renders that boundary problematic in order to reopen texts to a dynamic field of discursive play. Rather than solve the problem of history, such analysis works to keep it open.

· V ·

As invigorating as Greenblatt's strategy has proved for Renaissance studies, it is not without problems. One of the most obvious involves selection. If, as Greenblatt's narrative strategy implies, all social practices are on the same plane, on what basis does he select some social practices rather than others to juxtapose with particular literary texts? The very fact of their selection seems to imply their importance, just as my selection of Greenblatt to speak for this version of the new historicism implies his. But if some social practices are more important than others, are not we back in a position of assuming that some have at least relatively more independence than others? And if this is the case, should not we then try to offer an explanation as to why? To be sure, Greenblatt's response could be the pragmatic one that we need no foundational account of why his selections work. All that matters is that they work. Nonetheless, given Greenblatt's masterful style and his ability to find connections previously overlooked, it is easy to imagine that he could make numerous selections work. Indeed, as Walter Cohen has pointed out, in two separate essays Greenblatt brings Shakespeare's Henriad into relation with different social practices. The problem is, however, that the two draw opposite conclusions about its relationship to royal power.

Such contradictions have led Cohen to accuse the new historicism of a commitment to "arbitrary connectedness."[23] The charge is a serious one, and I will return to it in later discussions. For the moment, however, it is sufficient to note how it challenges Greenblatt's claim to undo the text/ context opposition. For if Greenblatt's narrative strategy creates the impression that he is reading history out of particular social practices and texts rather than first placing them in a context that predetermines how we will read them, Cohen's charge reminds us that his very selection of material already assumes a particular context. The dilemma is not new, and Greenblatt is aware of it. Nonetheless, its persistence suggests that even Greenblatt's mode of narrative presentation does not escape various versions of the hermeneutic circle formulated by old-fashioned historicists who, in trying to understand the past through its textual traces, realized that their reading of those traces could not begin without assuming some preliminary context for them. Since that context depends upon our sense of how the past relates to the present, the hermeneutical problem of text and context is intricately involved with the one of past and present. In diachronic narratives of progressive emergence the relationship between past and present is clearly spelled out, as the historian creates a usable past by selecting past material so as to identify a tradition leading to the present. In Greenblatt's synchronic analyses of Renaissance culture, the relation between past and present is not immediately apparent. Nonetheless, one is implied. For instance, it does not take much imagination to see why Renaissance new historicists were obsessed with displays of power and theatricality in the Reagan era; nor why scholars who experienced the radical promise of the late 1960s and are now in fairly comfortable academic positions pay careful attention to how subversive moments are contained. Indeed, there are moments in Greenblatt's work when a diachronic narrative about containment explicitly surfaces.

For example, in his attempt to historicize Bakhtin's analysis of the carnivalesque in Rabelais, Greenblatt asserts that "Rabelais's fantasy of perfect aristocratic liberty, like his fantasy of unending popular carnival, is generated in response to a culture increasingly intolerant of disorder in society, in the individual, and in art." The diachronic narrative that helps determine Greenblatt's selection of details to include in his synchronic analysis of the Renaissance is a Foucauldian one in which even forms of resistance become absorbed into an increasingly wider system of control, or as Greenblatt puts it, "the sense of a literary, social, and religious world hardening in its commitment to order, discipline, and decorum."[24]

Of course, Rousseau-like narratives of increasing social control and domination are not new. Marx's account of the rise of capitalism is one example. Many of the attempts to add new voices to the canon are others. After all, something has to account for why marginal traditions became marginalized. But when combined with a particular poststructuralist use of overdetermination a narrative of increasing control becomes different in kind from others. For instance, a marxist narrative of capitalist control can point to a determinate set of social and particularly economic forces that explain historical transformation. Furthermore, it posits the existence of a resistant group—the proletariat—that can be the agent of further change. Cohen's criticism of the new historicism's commitment to arbitrary connectedness is firmly lodged within this tradition. For instance, Jean E. Howard and Marion F. O'Connor describe it as an argument that "critical movements arise for *determinant* historical and political reasons, and *sustaining* the oppositional force of *emergent* critical practices remains a crucial theoretical and practical problem"[25] (my emphases).

Howard's and O'Connor's description helps focus on reasons for the tension between the reconstructive and poststructuralist aspects of the new historicism. An oppositional critical practice or voice sustains its force by referring to determinant historical and political reasons for its emergence. The notion of overdetermination reminds us, however, that in order to assess those determinant reasons it has to repress (or marginalize) other reasons. Once we adopt this perspective, the oppositional force of emergent critical practices or groups seems to depend upon narrative acts of repression that make them prone to charges of perpetuating the play of domination that they criticize. For instance, in his response to Cohen, Greenblatt focusses on Cohen's complaint that "new historicists are likely to seize upon something out of the way, obscure, even bizarre: dreams, popular or aristocratic festivals, denunciations of witchcraft, sexual treatises, diaries and autobiographies, descriptions of clothing, reports on disease, birth and death records, accounts of insanity."[26] That Cohen, "an intelligent Marxist critic," should consider these concerns bizarre is to Greenblatt an indication of "how narrow the boundaries of historical understanding have become" and "how much these boundaries need to be broken."[27]

Greenblatt's point, as always, is well-taken. But it fails to consider the risks involved in playing the role of a modern day Faustus by trying to break existing boundaries of historical understanding. That blindness surfaces as a contradiction in Greenblatt's brief response to Cohen. Greenblatt begins by describing the formalism that trained him to consider every part of a text important. "Thousands of pages," he laments, "were dutifully churned out to prove that the zany subplot of The Changeling was cunningly integrated into the tragic main plot or that every tedious bit of clowning in Doctor Faustus was richly significant" (155). As such Greenblatt's is a typical complaint against a previous generation's fidelity to the notion of organic form. What is strange, however, is that this complaint occurs only a few paragraphs away from his articulate challenge to the charge that the new historicism seizes on obscure or bizarre social practices for analysis. Could it be that a member of the present generation of graduate students might some day lament that thousands of pages were dutifully churned out to prove that every zany or tedious bit of social activity was richly significant?

In fact, Greenblatt's mode of analysis owes more to his formalist training than his attack on it would indicate. Starting with something that seems out of the way, a typical Greenblatt essay ends by making us adjust our sense of Renaissance culture so that what once seemed strange no longer seems so, just as formalists made us adjust our sense of a text in order to account for a detail that we originally found zany. To be sure, there is an important difference between formalists' confinement to the boundaries of a few classical texts and Greenblatt's expansion of the textual field to include all social practices. By showing significance in what was previously considered bizarre or out of the way he restores the importance of what previous historical accounts had repressed or marginalized.

But this very emphasis on the equal significance of all social practices comes into conflict with Greenblatt's expressed concern with contingency. Granted, Greenblatt remains concerned with contingency, but, as we shall see, his concern involves the marking of boundaries. In terms of the details of social practices, the effect of his analysis is not to stress contingency but to show how what was previously considered accidental is richly significant. If this were not the case, Greenblatt would be able to take Cohen's criticism of his choice of the bizarre much more gracefully. Something that is bizarre is, after all, eccentric; that is, something out of center. Greenblatt's power, however, lies in his ability to bring what seemed out of center into clearer focus by making us see new systems of relations. Or, as Joseph Litvak puts it, new historicism supplements post-structuralism by "motivating the arbitrary."[28] The problem is, of course, once the arbitrary is motivated, it loses its arbitrary status. What Greenblatt fails to see is that the real thrust of Cohen's complaint is not merely that the new historicism has a commitment to "arbitrary connection." Instead, he disagrees with the narrative of social connection that Greenblatt employs in order to grant significance to something *seemingly* arbitrarily chosen.

At first we might ask why this is a problem. After all, a marxist concerned with acts of repression should welcome efforts to grant significance to the previously marginalized. Just as formalist critics were able to redeem various inexplicable aspects of a text by fitting them into a significant pattern, so Greenblatt would seem to redeem aspects of the past previously considered eccentric or bizarre. To see why Greenblatt's is not an act of redemption we can briefly extend the comparison between the new historicism and Auerbach and Spitzer that I began last chapter.

If Greenblatt remains indebted to his New Critical formalist training, his way of proceeding more closely resembles that of these two philologists. Suspicious of how preconceived contexts can limit our readings, both Spitzer and Auerbach, like Greenblatt, proceed inductively, starting with a detail and reading outward. According to Spitzer this procedure grows out of his philological training. In what could almost be a description of a Greenblatt essay, Spitzer notes that "my personal way has been from the observed detail to ever broadening units which rest, to an increasing degree, on speculation." Dealing with "the all-too-human, with the interrelated and intertwined aspects of human affairs," philology proceeds by "the inductive way, which seeks to show significance in the apparently futile." Assuming "the attitude which sees all manifestations of man as equally serious," it attempts "to discover significance in the detail."[29] As I noted last chapter, Spitzer's brilliant analysis of a Sunkist orange juice ad and his early book on Italian slang indicate that his attention to detail did not stop with the boundaries of literary texts. In Auerbach the philological concern with detail led to his celebration of realistic works that make visible "the unprejudiced, precise, interior and exterior representations of the *random* moment in the lives of different people".[30] (my emphasis)

To note similarities between Greenblatt and Auerbach and Spitzer is, however, immediately to call attention to differences. Both philologists continued to assume an organic unity of great works of art. More important for present purposes, both maintained an older historicist's faith in the progressive emergence of truth through history. According to Spitzer, the philologian will "continue the pursuit of the microscopic because he sees therein the microcosmic; he will practice that Andacht zum Kleinen which Jacob Grimm has prescribed; he will go on filling his little cards with dates and examples, in the hope that the supernal light will shine over them and bring out the clear lines of truth."[31] Less prone to theological metaphors than Spitzer, Auerbach places his faith in the emergence of the common man, in a "common life of mankind on earth" in which random moments of "daily life" are "comparatively independent of the controversial and unstable orders over which men fight and despair."[32] To abandon such visions for Greenblatt's Foucauldian one is to produce a very different sense of what an attention to random detail will reveal.

Greenblatt's attraction to Foucault grows out of his distrust of marxism's totalized worldview. Claiming to be a force of liberation, marxism, by fitting all into a master narrative, too easily became one of the repressors. Against its determinant narrative of social formation, Foucault adopts an overdetermined one that makes room for the marginalized, the bizarre, the excluded. The argument that all acts of representation produce exclusions may seem pessimistic, but the very structure of repression guarantees the existence of a marginal that resists absorption into a culture's master narratives. A problem occurs, however, when, as Greenblatt's narratives attempt to do, the marginal is granted significance. This problem can be seen in terms of the lapse into organicism that I described in the last chapter.

An overdetermined model of texts and society is at odds with an organic one. Starting with an overdetermined model, Greenblatt champions the marginalized. When his marvelous talent for establishing connections grants the previously marginalized new significance, however, he too often lapses back into organicism. To put it another way, to motivate the arbitrary is, in Alan Liu's words, not to "diminish formalism so much as to amplify it—to the scale of the world."[33] Discontent with the narrowness of New Critical formalism, Greenblatt makes a move similar to the one made years ago by Northrop Frye. In *The Anatomy of Criticism* Frye did not so much abandon the New Critics' organicism as extend it to the entire body of the field of literature. Similarly, Greenblatt does not so much abandon organicism as extend the organic text to society-at-large. When combined with a Foucauldian vision that locates resistance in overdetermination such a "cultural poetics" produces a diachronic narrative quite different from the organic visions of Spitzer and Auerbach.

For Spitzer and Auerbach to create organic connections that grant significance to the previously excluded is to produce a narrative revealing the emergence of truth or the common man. From a Foucauldian perspective, however, such narratives expand the sphere of domination. Or, as Cohen puts it, Greenblatt's commendable desire to show the significance in what was previously considered bizarre or out of the way "ends up, if not with something like a totalitarian model, then at least with a sense of the almost inevitable defeat of the poor, the innocent, and the oppressed."[34] So long as this is the case, it is worth considering whether there might be important strategic reasons for maintaining certain boundaries, such as those between the oppressed and dominant, for when that boundary is broken it is all too clear who wins. At the same time, as I will argue next chapter, even that boundary can too easily imply a simple binary opposition.

In his obsession with breaking boundaries, Greenblatt seems to forget that boundaries played a double role in Renaissance culture. In his introduction to *Representing the Renaissance* he notes that "a heightened interest in boundaries emerged in Western Europe in the late sixteenth and early seventeenth centuries." It is regarding these boundaries that Greenblatt's concern for contingency is felt, as he attempts to restore the moment in which the "precise marking of borders was still in its early stages," so that "for the most part the period made do with frontier-regions rather than linear boundaries." In returning us to that contingent moment when many of our current boundaries were being drawn, Greenblatt, while still keeping an "eye out for boundary stones," invites us to rethink boundaries, not only boundaries between nations and between literature and other discursive systems, but also between normal and bizarre activities.[35]

We should remember, however, that the Renaissance was also a period noted for challenging accepted boundaries. In terms of global politics this resulted, not only in the marking of boundaries, but in their expansion to bring strange and bizarre "new worlds" under European control. When Greenblatt combines his effort to break existing boundaries of understanding with a Foucauldian notion of power, the result too closely resembles the logic of imperialism to be of use to those intent on preserving an oppositional space. Or to cleanse my language of suggestions that Greenblatt is motivated by a will to power, in making our understanding of history so diffuse, Greenblatt's breaking of boundaries risks defusing attempts at organized resistance.

I am fully aware that I will be accused of misreading Foucault, who has been celebrated precisely because he works against marxism's totalized sense of history.[36] But it is not merely a case of resentful revenge that causes a marxist like Cohen to accuse Foucault himself of totalizing. As I will try to establish, one of the biggest problems with poststructuralism in general is that despite explicit claims to the contrary, many of its disciples lapse back into totalizing visions from which they would break. Aware of this problem, Greenblatt himself has worked hard to combat criticism of the sort I have leveled against him. In the last chapter I will turn to his efforts to do so in his latest book, *Shakespearean Negotiations*. Part of the difference between the earlier and later work has to do with boundaries.

As Greenblatt acknowledges, boundaries between foreground and background, text and context, bizarre and normal do exist, "but they are not intrinsic to the texts; rather they are made up and constantly redrawn by artists, audiences, and readers."[37] It is this redrawing of boundaries that a rigorous adherence to poststructuralist assumptions renders so problematic, and it is the redrawing of boundaries that someone like Cohen finds lacking in Greenblatt's work. In this regard, one function of narratives of progressive emergence for those intent on maintaining oppositional status is clear: like the nationalistic narratives of an older historicism, they mark boundaries between themselves and others. If they risk labelling some social practices bizarre or out of the way, by establishing boundaries they are able to identify both an agent to transform the way things are—a repressed class or group—and the particular social institutions that most help keep particular oppressive groups in power—the legal system, for instance, as opposed to descriptions of clothing. In short, they help produce an account of what Cohen calls the "necessary and sufficient conditions for either containment or subversion."[38]

In contrast, Greenblatt at least implicitly calls into question the possibility of producing such determinant accounts because the very border between containment and subversion is subject to historical contingency and thus always prone to shifts and redefinitions. Oppositional movements depend on identifying a seat of power to oppose. But notions like Gramsci's of hegemony call attention to how difficult it is to oppose the ruling order when power is dispersed throughout society. The task is even more difficult, if recognizing the abuses made in the name of opposition, we, along with Foucault, distrust even the Gramscian call to organize oppositional power into a political party. For instance, in contrast to the slogan, "Down with the king," Foucault's "We have to think power without the king" is not so much a call to action as a cautionary reminder of how difficult it is to achieve an oppositional position. The two aspects of the new historicism that I have identified can be characterized by their opposite responses to this dilemma.

The Foucauldian aspect tries to avoid perpetuating the play of domination by exposing what power has repressed. In continually calling attention to the costs involved in instituting any discursive system, this strategy has a certain moral attraction as it tries to avoid any positive statements that would make it part of the existing power structure. But one thing that it seems to avoid asking is: what are the costs involved in its own mode of discourse? An obvious one for excluded groups, who want to seize or at least share power, is that by positioning itself on the margins, it virtually guarantees its own failure. "Perhaps the humility of failure," Paul Bové tells us, "is the only ground for being in opposition since success depends on a very complex knowledge of and ability to manipulate determinative politics, discourses, and institutions—on professional competencies and social privileges. . . ."[39] If, as Bové argues, the radical Foucault is one who demands that we "put aside" the "temptations to build a better world, to discover the truth about human life,"[40] to become a disciple to his thought is, to my mind, to pay too high a cost. Indeed, whereas Bové claims that Foucault's radicalism negates any utopian impulse, his reading comes very close to a politically naive utopianism. The only way that a practice of failure could have a substantive political effect would be for those in power to play "fair" by halting their admittedly successful present practices. What, we need to ask, is going to compel them to do so? Certainly not a moral yearning for failure.[41]

Not feeling able to afford the luxury of failure, many claiming to speak for those excluded work to achieve their oppositional position, not through negation, but by constructing a clear-cut target to oppose and clear-cut targets to work for. Starting from the position of the already marginalized, they do not waste much time agonizing over what new marginalizations their positions will create, and instead seem perfectly willing to share the costs and risks involved in holding power.

As in the case of Tompkins, these two aspects of the new historicism—critical acts of negation and redefinition—often exist side by side so that we can clearly see the tension that I have been trying to describe. To be sure, that tension can be explained within a poststructuralist framework. Any creation of a new history, we are told, involves an act of repression. What seems to be repressed in new historicists' efforts at reconstruction are the very poststructuralist assumptions that are of use in their deconstruction of existing histories. As a general account this poststructuralist reminder of the inevitability of repression is hard to dispute, and it would be relatively easy to accept it and conclude that the tension between the reconstructive and poststructuralist wings of the new historicism is inevitable. Tension is not really tension, however, if we rest content with it.

Continuing to wrestle with it, inevitable or not, I want to suggest a third alternative by focusing on what poststructuralists' accounts of Western history themselves seem prone to repress. To do so is to emphasize why, despite their obvious tension, the two wings remain compatible.

· VI ·

For an example of what too often gets repressed in poststructuralist accounts of history, we can turn to what would seem to be an illustration of how a Foucauldian commitment to the contingency of history undercuts Cohen's dream of arriving at the "necessary and sufficient conditions for either containment or subversion." In Renaissance England there was an acknowledged conflict between the Crown and Parliament. Generally representing the interests of the rising middle class, Parliament insisted on rule by law, which has turned out to be one of the middle class's most effective means of maintaining power in today's Western democracies. At the time, however, it was a powerful weapon to oppose the authority of the Crown. How, then, are we to interpret something like Chief Justice Coke's judgment that the courts, not the King, have the authority to interpret common law? Is it to be seen as a subtle way to contain opposition through appealing to the authority of rule by law, or an act opposing the power of the King? Is it an act of containment or subversion?

No set of determinant conditions, I would argue, would be able to decide that question for us, because, depending on what historical perspective we adopt, it is both. But our ability to consider it both an act of containment and an act of subversion does not mean that at a particular historical moment it did not have a subversive force. To fit Coke's challenge to the Crown into a diachronic narrative in which the West progressively hardens in its commitment to order is to repress the oppositional force that it had at a particular moment in history. Unfortunately, such repressions all too easily accompany the effort to display power in all segments of Renaissance life. For, whereas that effort can, on the one hand, confirm the Foucauldian notion that power is dispersed throughout society, it can, on the other, give the impression that power emanates from a single source—the Crown. In the Renaissance, however, it still makes sense to identify at least two competing seats of power, rather than to imply either a total dispersal or centralization of it.[42]

The problem I have with much poststructuralist analysis is this tendency of the anti-totalizers toward totalization. It varies from claims to know what "always already" will be the case to tracing the root of all evil to Western "phallogocentrism." Granted, this is only a tendency and not an inevitability, and both poststructuralists and new historians can claim that the tendency violates their own emphasis on "differance" or contingency. Nonetheless, the tendency is widespread enough to demand explanation. It is in part, I suspect, an overreaction to the failure of the Western tradition to live up to its modernist promise of emancipation and enlightenment. Emphasizing the failure of narratives of progressive emergence, poststructuralist discourse too often encourages the implicit adoption of a narrative of digressive emergence, in which increasing control replaces the dream of increasing emancipation. So far I have stressed how these narratives' capacity for infinite containment puts them in tension with efforts to establish an oppositional tradition. What I want to stress now, however, is how, with a little adjustment, such totalized accounts can serve the needs of those attempting to preserve an oppositional position. Needing to construct a monolithic "other" to oppose, such critics can easily buy into Greenblatt's diachronic narrative about the West's commitment to order. All that they need to do is evoke the privileged position of marginalization to exempt the new voices that they champion from the West's totalizing logic.

If I am correct to see the new historicism united by a tendency to adopt totalized accounts of the West's failed project of modernity, a slightly different explanation for the tensions that plague it presents itself. Rather than explain that tension by the truism that any attempt to produce the new involves an act of repression, we can look at one specific thing that is repressed; that is, a much more complicated account of modernity. Indeed, as my juxtaposition of modernism and new historicism suggested, despite the new historicism's acknowledged debt to poststructuralism, its very label reveals a deeper, if less acknowledged, debt to the tradition of the modern that it places into question. Caught in the ironic situation that in order to stay true to its desire to help bring about the new it must somehow remain within the tradition of the modern, the new historicism finds itself in tension with accounts of the modern typically produced by proponents of postmodernism. For instance, William Spanos sees the postmodern as resisting "the West's Re-collective mania to recuperate the One" by providing a "destructive projective impulse" that cannot promise something "new" or a "truly new epoch."[43]

To be sure, Spanos cannot speak for all postmodernists. Nonetheless, his own recuperation of "the One" when speaking of the West represents a tendency that I find all too prevalent, even if, as in the case of poststructuralist and reconstructive new historicists, it can take different forms. If those different responses help to account for the tension between the two aspects of the new historicism, to recognize their common tendency to totalize is to suggest a different way to interpret reconstructionists' seemingly forgetful reoccupation of discredited historicist narratives. As we have seen, the use of such narratives to exempt reconstructionists from the totalized account of the West produces glaring contradictions. But those contradictions point to the possibility that the project of modernity is not, after all, totally discredited, since it is precisely in drawing on that tradition that oppositional movements gain much of their positive power. Precisely in their contradictions, then, reconstructionists suggest how important it is for a "new" historicism to avoid discrediting the entire project of modernity.[44]

This is not to say that their use of historicist narratives is without problems. But those problems may have less to do with the fact that such narratives inevitably produce a sense of identity than the particular "others" that they construct in order to achieve their identities. Perhaps even poststructuralist attacks on identity *per se* need to be reconsidered, since such attacks depend upon identifying something called "identity" to oppose. Indeed, my own procedure indicates how important I feel identifying certain traditions or movements is for historical understanding. Such identifications need not imply that traditions or movements are fixed, essential entities, and they can be made with the self-conscious awareness that they are in part heuristic constructs of the historian. But only in part, for it would be ahistorical to deny that people have self-consciously constructed their own traditions and movements. As E. P. Thompson's title, *The Making of the English Working Class*, should remind us such traditions and movements are not given but result from acts of making, acts that contribute to the making of history.[45] Furthermore, the historian's acts of identification can be contributions to or interventions into debates about the directions that such traditions or movements will take, just as Thompson's was in regards to the English working class and as I hope mine might be in terms of the new historicism. All the more reason, then, that present day historians of the previously marginalized resist the tendency to construct monolithic models of the Western project of modernity.

To illustrate how even important work can be flawed by the construction of such monolithic models, I will start the next chapter by examining the spirited debate sparked by a collection of essays edited by Henry Louis Gates, Jr. entitled 'Race,' Writing, and Difference. I will use that debate to pose two challenges to the new historicism: (1) to imagine narrative strategies that will appropriate for its use the dominant ideology in present day Western democracies, an ideology, not of monolithic exclusion, but pluralistic inclusion, (2) to conceive of an impulse to the modern that it can use in its efforts to construct histories that create a space in which to imagine a new future.

CHAPTER 3.

A Postmodern Modernity?

· I ·

THE TITLE, 'Race,' Writing, and Difference signals that contributors come to their task equipped with poststructuralist armature. It also indicates that their task is to examine connections between writing and the construction of racial categories that have contributed to and enabled historical acts of domination and repression. But their concern for the historical victims of racism, who for these authors have been people of color, comes into tension with the logic of some of the particular poststructuralist assumptions that they adopt.

Those tensions are noted by Tzetan Todorov in his response, which points out some of the problems that I did in examining Jane Tompkins's use of poststructuralism. Poststructuralism proves most valuable when the focus is on the writings of Western colonialists. In these essays the reason for placing race in quotation marks is clear. The concept of race is under erasure. It is a social, not natural, construct, and in examining the documents of colonialism we see how "race" was written into contemporary culture. The problem Todorov sees, however, is that more often than not attempts to establish countertraditions of indigenous voices end up by writing race back into existence. This deconstruction of "race," on the one hand, and its reconstruction, on the other, causes Todorov to lament the preponderance of totalized narratives about the West. For instance, according to Abdul R. JanMohamed, colonialist literature served colonial domination by producing "manichean allegories," "a field of diverse yet interchangeable oppositions between white and black, good and evil, superiority and inferiority." But, as Todorov notes, the contributors too often produce "similarly manichean interpretations, with good and evil simply having switched places." Indeed, JanMohamed ends his own essay by announcing the progressive emergence of a superior group in the process of cornering the market on a desirable form of discourse. "[T]he domain of literary and cultural syncretism," he concludes, "belongs not to colonialist and neocolonialist writers but increasingly to Third World artists."[1]

As might be expected, contributors often attack precisely the values of modernity, especially its Enlightenment version, once celebrated as the particular possession of the West. Universal and humanistic values, the faith in rational, disinterested inquiry, the quest after truth itself are linked to a will to power and domination. Todorov's response to such attacks, like that of Jürgen Habermas, is to see poststructuralism as an extension of historicism's relativism rather than, as I have argued, a reaction to its limitations. As a result, he urges a return to the very enlightenment values of universalism and egalitarianism under attack. Todorov's celebration of those values is no more naive than that of Habermas. He admits that the Enlightenment rarely lived up to its ideals and that "what has been presented as universality has in fact been a fair description of white males in a few Western European countries." Nonetheless, he argues, previous failures "should not lead us to abandon the idea [of universalism], for such an abandonment would lead us to renounce the very idea of shared humanity, and this would be even more dangerous than ethnocentric universalism" (374).

Todorov's insistence on the ideal of a shared humanity is attractive. As he points out, it is an ideal that Gates himself appeals to in his introduction. Nonetheless, Todorov's particular way of maintaining that ideal raises familiar problems. If Todorov complains about the contradiction involved when contributors produce their own manichean allegories, he too seems guilty of contradictions. For instance, Todorov claims that the universalist and egalitarian ideology of the Enlightenment is "as far removed as possible from racialism" (373), only to remark on the same page that "racialism has affinities both with relativism and universalism" (373). This contradiction plays itself out when Todorov draws on his universalist assumptions to dispute Gates's claim that rather than apply existing critical methods to vernacular literature, "we must turn to the black tradition itself to develop theories of criticism indigenous to our literatures." "Is this not," Todorov asks, "to say that the content of a thought depends on the color of the thinker's skin—that is, to practice the very racialism one was supposed to be combatting? This can only be described as cultural apartheid: in order to analyze black literature, one must use concepts formulated by black authors" (376).

But Gates's point is not, as Todorov mistakenly contends, that we must use concepts formulated by black authors to understand the black tradition. Indeed, within African-American studies Gates has been challenged for relying too much on theories borrowed from the white, European tradition. Instead, he argues that the concepts we use should grow out of observation of a tradition and its particularity. Since in his attack on the links between racialism and universalism, Todorov admits that such things as "Japanese culture or Near Eastern traditions" exist and that it is possible to describe them, why not grant Gates his point that an African-

American tradition exists and that the concepts used to discuss it should come from a knowledge of it?

Gates clearly catches Todorov misreading him on an important point. Nonetheless, Gates's response also highlights contradictions similar to the ones we found in Tompkins when a critic simultaneously employs poststructuralist discourse while defending the need to establish critical categories based on indigenous traditions. For instance, it seems strange for someone who attacks universalism to defend his position, as Gates does, by claiming that he is merely doing "what all theorists do" (406). Furthermore, his argument that "One must *know* one's textual terrain before it can be explored; one must know one's literary tradition before it can be theorized about" (406), would seem to contradict the poststructuralist assumption that reading always already takes place within an ideological field. Does Gates really believe in the unmediated existence of a textual terrain that can be explored prior to theorization about it? Or does the very definition of the terrain involve theoretical assumptions? These contradictions, to the side, Gates does zero in on the major weakness in Todorov's effort to defend Enlightenment values.

According to Hans Blumenberg, the Enlightenment evaluated all from "the perspective of the *terminus ad quem* [the point at which the process terminates]" and thus "was incapable of turning its attention to the *terminus a quo* [the point from which the process takes its departure]."[2] Blumenberg makes this observation while discussing the Enlightenment's response to myth and religion. His point is that in understanding history as culminating in its demystified state, the Enlightenment could not understand the unique character of previous ages in terms of what their myths and beliefs had overcome. This inability, Blumenberg argues, made way for the Enlightenment's defeat by historicism.

Similarly, Todorov argues that "concepts are a little bit like workers: in order to measure their real value, one has to know what they can do, not where they come from" (376). Discounting the historical particularity to which a concept responds, Todorov evokes the category of universalism in order to dismiss all narratives that posit the concept of race, a concept that from his enlightened perspective is the product of mere superstition. Ironically, Todorov's method of evaluation has affinities with the sort of dogmatic ideological criticism that elsewhere he opposes. Also a product of the Enlightenment, such criticism assumes a position of knowing the truth from which it can judge all other false claims to truth. To make this point is not to deny Todorov's reasons for questioning narratives that assume the existence of race. To be sure, there are good reasons for his judgment, since similar narratives have proved extremely dangerous. But there is also a danger in judging narratives and concepts without paying attention to what they are trying to overcome. Such an understanding need not lead to a relativistic inability eventually to judge, but it will be impossible to achieve if we are not willing to relinquish the perspective of the *terminus ad quem* as our point of judgment. For instance, judging from the perspective of universalism, Todorov seems unable to hear differences in what to him appear to be the same narrative. But whereas it is important to call attention to the risks involved in reoccupying narratives previously used in discredited ways, it is also possible that when put to use to overcome previous exclusions old-fashioned narrative structures might have different functions from their original ones. Of course, if this is true, as Todorov himself argues, the notion of universalism need not be abandoned just because it has previously been put to improper uses. What is dangerous is a premature evocation of it.

For an example of how premature use of universalism as a standard of judgment can deny voices that should be heard, we can turn to the debate in the United States over affirmative action legislation. Relying on values of universalism and egalitarianism a number of respected legal figures argue that such laws are unconstitutional examples of "reverse discrimination." In doing so they see themselves in the tradition of Justice John Marshall Harlan, who in his dissent in the segregation case of *Plessy v. Ferguson* (1896) countered the racism of a Louisiana "Jim Crow" law by appealing to the ideal of a "color-blind" Constitution.[3] In judging present legislation according to the universal standard of a color-blind Constitution the opponents of affirmative action certainly seem to have placed themselves in a consistent tradition of combatting discrimination based on race. But to adopt such universal standards as an achieved condition from which to judge rather than as an ideal to be worked for is to deny the point of view of nonwhites whose present conditions are at least partially the result of discrimination made possible when the Constitution was not interpreted as color-blind. As a result, nonwhites face the possibility that a color-blind Constitution will be interpreted as the law of the land just in time to deny them a chance to overcome conditions allowed when the courts were less enlightened. In order "to measure [concepts'] real value" by "what they can do," it is very important to know where those concepts, like affirmative action, come from, for part of what they can do is work to overcome past conditions of inequality.

This appeal to historical understanding should not be misconstrued as a claim to have solved the heated debate over affirmative action, although my own position should be clear. Instead, my point is that prematurely to adopt a standard of universalism is to prejudge the outcome of the conflict because it renders even people as intent as Todorov is on hearing other voices incapable of discriminating between important differences. Todorov's ahistorical universalism is especially apparent in his misunderstanding of what it means to put race in quotation marks. Todorov assumes that the erasure of race implies that race does not exist. As a result, he puts the project of the entire collection into question when he asks, "If 'racial differences' do not exist, how can they possibly influence literary texts" (371)? But the point of putting race in quotation marks is not that race does not exist. To be sure, putting race under erasure implies that it is not a natural category. But just because it is not a natural category does not mean that it does not exist. Race is, after all, a real construct in our world, one that the contributors hope to alter. In appealing to universalism to deny its historical existence, Todorov risks ignoring the historical problems that accompany its constructed reality. Indeed, a wiser argument might be that it is universalism that does not yet exist. It can still, however, remain a goal to work for as a way of overcoming the constructed racial differences that do. There is a crucial difference between striving for universalism and assuming that it is an already existing condition upon which we can base our judgments. In terms of race what universalism entails remains to be imagined.

· II ·

Todorov agrees that race should be put in quotation marks because he (mistakenly) believes that doing so implies a universal state in which race does not exist. The problems with that position are made even clearer when we look at the argument of another respondent, Houston A. Baker, Jr. Concerned that putting race in quotation marks gives a misleading sense about the nature of racialism in present day societies, Baker notes that calling attention to race as a cultural, not natural, construct does not explain why New York cab drivers refuse to pick him, a black man, up. Race not only has real effects in the world; it also is linked to recognizable physiological differences, like skin color. Rather than join liberal white critics in placing the notion of race under erasure, Baker feels that a black critic is justified in evoking the very category used previously to exploit blacks in order to produce a "unifying discourse" to identify and celebrate their tradition. Baker is fully aware that to do so invites charges of reverse racism, and he refers to a symposium where two leading anthropologists at the University of Pennsylvania insisted that "talk of 'racial' difference as a *positive* aspect of Afro-American life sounded like biology 'some two hundred years ago'" (385). Such talk, Baker insists, is not a return to old racial categories but "inversive discourse" designed to turn the "bad joke of 'race'" (386) to its advantage. What Baker misses in the various essays that Gates collected is the presence of the indigenous voices that Gates himself feels must be attended to.

Baker clearly counters Todorov's Enlightenment refusal to consider the point from which a process takes its departure. For Baker narrative structures and concepts once used to exclude can now be put to use by the excluded. To be sure, rigorous poststructuralists will always be able to point to new exclusions created by Baker's inversive discourse. But in making that argument they reveal their affinities with ahistorical universalists who argue that affirmative action is reverse discrimination. Yes, exclusions take place, but they are not necessarily the same in kind. The exclusions of African Americans caused by segregation were much more absolute than the exclusions of white males caused by affirmative action, which is not to say that we should pretend that they do not take place. Indeed, it may be more than an irony of history that precisely at the moment when women and ethnics in this country sense the possibility of emergence and the establishment of a somewhat autonomous identity, a theory arises from the still predominantly white, male European academy declaring that notions of emergence and a centered self are bourgeois and reactionary. Perhaps those that have previously been denied representation feel a need for narratives of emergence that continue to prove so effective in drawing people into a united movement, narratives that continue to move people.

Baker's argument raises an important challenge to criticism leveled against revisionist histories that reoccupy old-fashioned narrative structures. For him it is the uses put to those structures, not the structures themselves, that are discredited. In responding to him I can clarify my own position, which is by no means to deny the historical importance of such revisionist narratives. It is, however, to challenge his celebration of "inversive discourse." We can start to see why by articulating an important difference between Gates and Baker.

Baker is as critical of Gates's reliance on poststructuralist discourse as is Todorov, although for different reasons. Poststructuralism, he argues, inherits the dualism of the Enlightenment that produced both debunkers and rationalists. Celebrating the debunker, he distrusts the rationalist and associates Gates's faith in the "development of subtle and searching modes of 'reading'" with an attempt to achieve a "transcendent academic (rationalist?) discourse which escapes the pitfalls of error and anachronism." Nonetheless, he admits that even this version of European discourse can be appropriated for indigenous use. In using poststructuralist discourse to his advantage Gates has produced his own inversive discourse. Gates is, according to Baker, "invading the territories of the Western Enlightenment and appropriating to his own *vale* the entire panoply of issues held in trust for so many years by white males" (395). This act of appropriation, what Baker calls "Caliban's triple play," "clears the (U.S.) bases in Third World geographies, providing space for poetry, a song, a sound rather than a sight, cite, or site for further Western duels—and dualities" (395).

This final image highlights the problems that I have with Baker's solution. As Baker well knows, a vision in which duels and dualities were to be overcome in order to clear out an open space was one often appealed to in order to justify the colonization of indigenous cultures whose difference was read as a duality. Just as JanMohamed's manichean allegories are too easily merely reversed, so Baker's inversive discourse seems to perpetuate the very dualities that he condemns. If this complaint sounds like the one charging affirmative action with reverse discrimination, there is an important difference. Affirmative action is still guided by a universal goal to eliminate exclusions based on race. To be sure, Baker's vision of a clear space for unencumbered song may act as such a goal. But if so, he depends upon the very non-debunking, Enlightenment attitudes that he claims to distrust. Indeed, Baker's characterization of the Enlightenment as the producer of dualities followed by his clear choice of one over the other makes me wonder if the cleared space he imagines will make room for different voices or only one. Put another way, can Caliban's triple play be separated from his call to burn books?

To put the question this way is to emphasize that my problem with Baker is not his call to listen to indigenous voices. Even Todorov, who claims that race does not exist, admits that he learned the most from the contributions "devoted to writings by Afro-American authors" (371). Their voices need to be heard. But when I listen to them, I hear more than an inversion of dominant discourse. This is because the most complex do not perpetuate the dualisms that Baker's notion of inversion depends upon. For instance, one way to challenge the dualism that Baker constructs between West and non-West is to remember that in our present historical moment the most celebrated call to burn a book originated in the Third World, while the book's postcolonial author seeks protection under a Western power's vow to defend the right to produce unencumbered song.

To point to this celebrated modern instance of book burning is not to deny the existence of (U.S.) bases in Third World geographies. Nor is it to imply that this one incident is typical of non-Western cultures. But it is to remind us that the West is not the only site of duels and dualities. It is further to remind us that, despite the implications of some cultural critics, there is a danger in uncritically linking those bases to Western logocentrism. I understand the desire of academics to believe that what they study is important, but domination cannot be explained by simple reference to a philosophical system. I do not say this to champion logocentrism. If connections between it and Western domination can be established, they should be. But the history of domination is clearly different from, if overlapping with, that of logocentrism. To take the new trinity of class, race, and gender, my limited knowledge of non-Western cultures does not convince me that cultures free from Western thought are necessarily superior. Asian women are very familiar with patriarchal domination. Some societies have such firmly entrenched class hierarchies that the introduction of Western thought is welcomed as liberating. And racism is not confined to the West.

The new historicism will make a strategic mistake if it perpetuates the totalizing discourse it claims to challenge by accepting a version of Western history in which logocentrism is the root of all evil. Instead, it needs a more complicated account of that history and how it led to forms of domination. Such an account needs to face the difficult issue of Western pluralism, which both undercuts narratives of rigid exclusion and poses more subtle questions of domination. One way to present such an account is to draw on Ernst Bloch's notion of "nonsynchronism."[4] Nonsynchronism also allows us to reconsider the historical importance of today's narratives of progressive emergence. Related as the two questions are, we can start with the one of narrative.

Baker's inversive discourse is similar to Bakhtin's appropriation. According to Baker marginalized discourse appropriates existing structures and concepts from dominant groups by performing an ironic reversal. Nonsynchronism implies a different possibility. Instead of a simple opposition between dominant and repressed groups, nonsynchronism implies a variety of different groups—often overlapping—existing in complicated relation to one another. These groups do not, however, conform to the same temporal logic. Thus when previously excluded groups employ narratives of progressive emergence, they are not necessarily ironically inverting them. African-American women, for instance, may subscribe to narratives of self-assertion and autonomy, not ironically and not even because they are theoretically outdated, but because their temporal logic is not identical to that of white, middle-class males for whom such narratives are worthy of ironic undercutting or deconstruction. This is not to provide a ready-made apology for all such narratives, but it is to insist that when previously excluded groups employ them they are neither inherently contestatory, as Baker's theory of inversive discourse would have it, nor retrogressive, as certain poststructuralists might argue. What matters is how they position themselves in relation to other existing narratives, including those whose structures they reoccupy. My own criticism of many reconstructive narratives has to do with their relational positioning. Working so hard to create a sense of autonomy, they too often feed the logic of pluralism. A marked failure of both the revisionist and deconstructive aspects of the new historicism to date has been their failure to confront the challenge of pluralism. In drawing on the notion of nonsynchronism to complicate accounts of Western domination, we can better see why narratives of pluralistic inclusion carry with them their own dangers.

As important as the notion of nonsynchronism is, it too has a possibly discredited history. The frequently evoked metaphor of "underdeveloped" reminds us that history was first considered the *Gleichzeitigkeit der Ungleichzeitigen* (the synchronicity of the nonsynchronic) as a result of Europe's overseas expansion. Exposed to many different cultures, Europeans had to admit the inadequacy of a singular notion of culture. Rather than one Culture there were many cultures. Rather than a unified *Historie* there was *Geschichte*, a word stressing the plurality of history's stories. Trying to explain the otherness of these various cultures, Europeans could rely on Herder's argument that each culture had its own internal temporal logic. If this notion granted each culture its uniqueness, the point of comparison remained European. Non-European cultures were in a less advanced state of temporal development. In this way the *Gleichzeitigkeit der Ungleichzeitigen* became a framework allowing the absorption of other cultures into the growing unity of a progressive, Eurocentric world history.[5]

If the West's ability to absorb non-Western cultures into a Eurocentric narrative of world history would seem to confirm Spanos's identification of "the West's Re-collective mania to recuperate the One,"[6] it also complicates the commonplace assumption that the West legitimated its imperialistic domination by constructing monolithic narratives of exclusion. On the contrary, it seems to have worked most effectively by constructing narratives of inclusion rather than exclusion. Today the most powerful version of control through inclusion is pluralism.

The failure to confront the complicated logic of pluralism helps to explain limitations in new historical appropriations of Bakhtin. Bakhtin's argument that official discourse is monological is extremely attractive to new historicists intent on listening to the voice of the "other" because it implies that dominant ideologies exclude such voices. For instance, as we have seen, Greenblatt insists that the historical force of Bakhtin must be understood in terms of a "culture increasingly intolerant of disorder in society, in the individual, and in art." This increased desire for order means that "what was once acceptable in the central zone of the social system was pushed out to the periphery, and what was once tolerated on the periphery was declared altogether unacceptable."[7] But this narrative of how order was consolidated in Europe cannot explain the workings of pluralism. Rather than expand its control by pushing what was acceptable further and further to the periphery, it operates by including more and more peripheral voices.

To historicize Bakhtin it is equally important to remember that he lived in a society in which it makes more sense to posit the existence of a monological, official discourse. In such a situation, appropriation of official discourse is subversive because it creates a doubleness where before there was a singularity of voice. What happens, however, when Bakhtin's theory is exported to Western democracies whose official voice of pluralism domesticates subversive voices by appropriating them? In such a context, acts of appropriation themselves can take on a doubleness. To be sure, there is an important difference between Bakhtin's notion of dialogism and pluralism, since the latter lacks the former's dialectical or conflictual edge. Nonetheless, the project of oppositional criticism is not served by assuming that the existing order functions monologically, so that all one needs to do to subvert its discourse is to invert it.

For an example of how that assumption can fail to confront the problems raised by pluralism we can return to Tompkins's construction of a "cultural elite" who have conspired to exclude popular writers from the canon. As a modern day example, Tompkins notes the failure of Sacvan Bercovitch to treat *Uncle Tom's Cabin* in his *The American Jeremiad* even though, according to Tompkins, Stowe's novel perfectly fits the jeremiad as described by Bercovitch. What she fails to recognize is that Bercovitch's work is perhaps the most powerful account that we have of how power in the United States has been maintained, not through an ideology of monolithic exclusion, but through one of pluralistic inclusion.[8] If *Uncle Tom's Cabin* really does fit the pattern of the jeremiad, it cannot offer the radical vision of American society from a feminine perspective that Tompkins claims for it.

My argument about pluralism would be as mistaken as the one it opposes, if it were to imply that pluralism was always already there. Clearly, pluralism was not always, nor does it always remain, the mode of maintaining an existing order. Postcolonial critics, for instance, frequently seem more justified in constructing a monological opposition, although, as we have seen, even they need to be careful about making claims about the totality of the West. To take another example, it would be a major mistake to imply that Renaissance England was a pluralistic society, although one reason that the Renaissance remains fascinating is that the rise of rule by law in the period establishes a framework within which Anglo-American pluralism will function. But precisely because Renaissance England was not a modern society, applications of Gramscian notions of hegemony or Foucauldian notions of the dispersal of power are somewhat anachronistic. After all, those theories were developed as explanations of the vexing problem of how power is maintained in modern industrial states in the West. To be sure, Gramsci was not concerned with the problem of pluralism itself. Furthermore, new historical analysis *has* allowed us to see power on display in the Renaissance in areas in which we failed to see it before. But we should be alert to the possibility that such displays have a very different significance from similar displays in Reagan America.

Finally, my point about the inclusiveness of pluralism does not mean that Greenblatt's narrative about increasing standardization of life in the West is completely wrong. The general rise of hegemonic rule by the middle class is loosely connected with the consolidation of power in a centralized state. But it would be a mistake to equate that standardization and centralization with a monological process of exclusion. Instead, we need to understand how standardization and centralization go hand in hand with a modern, as opposed to say medieval, dispersal of power. How, in other words, has pluralism's ideology of inclusion operated to exclude?[9] Or to pose that question as a challenge, if it is relatively easy to imagine appropriating an official, monological voice, how can we appropriate the voice(s) of pluralism?

But before trying to answer that question, we should first ask whether such an effort is necessary. Is pluralism really so bad? After all, the fact that pluralism makes the task of oppositional criticism harder can be interpreted as a good sign rather than a cause to despair. There may simply be fewer grounds for opposition. Without a doubt, there is much to be said for an ideology that rules by inclusion rather than exclusion, and recent developments in Eastern Europe where citizens demanded pluralistic political institutions indicate pluralism's attraction over monolithic rule. If existing forms of pluralism have excluded certain voices, the defenders of pluralism can always respond that the only answer is a more inclusive pluralism. For instance, the example of affirmative action that I evoked is one illustration of how a pluralistic society tries to correct for past exclusions. Moreover, if critics of pluralism argue that pluralism represses conflicts between various voices, they need to ask themselves if their criticism itself is not a luxury allowed those in pluralistic societies. How far are advocates of a conflictual as opposed to a pluralistic model willing to go? Are they advocating a conflict of ideas and interpretations, or the sort of conflict that can arise in countries where dissenting voices are forced to take arms? In short, there are far worse systems than pluralistic ones.

These positive aspects of pluralism make it difficult to imagine non-monological alternatives to it. Yet there are those, like me, who feel that the answer to pluralism's exclusions is not a more inclusive pluralism. This is because the price paid for assimilation is precisely the standardization that worries Greenblatt. Various voices are allowed to speak, but only if they have made a prior commitment to consent to a larger unity—*E Pluribus Unum*. Though different, the various voices within pluralism have a way of sounding the same.

Pluralism works most effectively by flattening the temporal differences Bloch insists upon in his notion of nonsynchronism. Differences are acknowledged but they are absorbed into a master logic that rules at any synchronic moment. It is in this way that pluralism helps perpetuate the Western tradition of logocentrism. For a spatial image of how this works we can return to the metaphor of boundaries continually evoked by Greenblatt. On the one hand, pluralism respects boundaries between diverse, autonomous groups. On the other, it operates through a capacity infinitely to extend its boundaries to include more diversity through a logic of addition.

It is this ability to respect boundaries between groups while simultaneously expanding its boundaries to absorb more groups that makes pluralism so difficult to oppose. If, for instance, we adopt the reconstructionist strategy of constructing separate, oppositional traditions, we feed the pluralist logic. Whether they unconsciously reoccupy old-fashioned narrative structures or self-consciously appropriate them through inversive discourse, such histories do not challenge the boundaries established by pluralism, but work within their framework. After all, the challenge of dealing with a myriad of competing voices is not new to pluralism, for it developed in response to it. Thus, if it is indeed the case that pluralism maintains order by excluding radical voices, given the present alignment of power, there is little doubt as to which voices will not be tolerated in a new pluralistic consensus. At the same time, to construct a separate tradition whose voice, along with others, will be heard is to submit to pluralism's logic that controls by assimilation.

More effective than either of these strategies would seem to be a strategy like Greenblatt's that challenges the way in which existing boundaries are constructed. But if reconstructionists' efforts conform to pluralism's logic of respecting boundaries between separate groups, the early Greenblatt's Foucauldian narratives have an uncanny resemblance to pluralism's capacity to extend its boundaries to absorb more and more of what was once considered marginal. As we have seen, Foucauldian narratives can easily be turned into descriptions of how opposition is contained rather than acts of opposition themselves. What is needed is not merely inversions, additions, or expansions of existing boundaries but a realignment of them by bringing various voices into relation with one another. For a suggestion of how such narratives might be constructed we can turn to an essay that I mentioned in the introductory chapter, Erich Auerbach's "Philology and *Weltliteratur*."

· III ·

First published in 1952, this essay takes on added significance because, as I noted, it was translated into English by Marie and Edward Said. Expressing Auerbach's awareness of the dead end of philological historicism based on national traditions, it clearly influenced Said, who has done as much as any recent critic to expand the West's engagement with non-European literatures. In many respects Auerbach appeals to values that someone like Todorov struggles to maintain, which is not surprising since his notion of *Weltliteratur* is borrowed from Goethe and carries with it an

Enlightenment vision of a shared humanity. Furthermore, at times he seems to be advocating nothing more than an inclusive pluralism with its ideal of unity in diversity. *Weltliteratur*, for instance, is concerned with the "diverse background of a common fate."[10] What distinguishes Auerbach, however, is his attempt to combat the standardization that pluralism brings about, despite its claimed respect for diversity. As a result, there is a crucial difference between Auerbach's way of proceeding and Todorov's.

Starting from a position of universality, Todorov, despite his best intentions, is too often deaf to crucial distinctions within various voices. Auerbach's *Ansatzpunct*, or point of departure, is different. He too has a universal vision. Nonetheless, his starting point remains, as it does with the best of his generation's philologists, the tradition into which he was born and the pressures brought to bear upon him by his particular historical situation. As Ernst Curtius acknowledges at the start of his major work, "My book . . . is not the product of purely scholarly interests. It grew out of vital urges and under the pressure of a specific historical situation."[11] Auerbach himself writes that "my own experience, and by that I mean not merely my scientific experience, is responsible for the choice of problems, the starting points, the reasoning and the intention expressed in my writings."[12] Thus in *"Weltliteratur"* when he writes, "Our philological home is the earth; it can no longer be the nation," he immediately cautions, "The most priceless and indispensable part of a philologist's heritage is still his own nation's culture and language." Unlike reconstructionists, however, who more often than not stay lodged within an individual heritage, Auerbach insists, "Only when [the philologist] is first separated from this heritage, however, and then transcends it does it become truly effective."[13] Auerbach's call for critics to transcend their heritage might seem to be an escape to a position outside of history. But it need not be so. Instead, it can involve an attempt to cross the boundaries of one's inherited tradition to understand another, just as Auerbach studied Romance not Germanic philology. This crossing of boundaries not only alters the point of view of the critic, it can also contribute to a realignment of existing boundaries, not from an omniscient perspective above history, but through a productive process of cross-fertilization of existing traditions.

Granted, the task of present critics is more complicated when they take the earth as their home. I do not want to imply that Auerbach's selections are necessarily the model for those intent on breaking a Eurocentric grip on the study of literary history. As people, like Said, have pointed out, many of his assumptions remained Eurocentric, and his attention was almost exclusively on European texts. Indeed, his mention of Pearl Buck's Chinese peasants as an example of "an economic and cultural leveling process"[14] may seem somewhat embarrassing. As Geoffrey Gorer astutely noted, much of the success of Buck's work grows out of her portrayal of the "economic and social rise of a Chinese family through the exercise of private enterprise and its subsequent disintegration in terms with which American readers could identify themselves with the greatest of ease." In her books "one would imagine that only the most superficial differences distinguished the valley of the Yangtze from that of the Mississippi."[15]

Nonetheless, I can imagine worse goals than for a North American critic to use *Mimesis* as a point of departure in an attempt to bring together the multiplicity of voices and traditions of that continent in the way that Auerbach does for Europe. More important for the new historicism, however, are the suggestions he makes while wrestling with the dead end of the nationally based historicism, that still partly informs his work in *Mimesis*. There is much to be learned from Auerbach's observation that I quoted in chapter 1. "The more our earth grows closer together, the more must historicist synthesis balance the contraction by expanding its activity."[16]

Auerbach's insistence on the need to expand our activities is generally acknowledged by new historicists. One result is the increasing number of collective histories that widen the range of material covered. More controversial is his implication that such expansion should go hand in hand with continued efforts at synthesis. Synthesis for many implies monological narratives of exclusion. Thus we have new collectivist histories that try to create a dialogical effect by merely placing a variety of different voices under the same cover. But in refusing to synthesize, their editors forget that dialogic history results from the interaction of different voices, not just their separate but equal representation. Rather than reject efforts at synthesis as inevitably monological, we need to distinguish between different kinds of synthesis. In this regard Auerbach remains exemplary because he implies that we can work toward synthesis from a specific position within history, not by imposing a unity from above. A diverse, yet shared, humanity is not a given, as the ideology of pluralism implies, but something that human beings must work for. One way for the new historicism to work for that goal is to pay careful attention to the point of view it adopts to construct its histories. The new historicism can profit by what Auerbach learned in "*Weltliteratur.*"

Auerbach's argument that critics' points of departure are always their own cultures and languages would seem to confirm recent calls that new historicists need to acknowledge their point of view. As Auerbach's work demonstrates, this does not mean turning historiography into narcissistic confessionals. Instead, it merely means recognizing that the questions historians find urgent result from the particular identities pressed upon them by their place in history. That recognition can lead to eloquent moments such as Raymond Williams's autobiographical beginning to *The Country and the City* in which by situating himself historically he is able to explain the pressing nature of the questions that inform his study as well as his authority to deal with them.[17] But it need not. Nor does it necessarily confirm Jean Howard's call for the new historicism to theorize itself.[18]

Without a doubt, we should try to be as aware of our theoretical assumptions as possible. But the very specificity of the historian's position within history works against the dream of having a general set of theoretical assumptions or a methodology that will cover all situations. As a poststructuralist would remind Howard, no matter how clear we make our assumptions, that clarity will depend upon an act of repression. Or, perhaps more importantly, as a radical historicist would remind her, any set of assumptions is prone to correction and adjustment by a new historical situation and every historian's starting point is somewhat different. Indeed, the call for theoretical and methodological clarity has bizarre affinities, on the one hand, to a 1960s' call to be "up front" by letting people know where you are coming from and, on the other, with positivistic efforts to found literary criticism as a science with clearly-established principles and methods. It was from the latter perspective that René Wellek faulted Auerbach for not making his methodology in *Mimesis* clear enough.[19]

The inability to found histories on a lucid theoretic foundation should not, however, become an excuse to rest content with the limitations pressed upon us by our particular places in history. As Auerbach argues, our individual heritages may be indispensable, but they are most effective when we are separated from them. Part of the task of the historian might be, then, not only to attempt to understand different points of view, but also to incorporate them into his narrative. Not to do so is to fall prey to charges of monologism, and it is monological histories that are most easily absorbed by pluralism's logic of addition.

One of the most popular revisionist strategies used to avoid constructing monological histories while placing theirs in relation to others has been to draw on the Bakhtinian notion of appropriation. But, as Baker's "inversive discourse" indicates, Bakhtinian appropriation can be appropriated in such a way as to perpetuate existing dualities. If confined to this binary logic, the alternative can invert the dominant, but the dominant can respond by appropriating the alternative. The first we call subversion; the second co-optation. Auerbach provides a model for how to bring various traditions together that neither places them side-by-side in a relation of pluralism nor establishes a binary logic of endless subversion and co-optation.

Auerbach's work clearly does not rule out the desire of reconstructionists to construct narratives identifying distinctive traditions similar to the one of the common man that he identified in *Mimesis* and associated with realism. In fact, Auerbach's philological orientation provides a useful analogy to help us understand the nature of such traditions. Even though in a very general sense languages share certain similarities, individual ones clearly operate according to their own logics. Despite these different logics, however, the boundaries between them are in perpetual flux, as languages come into contact with one another. That contact is historically conditioned, so that some are more closely related than others; for instance, those making up Indo-European languages, or in an even closer relationship, Romance languages. Similarly, identifiable literary traditions exist. But they are formed and shaped by pressures and interactions with other traditions, and not just a single dominant one. Whereas it is impossible to detail all such interactions, historians of individual traditions willing occasionally to abandon an interior point of view would help to destroy the illusion that any one tradition is an autonomous creation. In doing so they would make it clear that such traditions do not unfold according to an internal teleology. Furthermore, such boundary-crossing would both suggest historical pressures that produced the tradition in question *and* indicate how it shaped and influenced other traditions, dominant or not. Rather than merely adding previously excluded traditions, we need to use those traditions to redefine accepted ones.

Variation in point of view will be disorienting for some. In my work cross-examining law and literature in antebellum America I shifted not so much from one literary tradition to another, as from legal to literary history and various points of view within each. This strategy, designed to avoid a teleological narrative structure, caused one reviewer to complain of my "constantly shifting methodologies" and the impression he had "of being afloat without moorings or ports in sight."[20] This complaint may be accurate, the result of my limitations as a writer (ones that present readers may be feeling.) But it does not rule out the importance of attempting to find a narrative form to accommodate shifting points of view.

A successful recent example is Taylor Branch's *Parting of the Waters: America in the King Years 1954–63*. Branch, a white man, adopts an inside point of view by writing a "history of the civil rights movement out of the conviction from which it was made," the conviction that "truth requires a maximum effort to see through the eyes of strangers, foreigners, and enemies." Thus Branch recounts events from the perspective of King, other members of the movement, southern whites, the Kennedy administration, and J. Edgar Hoover. In doing so he, like King himself, "attempts to rise from an isolated culture into a larger history by speaking more than one language."[21] As King knew, that requires a willingness to try to communicate with an audience that does not necessarily share one's own background. To evoke the linguistic example again, even though boundaries exist between languages, it is possible to learn to communicate in a language not one's own. Doing so, however, requires attention to one's audience.

An inside point of view is immediately altered when it addresses an audience that does not share its point of view. To be sure, something is always lost in translation, but something important can be gained. After all, it is through attempts to cross linguistic barriers in order to communicate that languages are shaped and altered. There are boundaries between languages, but they are not fixed. To write histories of individual traditions that are shaped by what Greenblatt calls "frontier-regions" rather than "linear boundaries" is, not only to record more accurately how distinctive traditions are created, but also to make self-conscious efforts to have these traditions shape others by helping to redefine existing boundaries. New histories that suggest how various traditions can be interwoven and cross-examined would restore the dialectical tension to the dialogical that gets lost in celebrations of liberal pluralism.

To cite Greenblatt's concern with frontier regions and the crossing of boundaries is to acknowledge how close his narratives come to adopting a mode of narration that combats the logic of pluralism. Nonetheless, as we have seen, despite Greenblatt's remarkable capacity to interrelate various social practices and discourses, the tendency of his early work to contain all within a totalizing logic has an uncanny resemblance to pluralism's ability to absorb various voices into a single unity. Greenblatt's tendency to totalize, despite his expressed antipathy to totalization, is, I would like to suggest, related to the point of view that he adopts.

The older historicism against which Greenblatt reacts adopts a narrative point of view similar to nineteenth-century Balzacian realism that situates a text, like a character, within a historical environment. Reconstructionists tend to adopt another nineteenth-century technique: that of the interior point of view of the *Bildungsroman*, as they trace the development of an individual tradition, not an individual self. In contrast, Greenblatt's narrative point of view has affinities with the modernist technique of montage, as he eschews background by juxtaposing a particular historical event with a particular text or performance. Montage, however, still implies the existence of an omniscient narrator, a camera eye, that selects and arranges which details are to be juxtaposed. In pointing to Greenblatt's implied, omniscient point of view, I am not suggesting that we can escape the problem of selection. My point is that the narrative point of view that Greenblatt adopts might be at least partially responsible for his tendency to construct a totalized vision. Indeed, the question of point of view is one that plagued Foucault himself, since it could always be asked: from what point of view did he narrate his historical accounts? To be sure, a poststructuralist might respond that it was not Foucault who was narrating, but language speaking through Foucault. But, then, should we not ask: whose language? And when we do, we are forced to confront Auerbach's reminder that a critic's point of departure remains his own culture and language. After all, Foucault was writing in French, not some abstract, universal Language.

I would be unfair to Greenblatt if I did not admit that there are crucial and extremely effective moments in his work when he, much more than Foucault, acknowledges his point of view. My problem is with the position of omniscience that he then adopts. Rather than work to transcend his point of view by attempting to adopt other points of view within history, he adopts a position above history. To be sure, that position allows him to transgress existing disciplinary boundaries so that he can rapidly shift from social practice, to historical event, to theatrical performance with dazzling results. But if reconstructionists generally adopt an inside point of view, Greenblatt's generally remains that of an outsider. This reluctance to adopt an inner point of view helps to account for why Greenblatt's narratives so often end by containing the oppositional force of emergent groups or institutions. Rather than abandon himself to an inside point of view in order to see what such groups are attempting to overcome, he maintains his omniscient point of view that knows from the start how they were overcome.

There are good reasons for Greenblatt's reluctance to empathize with even emergent groups in the past. In leftist circles, the notion of historical empathy has been attacked by both Brecht and Benjamin. In *Renaissance Self-Fashioning* Greenblatt offers his own version of that attack. Bourgeois critics consider empathy an act of imaginative generosity necessary for the understanding of a tradition or work from a culture or period other than one's own. For Greenblatt, the Western capacity for empathy is intricately linked to improvisation, which is the "ability both to capitalize on the unforeseen and to transform given materials into one's own scenario." As Said in *Orientalism*, Todorov in *The Conquest of America*, and Greenblatt himself demonstrate, empathetic improvisation was an important tool in Western imperialism. Tainted with imperialism, empathy can scarcely be considered "wholly disinterested or benign."[22]

It is hard to dispute Greenblatt's argument. But does it follow that we should discard such notions as empathy and improvisation? If empathy is such a crucial element in an improvisation allowing us to capitalize on the unforeseen and transform material to our own uses, why abandon such effective techniques? Indeed, Greenblatt's definition of improvisation sounds surprisingly like Bakhtin's description of how oppositional voices appropriate official discourse for their own use. If the official voice of pluralism makes such acts of appropriation more difficult to imagine, all the more reason to use all of the tools at one's disposal. The very success that the West has had in employing such tools makes it imperative that those intent on questioning Eurocentric domination should not reject them out of hand. This is not to imply, as Todorov does, that we can simply dislodge them from their complicated history. As Derrida has poignantly argued, we cannot simply turn the page of philosophy and use the concepts and strategies developed by Western culture to question the consequences of that culture, as if they were not intricately entangled with its history.[23] Nonetheless, as I have tried to argue, those consequences have not been universally bad. Furthermore, the use put to concepts and strategies needs to be situationally (historically) considered. It is for pragmatic reasons, then, that the new historicism should find it in its interest to abandon totalized accounts of Western history, especially the project of modernity. In its place we need ones that identify subtle, but crucial, distinctions. One of the ironies of my argument is that the mode of narrative presentation that I advocate for doing so is one associated with postmodernism, a continually fluctuating point of view moving from inside to outside, without implying a point of omniscience. It is not an irony of my argument that I find one of the most subtle accounts of modernity in Hans Blumenberg's *The Legitimacy of the Modern Age*.

· **IV** ·

Blumenberg may seem to be a strange person to turn to for someone concerned with the project of the new historicism. He addresses neither the question of writing histories of excluded groups nor social, materialist, or "textual" history. Instead, his field, like Derrida's, is the history of traditional philosophy. Unlike Derrida, however, whose major historical work traces the persistence of a particular tradition within Western thought, Blumenberg is interested in breaks as well as continuities within that tradition. Rather than demonstrate the persistence of "differance," Blumenberg attempts to analyze differences within history. If, like Todorov, he ends up defending certain notions associated with modernity, he avoids Todorov's tendency toward hasty universalization by basing his defense on a detailed account of what such notions were used to overcome.

Written before the term postmodern was widely used and before the rise of poststructuralism, *The Legitimacy of the Modern Age* does not directly engage either. Nonetheless, in directing his argument against a widely accepted account of modernity, Blumenberg can help us to recognize flaws in blanket attacks against it. The target of Blumenberg's attack is the argument that the modern is merely a secular version of the Judeo-Christian eschatological worldview. According to such thought the modern era's self-proclaimed break with the past is an illusion. For instance, the modern idea of progress is not new but a disguised version of the Judeo-Christian faith in the fulfillment of world history through either the coming of the Messiah or the Last Judgment. Countering this "secularization" thesis, Blumenberg proposes a reoccupation thesis.

The modern, according to Blumenberg, inherited from the medieval period a set of questions about "the great and the all too great."[24] Medieval thinkers were able to pose these impossible questions, as Nietzsche argues, because their theological system already provided the answers. The first thinkers of modernity did not have that luxury. Nonetheless, having inherited a set of questions, they "reoccupied" the positions created by them with mixed results. On the one hand, the reoccupation of these positions means that the modern did not make the complete break with the past that it claimed for itself. As numerous historians and philosophers have noted, in order to have reached a point marking a new departure, someone like Descartes had to conceal his indebtedness to the past. On the other hand, modernity's inability to achieve a total break with the past is not proof that it contributed nothing new. If modern philosophy reoccupied the function of Christian theology, in answering the questions that it inherited its attempted solutions are at times legitimately new.

Blumenberg's reoccupation thesis is extremely important for my argument because it allows us to see how the new can be brought about without lapsing into either the liberal belief in temporal continuity or that of a radical, but impossible to achieve, total break with the past. History for Blumenberg is not continuous but discontinuous. Furthermore, like poststructuralists, he links those discontinuities and the efforts to overcome them with a rhetorical transaction.

In our tradition's system of the explanation of reality there is a "position" for [the] historical subject, a position to which vacancy and occupation refer. The accomplishment and establishment of the reoccupation are rhetorical acts; "philosophy of history" only thematizes the structure of this process, it is not the agency responsible for it. Not accidentally, the act by which the subject of history is determined and legitimized has borne the name of a fundamental rhetorical figure, as *translatio imperii* [transfer (or: trope, metaphor) of power]. "Carryings over," metaphorical functions, again and again play an essential role here. Alexander conceives his historical project by reversing Xerxes' march across the Hellespont. The God of the Old Testament transfers his sovereignty in history by means of a covenant. The citizens of the National Convention, in the French Revolution, take metaphors of the Roman Republic literally, in their costume and their speech. "Men make their own history, but they do not make it just as they please; they do not make it under circumstances chosen by themselves, but under circumstances directly encountered, given and transmitted from the past," Marx writes in the *Eighteenth Brumaire*. The deeper the crisis of legitimacy reaches, the more pronounced the recourse to rhetorical metaphors becomes—it is not inertia that makes tradition but rather the difficulty of living up to one's designation as the subject of history.[25]

Blumenberg stresses the rhetorical nature of this historical subject's position, but he differs from poststructuralists on the possibility that human beings make history, one "on which, after detours through philosophy of history, the modern age has wagered." In announcing the death of "man" and the deconstruction of the subject, poststructuralism, from a Blumenbergian perspective, risks turning us toward a new detour by failing to face "the difficulty of living up to one's designation as the subject of history." Nonetheless, his recognition of the rhetorical transaction involved in the transmission or *uberliefern* of history lets us see why this detour is so plausible. So long as the act by which the subject of history is determined and legitimized bears the name of a fundamental rhetorical figure, it is easy to see why someone would conclude that rhetoric, not human beings, makes history. If that argument tends to relieve human beings of their responsibilities as historical subjects, it is not necessarily illogical. As Blumenberg notes, "Rhetorically, both attributions of responsibility and excuses are always equally readily available."[26] Blumenberg, however, continues to wager—the allusion is clearly to Pascal—on the prospect that human beings, not rhetoric, make history. As such, he remains a defender of the impulse toward the modern and its attempt to bring about the new.

At this point it is important to point out that Blumenberg's argument for modernity's legitimate claim to newness is not necessarily an argument to legitimize the chronological period that we call the modern age. As one of Blumenberg's best critics writes, "There is a small but vital difference between defending a development because it started from legitimate ground and the legitimation of what it has become."[27] Blumenberg, for instance has much in common with poststructuralist criticism of what it takes to be modernity. If Blumenberg still takes historical epochs seriously, he is completely opposed to a teleological philosophy of history that sees each epoch as a stage leading to an ultimate goal. His later *Work on Myth*, for instance, is an attack on the notion that history is the progressive development from primitive "mythos" to modern "logos."[28] It is in this work that Blumenberg's difference with Habermas's defense of modernity as an unfinished project is most clearly evident, for Habermas's reliance on critical reason can too easily evoke the notion of an ahistorical "right reason" that falls prey to the Enlightenment tendency prematurely to universalize. More of a historicist than Habermas, Blumenberg admits that the very question of legitimacy is a modern problem. "The problem of legitimacy is bound up with the very concept of an epoch itself. The modern age was the first and only age that understood itself as an epoch and, in so doing, simultaneously created the other epochs. The problem of legitimacy is latent in the modern age's claim to carry out a radical break with tradition, and the incongruity between this claim and the reality of history, which can never begin entirely anew. Like all political and historical problems of legitimacy, that of the modern age arises from a discontinuity, and it does not matter whether the discontinuity is real or pretended" (116). As Blumenberg frequently points out, "Legitimacy becomes a subject of discussion only when it is disputed" (97). The modern era created the possibility for the debate over its legitimacy, and yet the very fact that its legitimacy is disputed signals a shift. If we were completely locked within the assumptions of modernity, its legitimacy could not be questioned. It is precisely this questioning that puts modernity's assumptions into focus. Indebted to the argument that questions modernity, Blumenberg does not blindly defend the modern.

Like the poststructuralists, Blumenberg acknowledges Nietzsche as a key figure in the criticism of modernity. His difference with them comes in the relationship he establishes with Nietzsche. Rather than adopt a Nietzschean perspective, Blumenberg uses it to detect what can be salvaged from the system Nietzsche attacks. "This whole theory interests us here only for the implications that it allows to become visible in a retrospective view of the foundation of the modern age" (141). What the Nietzschean and other perspectives allow Blumenberg to see is that progress and the accompanying beliefs in modern reason and human self-assertion are not inherently teleological. Through his metaphor of "reoccupation" he is able to defend humanistic beliefs in reason and self-assertion by severing them from the modern era's sense of inevitable temporal continuity. What remains to be defended is a much more limited sense of both reason and self-assertion.

As Blumenberg notes, the modern age gave rise to a Faustian image of reason as demonic. But Blumenberg denies that there exists some spontaneous will to knowledge that inevitably drives reason to overexertion. Instead, modern reason appears demonic because, in accepting the challenge of all too great medieval questions, it found itself overextended. "The modern age," Blumenberg argues, "found it impossible to decline to answer questions about the totality of history. To that extent the philosophy of history is an attempt to answer a medieval question with the means available to a postmedieval age" (48–49). It is important, therefore, to recognize that "the formation of the idea of progress and its taking the place of the historical totality that was bounded by Creation and Judgment are two distinct events" (49). Taken as an assertion about the totality of history "the idea of progress is removed from its empirical formation in the more modest task of extending the boundary of reality accessible to and manageable by theory . . . and forced to perform a function that was originally defined by a system that is alien to it" (49). It is this overextended,

teleological idea of progress that both poststructuralists and new historicists find so suspicious. Nonetheless, there remains a less ambitious notion of progress and self-assertion that is still of use in humankind's efforts
to free itself from the constraints of necessity.

The moment that we distinguish between an authentic modern idea of
progress and an overextended one, we are no longer dealing solely with
historical description. Clearly, the chronological period that we call the
modern age contained both notions of progress. When Blumenberg defends the legitimacy of a less ambitious, non-totalized idea of progress, he
is trying to salvage its usefulness for an age that is already experiencing the
dismantling of the "modern" worldview. To phrase this in a way that does
not do justice to Blumenberg's skeptical tone: we might hope that in the
age to follow the modern, the authentic—non-teleological—idea of progress might finally have its day. Paradoxically, then, the only hope for a
truly legitimate modern age is in what is commonly referred to as the
postmodern.[29]

Blumenberg's account of modernity has the advantage of explaining
both why postmodern responses to the modern are at least partially justified and why those responses themselves have a tendency to totalize. On
the one hand, there is a teleological trend in modernity worthy of criticism. On the other, postmodernism and poststructuralism are as prone as
modernity to reoccupy inherited questions that lead toward totalization.
Even the poststructuralist activity that is least prone to totalization—the
deconstruction of attempts to establish rational foundations—acquires its
force from modern thinkers' efforts to have rationality answer questions
that only theology could afford to ask. The extent to which this is true is
indicated by Blumenberg's qualification of his defense of rationality in
Work on Myth.

It can be rational not to be rational to the utmost extent. . . . [R]ationality is
all too ready to engage in destruction when it fails to recognize the rationality
of things for which no rational foundation is given, and believes it can afford
to get carried away by the process of establishing rational foundations. Descartes thought that the best way to build cities rationally was to begin by
razing the old cities. Not even World War II yielded proof of this prospect for
rationality. There are moments in which the outcome of centuries and millenniums are thoughtlessly sacrificed. What had been held fast and passed on
by a loyalty shielded from all reflection becomes a source of offense and is
gotten rid of. One does not need to be conservative, however, to see that the
demand for 'critical' destruction, and then for a final rational foundation,
leads to burdens of proof that, if they were really accepted and undertaken as
seriously as they are asserted and demanded, would no longer leave room for
what is supposed to be gained, by this process, for the intelligent movement
of existence.[30]

It may be that the current fascination with deconstructing logocentric foundations follows the logic of logocentrism to its most extreme form.

Indeed, for all the subtlety of his thought and his marvelous capacity to avoid the types of totalization that I have been criticizing, Derrida himself seems to have adopted a very general version of the secularization thesis, in which the Judeo-Christian concern with the logos can be traced, without interruption, to the logocentric thought that he hopes to supplement. Recognizing the similarity between his way of proceeding and negative theology, Derrida continually struggles to resist its logic.[31]

That struggle can be fascinating to watch, and Derrida's narrative strategy of acknowledging his point of departure while shifting perspectives in a struggle to overcome its limitations is exemplary. Even so, Blumenberg suggests that there are questions to ask other than philosophical ones about foundations. Having conducted some early canon bashing of his own, Blumenberg argues that "We are going to have to free ourselves from the idea that there is a firm canon of the 'great questions' that throughout history and with unchanging urgency have occupied curiosity and motivated the pretension to world and self-interpretation" (69). The dilemma of deconstruction, indeed of much of poststructuralism, is that, recognizing that we will never be able to construct rational foundations to answer questions inherited from theology, it finds no way of freeing itself from them. To be sure, that is no easy task. As Blumenberg admits, "In history the price we pay for our critical freedom in regard to answers is the nonnegotiability of the questions" (69). Having inherited certain questions, we cannot merely make the problems that they raise disappear any more than trying, as I and others have, to understand poststructuralism historically will make the problems it raises disappear. Nonetheless, we can recognize moments when the lucid awareness that certain "fundamental" questions will never be answered serves to block the impulse to conduct historical investigation. It is one thing to recognize the existence of such questions. It is another to continue to grant them the privileged status that some poststructuralists seem to do.

For an example we can turn to the first essay in *Allegories of Reading*. Anticipating the coming of a new historicism, de Man questions the increased stress "on the interplay between [literary] fictions and categories that are said to partake of reality, such as the self, man, society, 'the artist, his culture and the human community,' as one critic put it." Such criticism is misguided, he argues, because it is precisely through a close reading of literature that we best learn about such "real" categories. "Literature," de Man asserts, "as well as criticism—the difference between them being delusive—is condemned (privileged) to be forever the most rigorous and, consequently, the most unreliable language in terms of which man names and transforms himself."[32] My problem with de Man's argument is not the implication that the attempt to construct a permanent rational foundation for historical investigations is doomed to failure. It is instead the implication that because those investigations are forced to rely on inherently unreliable language they cannot get started until they have answered fundamental questions that by nature are unanswerable. We are being prodded not only continually to reinvent the wheel, but also to invent it knowing that it will be asked to serve the function of a firm and stationary foundation. Meanwhile, numerous other questions of historical importance go unexplored.

If I am correct, the new historicism arose in response to the urgency of such questions, and if those questions are not determinant in number, we can at least attempt to identify some of the most urgent. To be sure, that some of them grow out of the persistent postmodern challenge to modernity's attempt to construct rational foundations complicates the situation. Foundational questions will not simply disappear. Nonetheless, the new historicism's ability to answer other pressing questions will be greatly hampered if it does not recognize that it was precisely modernity's failure to answer foundational ones that led to its overextended version. Rather than allow this overextended version of modernity to speak for the whole, the new historicism would be wise to recognize its debt to and the continued usefulness of the more modest version of modernity that Blumenberg describes. That act of recognition cannot eliminate the tensions arising from the effort to produce a new historicism in a postmodern age. But it can make those tensions more productive by suggesting a different vision of the postmodern itself, one in which such valuable modern tools and concepts such as rational inquiry, human assertion, and the ideal of a shared humanity still have a place. Indeed, as Nancy Fraser has poignantly argued, even Foucault's project gets its political force from the "reader's familiarity with a commitment to modern ideals of autonomy, dignity, and human rights."[33]

My defense of these products of modernity should not be construed as an argument that they have a transcendental, ahistorical value. Quite the contrary, it is precisely because they are cultural constructs that they need to be defended and reasserted, for they could easily be lost. To be sure, in their overextended, teleological versions they have also been party to much harm. All the more reason, then, to retain Blumenberg's notion of the modern as an open-ended sense of temporality that carries with it an uncertainty over what the future will bring, an open-ended temporality that renders teleological thinking as problematic as statements about what always already will be the case.

Such a sense of the modern reminds us that the most unreliable aspect of poststructuralism's rigorous criticism is its tendency to scale Olympian heights in order to make pronouncements about what *forever* will be the case. For instance, in "Nietzsche, Genealogy, History" Foucault summarizes Nietzsche on the will to knowledge. "The historical analysis of this rancorous will to knowledge reveals that all knowledge rests upon injustice (that there is no right, not even in the act of knowing, to truth or a foundation for truth) and that the instinct for knowledge is malicious (something murderous, opposed to the happiness of mankind.)" But when he quotes Nietzsche directly we read, "The desire for knowledge has been transformed among us into a passion which fears no sacrifice, which fears nothing but its own extinction."[34] The difference between the blanket statement that "*all* knowledge rests upon injustice" and the historical one that "the desire for knowledge *has been transformed* . . ." is essential. The former implies a deterministic inevitability; the latter a chance for further transformation.

A sense of temporality in which existing realities are always prone to being rendered unreal presents both opportunities and difficulties for those intent on finding present uses for studies of the past. The major difficulty is that there is no guarantee that what we learn about the past will be applicable to the present, not to speak of the future. No study of the past, no matter how exhaustive, can be used as a firm foundation from which to control the direction of the future. But just because studies of the past do not provide a firm foundation, it does not follow that they have no uses. Indeed, if what happened in the past completely controlled the direction of the future, it would be useless to study it, since there would be nothing we could do anyway. The very impossibility of establishing a narrative of necessary causality from the past to the future opens up a realm of human action in the present.

Because that realm is at least partially conditioned by the past, part of the task of human action concerned with trying to shape the direction of the future needs to involve an understanding of the past. Many concerned with returning to "history" in literary studies have discovered (once again) that such understandings are not disinterested acts, that the versions of the past that we construct are also interventions into political debates about what is possible in the present. Such a discovery need not, however, lead to a rejection of the goal of achieving disinterested inquiry, for so long as our situation in the world has been partially determined by the past, the most empowering studies will be the ones that come as close as possible to telling us how it really was or perhaps more importantly why it was the way it was. To state my point as a paradox: the present has an interest in maintaining a belief in disinterested inquiry into the past. Those inquiries will not establish a firm foundation for human action in the present, but if they did human action itself would be rendered meaningless, since it would be controlled by timeless structures that have always already been there. Furthermore, it is the very inability to use history to establish firm foundations for conduct that makes the intersection of literature and history so interesting—and so problematic.

I have argued that it is in our interest to maintain disinterested inquiries into the past. But those inquiries are not sufficient for a new historicism in literary studies. This is because the realm of the literary as socially and historically constructed is not primarily concerned with texts that make claims to tell it as it really was. In addition to being concerned with the uses of history, the new historicism also needs to be concerned with the uses of literature—or perhaps better—the uneasy relationship between them. But before turning to that thorny issue, I first want to turn to the relationship between today's new historicism and the pragmatic tradition of historiography within the United States. One of the limits of that tradition has been its inability to deal with the literary. Thus, after turning to a chapter on that tradition and one on a new historicist strongly influenced by it, I will return to the problem of the literary, a problem that I cannot promise to solve, but one that I insist on raising.

CHAPTER 4

The Uses and Abuses of a Pragmatic Past

The luminous fog of immediacy has a place in
nature; it is a meteorological and optical effect,
and often a blessing. But why should immediacy
be thought to be absolute or a criterion of reality?
The great error of dogmatists, in hypostatizing
their conclusions into alleged preexistent facts,
did not lie in believing that facts of some kind pre-
existed; the error lay only in framing an inadequate
view of those facts and regarding it as adequate.[1]
—(George Santayana)

· I ·

IN CHAPTERS 2 and 3 I presented a brief account of the new historicism's
relation to the history of historicism in order to explore the narrative dilemmas facing those intent on writing new, more inclusive histories in a
postmodern world. The project of a new historicism, I argued, while
clearly indebted to an engagement with postmodernism and poststructuralism, is also in tension with them because the very notion of a *new*
historicism reveals an often unacknowledged debt to the notion of the
modern. One challenge that I posed to the new historicism was to come
up with alternatives to the accounts of modernity offered by poststructuralism, a movement that can be understood as a response to a crisis in
historicism from which the Western world has not yet recovered.

It is important to note, however, that a number of those associated with
the return to history in the United States feel that they have found such an
alternative in a native tradition of pragmatism. The most obvious example
of this turn to pragmatism in literary studies is the "Against Theory" position proposed as a solution to the contradictions that a new historicist, like
Jane Tompkins, faces when trying to provide revisionist histories while
remaining true to poststructuralist assumptions. To restate that contradiction in slightly different terms, on the one hand, new historicists claim
authority for their reconstructions of literary history by appealing to historical evidence. Their histories correct previous histories by drawing attention to their exclusions. On the other hand, new historicists have to

admit that their evidence is itself inevitably a partial construction of the past from a present perspective, thus rendering their histories no more authoritative than those they would replace. Given this dilemma, the attraction of the "Against Theory" position is that it solves it by making it disappear. Such theoretical worries, so we are told, ultimately have no consequences for the practice of criticism, or to use Tompkins's words, "Arguments about 'what happened' have to proceed much as they did before poststructuralism broke in with its talk about language-based reality and culturally produced knowledge."[2] Such a position might be subtitled, "How I learned to stop worrying about theory by forgetting it," and it certainly provides an excuse to proceed full-speed ahead with a what-me-worry attitude.

But even though the "Against Theory" argument has been developed by people associated with the new historicism, it, like poststructuralism challenges the very possibility of a *new* historicism. Indeed, it confirms both traditional historicist and poststructuralist critiques of the new historicism. Traditional historicists can be reassured that there's nothing new happening anyway, since all that theoretical jargon does not really make a difference when it comes to the practice of history. Poststructuralists can watch with knowing eyes as their theoretical assumptions are actively forgotten in order to continue to produce different, but not really new, histories.

Clearly, not all new historicists would consider themselves neopragmatists, and not all neopragmatists embrace the "Against Theory" argument. Nonetheless, when critics as different as Walter Benn Michaels, Cornel West, Ihab Hassan, and Frank Lentricchia move from poststructuralism or postmodernism to pragmatism, we can speak of a trend even if a diverse one. Influenced by pragmatism, I am closer to West and Lentricchia, who want to revitalize pragmatism's progressive heritage in opposition to Hassan's neoconservative use of it or Michaels's appropriation of it to argue against the political consequences of theory.[3] Lentricchia even anticipates some of my criticism of the "Against Theory" position. Nonetheless, I differ from him and West in one important respect. They imply that, if we would only stay true to the *proper* strain within pragmatism, we could continue to use it as a radical vehicle for social change. In contrast, I argue that the usability of pragmatism, properly or improperly understood, is limited today precisely because of its assumed sense of progressive temporal continuity. As a result, even though I disagree with the consequences of the "Against Theory" position, its very existence is useful for me as an indication of the present limits of pragmatism for a critical historicism. The most powerful feature of pragmatism's progressivism was its claim to do work in the world by helping to engineer the direction of social change. When, as with the "Against Theory" position, the pragmatic tradition can be used against itself to deny that very possibility, it may be time to seek alternatives to it rather than campaign for its renewal.

The "Against Theory" position helps me to highlight another aspect of my argument. Many people, like Tompkins, attribute the new historicism's newness to a poststructural awareness of the constructed nature of historical knowledge. As we have seen, however, many of the new historicism's claims to newness do not turn out to be so new after all. Perhaps this is because much of what new historicists call poststructuralist is actually part of a native, pragmatic tradition. Mistaking homemade products for fancy imports, many new historicists seem unaware of their debt to that tradition. If so, the "Against Theory" argument, which uses pragmatic assumptions to conclude that even the new historicism is no more than an extension of business as usual, would help to explain why so much of the new historicism fails to live up to the adjective in its label. After all, there is nothing new about continuing in a timeworn tradition.

Whereas the "Against Theory" argument helps to emphasize the limits of the pragmatic tradition, its own limitation is that it is so firmly lodged within that tradition that it can see no alternative to it. This limitation is extremely important in terms of the new historicism. As I have argued, a major failure of the new historicism is to confront the challenge of pluralism. Pluralism, in turn, owes its most persuasive political expression to the pragmatic tradition. To be sure, neopragmatists like Michaels and Fish do not consider themselves pluralists and in many ways their self-image is correct. Nonetheless, despite their insistence on the historical constructedness of all knowledge, they persist in making universal statements that depend on assumptions that grow out of their membership in a pluralistic society; or so I will argue by offering an American supplement to my admittedly partial account of the new historicism's relationship to the tradition of European historicism.

My argument proceeds by proposing that the pragmatic response to late nineteenth-century conservative historicism and rationalism gave rise to a notion of truth, which (within an American context) implies a pluralistic mode of governance and use of the past for present purposes. Through a brief history of what I loosely term pragmatic history, I will suggest that for some segments in the United States faith in both this mode of governance and existing uses of the past experienced a crisis when in the sixties and seventies doubts arose about American exceptionalism. This delayed crisis in historicism was a precondition for the usefulness of poststructuralism for intellectual debates in the United States. In this context the "Against Theory" argument serves as a persuasive account of why pragmatism is not as politically useful as it once was in this country, but it is so much a part of that tradition that it has to admit that its own argument is inconsequential. A major difference between this version of pragmatic antifoundationalism and poststructuralism, both of which are anti-essentialist, is their senses of temporality. Pragmatism continues to posit a sense of temporal continuity, whereas poststructuralism insists on temporal gaps and discontinuities.[4] If poststructuralism challenges the mode of temporality assumed by pragmatism and old-fashioned historicism, pragmatism challenges the usefulness of histories that emphasize gaps and discontinuities. Having ended the last chapter by evoking Blumenberg's notion of reoccupation as an alternative to both modern and postmodern senses of temporality, I will end this one by turning to Walter Benjamin to suggest how discontinuity can be turned into a constructive rather than destructive principle in the making of histories. But first I want to place the new historicism within a tradition of what Cushing Strout has called *The Pragmatic Revolt in American History*.[5]

· II ·

To suggest that the new historicism owes a debt to a native tradition is, no doubt, to spark resistance from those new historicists who acknowledge their debt to poststructuralism in order to proclaim their break with Anglo-American predecessors. Nonetheless, the most obvious evidence that the new historicism needs to be seen within an American tradition is that it developed on American soil. Perhaps its debt to an American tradition better explains its difference from British cultural materialism than the argument, first put forth by Louis Montrose, that the difference has to do with the uses each puts to the past. As an example I can cite Walter Cohen's extension of this argument. "The British rather than the Americans," he writes, "consistently seek to recover a usable past, a potentially progressive Shakespeare."[6] Although Cohen is describing a British rather than an American brand of criticism, his very language betrays how much even an American marxist remains lodged within the pragmatic tradition. After all, the phrase "a usable past" was popularized by Van Wyck Brooks in a 1918 essay.[7] Furthermore, Cohen's use of "progressive" suggests an unacknowledged link between his marxism and his native progressive heritage.

That tradition's stress on the new helps to account for why the label the "new historicism" has proved so popular in the United States. And I refer to more than the adjective in the label. The need of Americans to stress "historicism" might result from America's notorious escape from history brought about in part by its stress on newness. Polemical calls "always to historicize" are most needed when there is a general tendency to do the opposite. But this explanation serves only to invite another question. If America has a tradition of escaping history, why in the late seventies and early eighties did the call to historicize suddenly reach such a responsive audience among literary scholars?

We can start to answer that question by noting that America's notorious escape from history is not, paradoxically, an escape from historicism. American exceptionalism, the belief that America breaks from Europe's repetition of hereditary wrongs, depends upon the metaphoric distinction between the "old" and "new" world. A precondition for that distinction is the modern notion of temporality that is also a precondition for the rise of historicism. Rather than break with European historicism, American exceptionalism is a product of the belief that history can be made new. Put more simply, the doctrine of American exceptionalism is not, after all, so exceptional. In fact, the belief, that America has broken with a European past is similar to the belief ushering in the modern era that the modern had broken with the ancients. Americans merely claimed that this break with the old did not really occur until the founding of the New World. Thus what is often seen as America's *escape* from history is better seen as a belief that it *culminates* history. It is only in America that history can truly be made new.

But if there is nothing exceptional about the mode of temporality that produced the doctrines of American exceptionalism, that mode of temporality did enable the spatial metaphor of the "new world" that does make a difference.[8] That difference manifests itself in a contradiction that inhabits both American exceptionalism and the modern self-definition of itself.

An important way in which the modern established its break with what went before was through a different notion of temporality, a belief that the linear progression of time brings about the new. Paradoxically, however, the very notion of progressive linear time rules out radical breaks in the future, since history unfolds in what Walter Benjamin called "homogeneous, empty time." Similarly, American exceptionalism depends upon a belief that in the "new" world the "old" world's repetitive cycle of hereditary sin will be replaced by a better future that gradually unfolds through time. Thus, once the original break with the European past has occurred, no more "revolution" is necessary to fulfill the promise of the new.

If these patterns are similar, their difference lies in the historical specificity of the moment and place in which they took shape. Absorbing the ideology of republican virtue and economic liberalism that constituted the foundation of the United States as an independent entity, American exceptionalism linked the progressive unfolding of time with American political institutions. In Europe, the situation was different. As in American exceptionalism, a belief in progressive temporal emergence structured narratives of nationalism and on a larger scale narratives of Europe's superiority over non-European cultures. Yet European narratives of temporal emergence were not necessarily linked to republican political institutions, a difference that was, as we shall see, extremely important when historicism started to experience its crisis. First, however, we need to establish the pragmatic influence on the current shape of progressive pluralism in the United States, for at the time that pragmatism arose the progressive version of American exceptionalism was at odds, as it often has been, with a conservative version. Pragmatism's conception of truth helps to sanction a pluralistic mode of governance.

Both Europe and the United States in the late nineteenth century were dominated by a conservative use of historicism. Intent on defusing the threat of radical social change, it stressed continuity and identity within history. It especially wanted to demonstrate the continuous identity of a nation's institutions and cultural heritage. A national or racial identity, so conservative historicists argued, was determined by a germ or seed at the beginning of history that then experienced its gradual unfolding within time. In the United States, where anxiety over the national identity grew with the rise of immigration, historians embraced a "Teutonic-germ theory" that traced the country's republican political institutions, through Britain, to their origins in Teutonic culture.[9] The uniqueness of American identity needed to be understood by reference to these institutions, just as these institutions could find their true fulfillment after having been transplanted to American soil.

Conservative historicism was allied philosophically with rationalism. According to William James, rationalists are backward-looking. This is because for them reality "stands complete and ready-made from all eternity." Truth for the rationalist "has nothing to do with our experiences. It adds nothing to the content of experience. It makes no difference to reality itself; it is supervenient, inert, static, a reflexion merely. It doesn't *exist*, it *holds* or *obtains*, it belongs to another dimension from that of either facts or fact-relations, belongs in short, to the epistemological dimension—and with that big word rationalists close the discussion."[10]

As described by James, rationalism's belief that reality is complete and ready-made might seem to come into conflict with the historicist belief that temporality is a component part of reality. It is important to remember, however, that for conservative historicists the Truth to which history leads already exists in an ideal realm outside of history. History could unfold to reveal this Truth only because its seed had been planted at the beginning of time. Thus a sense of history's telos was to be found in its origins, and conservative historicists, like rationalists, remained backward-looking.

If rationalism and conservative historicism look backward to eternal principles and existing institutions, pragmatism looks forward to the future. Eternal principles will not do for pragmatism because it assumes the existence of a historical world in which the passage of time renders previous realities potentially unreal rather than allowing an ideally existing reality to unfold. Nonetheless, pragmatists, like rationalists, continue to believe that for an idea to be true it must agree with reality. They simply disagree about what it means to agree with reality. Part of that disagreement involves a belief in essentialism. As John Dewey put it, "There are two radically different types of definitions; first, the type inherited from Greek logic reflecting a definite metaphysical conception regarding the nature of things. This definition proceeds in terms of an essential and universal inhering nature. There is another mode of definition which proceeds in terms of *consequences*. In brief, for the latter a thing is—is defined as—what it does, what-it-does being stated in terms of effects *extrinsically* wrought in other things. This logical method was first stated by Charles S. Peirce as the pragmatistic rule: 'Consider what effects, which might conceivably have practical bearings, we conceive the object of our conception to have. Then, our conception of these effects is the whole of our conception of the object.'"[11] This attack on essentialism led pragmatists to question a correspondence theory of truth.

Perhaps the clearest statement of pragmatism's difference from other ways of dealing with the question of truth is William James's "Pragmatism's Conception of Truth," which appeared in *Pragmatism: A New Name for Some Old Ways of Thinking*. Arguing against the "popular notion that a true idea must copy its reality," James claims that the truth of an idea is not "a stagnant property inherent in it. Truth *happens* to an idea. It *becomes* true, is *made* true by events. Its verity *is* in fact an event, a process: the process namely of its verifying itself, its veri-*fication*. Its validity is the process of its valid-*ation*" (160–61). Experience, of course, does not demand that we verify all ideas at all times. Nonetheless, there are numerous ideas that may someday be useful. Thus "the advantage of having a general stock of *extra* truths, of ideas that shall be true of merely possible situations is obvious. We store such extra truths away in our memories, and with the overflow we fill our books of reference. Whenever such an extra truth becomes practically relevant to one of our emergencies, it passes from cold-storage to do work in the world and our belief grows active. You can say of it then either that it is useful because it is true or that it is true because it is useful. Both phrases mean exactly the same thing, namely that here is an idea that gets fulfilled and can be verified" (162).

If James's attack on a correspondence theory of truth upset rationalists, his emphasis on verification seems to counter charges of relativism sometimes leveled against him. Nevertheless, in a historically changing world, verification must always take place in the future because what was once true may no longer be the case. It is pragmatism's future-oriented definition of truth that most distinguishes it from rationalism.

An idea agrees with reality when it is a useful guide to conduct. It is through this agreement, such as when a food agrees with the body, that it is verified. True ideas are those that do work in the world. They are, therefore, "*those that we can assimilate, validate, corroborate and verify. False ideas are those that we cannot*" (160). For James, agreement is "any process of conduction from a present idea to a future terminus, provided only it run prosperously"(162). Agreement, then, is essentially an "affair of leading" and the function of "agreeable leading" is what James means by an idea's verification. True ideas "work because they lead to consistency, stability and flowing human intercourse. They lead away from eccentricity and isolation, from foiled and barren thinking. The untrammeled flowing of the leading-process, its general freedom from clash and contradiction, passes for its indirect verification; but all roads lead to Rome, and in the end and eventually, all true processes must lead to the face of directly verifying sensible experiences *somewhere*, which somebody's ideas have copied" (167).

We can best see how this pragmatic definition of truth had political consequences in the United States by turning to its consequences for the country's most sacred institution: the law. An alliance of conservative historicism and rationalism helped to legitimate the formalism that dominated late nineteenth-century studies of the law. Concerned with maintaining precedent and preserving institutions, formalists believed that the law consisted of a set of eternal principles that could be abstracted from a logical study of particular cases. These timeless principles, discoverable through precedent, were the guide to legal adjudication.

The most famous challenge to formalist doctrine came from Oliver Wendell Holmes, Jr. Holmes developed his ideas of the law while attending meetings of an informal Metaphysical Club in Cambridge, Massachusetts, whose members included William James and C. S. Peirce. Pragmatism developed out of the club's meetings, as did Holmes's attack on formalism. The law, Holmes argued is not a "brooding omnipresence in the sky."[12] The life of the law is not logic, it is experience. It is not a set of principles, but the actual practices of judges and courts. The truth of a law is not to be measured by reference to a set of transcendental principles nor by its conformity with precedent, but by its consequences. According to Holmes, the only "real justification of a rule of law, if there be one, is that it helps to bring about a social end that we desire."[13]

Holmes is not unique in viewing the law as an instrument to bring about desired social ends. For instance, orthodox marxists also posit an instrumental role for the law. But there is an important difference, one that highlights pragmatism's association with pluralistic progressivism. Assuming a view of history generated by class struggle, marxists argue that law is the instrument of the ruling class. Their goal, therefore, is to gain control of the state so as to impose a legal system that reflects the interests of the proletariat, a move that should eventually lead to a classless society.

The law serves social interests, but until a classless society has been achieved, it is the ruling class's tool to maintain its particular interests.

Such class-based analysis of the law influenced Holmes and the legal realists that followed him. But they tried to overcome it. With the help of pragmatism they were largely successful, and their success coincided with the triumph of pluralistic progressivism as the dominant political ideology in the United States.

Pragmatism, it is important to remember, arose at a time of acute social conflict in the United States. If the memory of the French Revolution and the events of 1848 motivated a turn to conservative historicism in Europe, Americans added to that memory the regional conflict that culminated in the Civil War. The triumph of the industrial North in that conflict gave rise to sharpened conflicts between labor and capital. If, as Holmes argued, the justification of a law is that it helps to bring about a desirable social end, one end that pragmatists desired was a unified society free from violent conflict and rule by special interests. For them the radical response of socialist marxism and the conservative response of formalist rationalism were equally undesirable. Both failed because of their means of imposing unity. Marxism relied on violence to impose a dictatorship of the previously repressed proletariat. The formalist answer was to govern according to a set of eternal principles embodied in existing political institutions. To be sure, both the marxist and the formalist solutions ultimately claimed to be for the good of the entire society, but each seemed to be serving the interests of only one group, whether labor on the one hand or capital on the other. The charm of the pragmatic definition of truth as a model for political governance is that it refused to achieve unity by imposing one set of ideas or ideals—and therefore interests—upon the entire community. To see how, we need to return to pragmatism's problem with rationalism.

In a book by a rationalist James had read passages such as: "Justice is ideal, solely ideal. Reason conceives that it ought to exist, but experience shows that it cannot. . . . Truth, which ought to be, cannot be. . . . Reason is deformed by experience. As soon as reason enters experience it becomes contrary to reason" (173–74). For the rationalist, therefore, proper government consists of the impossible struggle to realize a set of ideal principles that are by nature unrealizable. In contrast, James would consider such ideals of justice false precisely because they cannot be validated by experience. As James puts it, pragmatism asks a very simple question: "What, in short, is the truth's cash-value in experiential terms?" (160). It is, he argues, "the nature of truths to be validated, verified. It pays for our ideas to be validated. Our obligation to seek truth is part of our general obligation to do what pays. The payments true ideas bring are the sole why of our duty to follow them" (174). James's argument that the only obligation that we have to seek truth is because it pays, combined with his definition of true ideas as those leading to "consistency, stability and flowing human intercourse," brings us to the heart of his pluralistic vision.

Confronted with a conflict of beliefs, pragmatism requires no higher authority to force people to give up certain beliefs. Instead, if their ideas are false, people will willingly give them up because it no longer pays to hold them. And what determines true or false ideas is not some abstract principle of reason but their ability to find agreement, or as Holmes put it in a famous freedom-of-speech case, their ability to withstand the "competition of the market."[14] Beliefs that find agreement are retained. Those that do not are abandoned. Thus social unity is achieved by letting people see that their individual interests are identical with the public interest. In turn, the public interest is defined, not by reference to a set of a priori ideas or ideals, but through a continual process of negotiation that balances the competing interests of the various groups and individuals making up a pluralistic society.

To link the pragmatic definition of truth with progressivism's pluralistic mode of governance is not to argue that all pragmatists or progressives held what today we would call progressive ideas. Holmes, for one, held many conservative, elitist views. Furthermore, William James aside, few of those whom we can readily identify as progressives of the period shared a current progressive's pluralistic vision of ethnic diversity. The Anglo-Saxon bias of many early progressives and pragmatists is easy to uncover. Nonetheless, part of the force of the pragmatic definition of truth is that it can account for these changes in belief. What I am interested in describing is the means of dealing with social conflict implied by pragmatism. Extremely adaptable, the pragmatic method has proved capable of both dealing with the problems raised by a multiethnic culture and shaping our vision of how that culture should be constituted.[15]

The progressive vision, it should be emphasized, did not question the possibility of truth or rationality. On the contrary, like laissez-faire formalists, progressives continued to believe in the possibility of a rational social order. Unlike laissez-faire formalists, however, their test for rationality was not to be found by reference to past truths but in continually changing experience, not in generality but in particularity. Since each social situation is unique, it required a balancing of interests tailored to its uniqueness. As Holmes put it in terms of adjudication, "General propositions do not decide concrete cases."[16] What then is to guide the delicate balancing acts required? The answer is efficiency. A rational social order is one that pays off in terms of social efficiency. In Robert Gordon's formulation, progressives conceived of social governance as expert management, "whose goal was to promote the efficient attainment of an immanent social equilibrium (the 'public interest') between the actual and potential conflicts of corporate interest groups." That goal of efficiency assumed that "buried in each social conflict or dispute was an efficient solution in terms of some universally valid harmony of the underlying social policies. To find it, of course, you needed to consult experts."[17]

The progressive reliance upon and celebration of experts points to another important aspect of the pragmatic vision. Pragmatism developed simultaneously with the rise of a culture of professionalism. As Thomas Haskell notes, those trained in various specialized professions were granted increasing authority.[18] If in antebellum America the criteria for truth rested in a set of transcendental laws to which, theoretically, each individual had intuitive access, more and more the authority for truth shifted to what Peirce called "communities of the competent" that oversaw each discipline and profession. According to Haskell, Peirce's pragmatic semiotics helped to grant this new form of authority philosophical justification. Clearly, professionally trained experts played an important role in progressive efforts to engineer a rational social order that embodied the public interest. The public interest is not a preexisting entity that governmental policy merely reflects. Instead, it is itself shaped and constituted through policy decisions. Experts were necessary, not only to measure an always-changing mix of social interests, but also to balance them in the most efficient manner. The very metaphor of balance implies a stable social order, but a historically changing world demanded a continual process of adjustment in order to maintain social stability. Furthermore, since progress was as important to achieve as stability, it was necessary to stop thinking of laws and policies as eternally binding. Instead, they demanded continual revision. As Dewey wrote, "Failure to recognize that legal rules and principles are working hypotheses, needing to be constantly tested by the way in which they work out in application to concrete situations, explains the otherwise paradoxical fact that the slogans of the liberalism of one period often become the bulwarks of reaction in a subsequent era."[19]

The pragmatic insistence on continually adjusting and accommodating ideas to agree with a historically changing world is clearly at odds with the conservative historicism against which it reacted. Nonetheless, just as pragmatism does not question the possibility of rationalism, so it does not question the basic historicist sense of temporality. On the contrary, by breaking historicism's bondage to rationalism and moral philosophy, it asserted a modern sense of temporality more forcefully. Accompanying the radical historicist belief that an always-changing reality demands a continual testing of truth by present experience is an emphasis on using history, not to legitimate the status quo, but to help respond to the new. It is to the pragmatic sense of the uses of history that I want to turn. To do so is to recover a tradition within this country calling for more usable pasts. It is also to examine how over half a century ago the historical relativists struggled with problems that some new historicists assume were first posed by poststructuralists. Finally, it is to recognize the changed historical circumstances that render the relativists' pragmatic solutions to those problems less usable. But, first, for an early example of the pragmatic uses of the past I turn once again to Holmes.

· III ·

In an essay with the new historicist-sounding title "Law in Science and Science in Law," Holmes urged jurists to turn to the authority of science and scientific experts in order to accurately measure social needs. Nonetheless, before turning to science he placed various laws under historical scrutiny. His use of history differs from the legal formalists whom he derides. Formalists, like conservative historians, used history to legitimate existing practices by establishing a continuity between past and present. The mere survival of a law over the years was a sign of its truth. Furthermore, since the germ of a nation's identity existed in the past, there was a moral obligation to maintain sacred, foundational laws and institutions. For Holmes, however, history had quite a different lesson. Since the needs of society are always changing, the persistence of a law is no guarantee of its usefulness. Historical inquiry, for Holmes, is a means of ascertaining a law's present fitness. "Some rules," Holmes argues, "are mere survivals. Many might as well be different, and history is the means by which we measure the power which the past has had to govern the present in spite of ourselves, so to speak, by imposing traditions which no longer meet their original end. History sets us free and enables us to make up our minds dispassionately whether the survival which we are enforcing answers any new purpose when it has ceased to answer the old" (452). Just as James argued that truth happens to an idea, so Holmes argued that truth or usefulness happens to a law. A law that was once useful may no longer be so, and history is an aid in verifying its present use. History helps the legal scholar measure a law's conformity to "social desires instead of tradition" by "clearing away rubbish" (452).

"Clearing away rubbish" could have been a slogan for the rise of the pragmatically influenced progressive historians who started to shake up the study of history in the early years of the twentieth century. Indeed, Holmes's combined uses of history and science to serve present social needs anticipates the rise of a movement known as the New History. The movement's popularizer was the Columbia University historian James Harvey Robinson, who in 1912 published an influential collection of essays entitled *The New History*. As a student Robinson had attended the lectures of William James, and like James he linked usefulness and truth. Robinson makes clear the enlightenment heritage of such notions of usefulness by linking them to Voltaire's concept of serviceable truths. Even so, he disputed the neoclassical belief that the past contained truths applicable to all ages. Instead, the most important truth to be learned from the past was that of change. Emphasizing historical process over product, he urged that Ranke's study of *wie es eigentlich gewesen war* be transformed into a study of *wie es eigentlich geworden ist*. The study of the past is necessary because without it, we have no understanding of our present situation that evolved out of the past.

Furthermore, Robinson, who was trained in Germany under the author of a famous book on American constitutional history, criticized most nineteenth-century histories for being too narrowly political, for telling the story of great leaders and wars while neglecting other areas of human life. In *The New History* he demanded that historians draw on the newly developed professional social sciences to give a fuller account of the past, an account that covered economic, psychological, and social life as well as political life. He wanted more inclusive histories that took into account the lives of more than an elite few. Most important Robinson urged the production of histories that would set us free from ideas and beliefs that no longer agree with present experience. Sounding very much like Holmes, he writes, "Our respect for a given institution or social convention may be purely traditional and have little relation to its value, as judged by existing conditions. We are, therefore, in constant danger of viewing present problems with obsolete emotions and of attempting to settle them by obsolete reasoning. This is one of the chief reasons why we are never by any means perfectly adjusted to our environment." The New History hoped to serve that process of adjustment by eliminating "anachronisms in conservative economic and legal reasoning" as well as in other areas of thought.[20]

A basic component of the New History was a faith in temporal progress. Progress for Robinson was the "greatest single idea in the whole history of mankind" (247). Charles and Mary Beard called belief in progress "the most dynamic social theory ever shaped in the history of thought."[21] Even the notion of progress itself had progressed. According to Robinson, humanity had been unconsciously progressing for hundreds of thousands of years. Only recently, however, progress had become an "ideal consciously proclaimed and sought" (*NH* 251). Part of the modern effort self-consciously to bring about progress, progressivism contributed to the early twentieth-century efforts to "make it new."

For instance, the progressive era saw not only the rise of the New History, it also reckoned with the new South, the new woman, the new Negro, and the new morality. Discussions of these phenomena could be followed in publications such as the *New Republic* and *New Democracy*. The political programs responsive to them were known as the New Freedom and the New Deal. This progressive sense of the new was dependent upon a pragmatic sense of the past concisely articulated by John Dewey. On the one hand, Dewey adheres to the historicist belief that the passage of time necessitates construction of new histories, so that he writes, "Changes going on in the present, giving a new turn to social problems, throw the significance of what happened in the past into a new perspective." On the other, a proper understanding of the past can serve as an important tool to help engineer a better society. It is "a lever for moving the present into a certain kind of future."[22] The pragmatic faith in the continuity between past and present leading to reform in the future is strongly felt in Robinson's *New History*. For instance, he describes events in Paris in 1789, not as a revolutionary, but as "one of the grandest and, in its essential reforms, most peaceful of changes which ever overtook France or Europe" (*NH* 63). In America, we might add, even "peaceful" reforms as momentous as the French Revolution were not necessary, since its unique history isolated it from the corruption of the European past.

Class struggle had existed and continued to exist in the United States, and progressive historians called attention to it. Both Beard and Robinson, for instance, learned Marx through the economist E. R. A. Seligman. Robinson went so far as to claim that "in the sobered and chastened form in which most economists now accept [marxist] doctrine, it serves to explain far more of the phenomena of the past than any other single explanation ever offered." But he prefaces that comment by recalling "the manner in which Marx's theory was misused by himself and his followers" (*NH* 50–51). Instead, he and Beard discovered a Marx usable to the American situation, one that did not necessarily endorse his socialism. The special conditions of the United States made it possible to achieve an equilibrium of conflicting interests that was identical with the public interest.

But not even American exceptionalism made progressives immune to the European crisis in historicism, although it is important to recognize the difference in their response from Europeans'. World War I caused special problems for progressives. Beard worried that the United States' entry into a European conflict risked contaminating the New World. The war itself strongly taxed progressive historians' belief in progress. Carl Becker called the war the "most futile and aimless, the most desolating and repulsive exhibition of human power and cruelty without compensating advantage that has ever been on earth. This is the result of some thousands of years of what men like to speak of as political, economic, intellectual, and moral Progress. . . ." Robinson, after the war, complained that history no longer seemed to present "a natural *terminus ad quem*."

"History does not seem to stop any more. . . . It is as difficult to tell where to start as where to stop. . . . I have come to think that no such thing as objective history is possible."[23]

Those words were written even before the worldwide depression further threatened the belief that the United States was exempt from problems affecting Europe. It was also written before European questioning of objectivity in history had an influence, no matter how small, on American historiography. In the thirties, however, Beard turned to Benedetto Croce and a book by Karl Heussi entitled *Die Krisis des Historismus*.[24] Soon after, he delivered his famous "Written History as an Act of Faith," which along with Becker's "Every Man His Own Historian" marked the ascendancy of the school of historical relativism.[25] Going beyond the New History's argument that histories should serve the present, the relativists questioned the belief that reliance on the methods of the social sciences could produce objective accounts of even *wie es eigentlich geworden*. The recovery of the past was based on an act of faith, not scientific objectivity.

A passage from a 1936 work by Beard provides a concise illustration of how his former scientific confidence had turned to relativism. Asking after the causes of America's entry into World War I, he responds, "A search for the causes of America's entry into [World War I] leads into the causes of the war, into all the history that lies beyond 1914, and into the very nature of the universe of which the history is a part; that is, unless we arbitrarily decide to cut the web and begin at some place that pleases us."[26] Beard's articulation of the historian's dilemma in terms of an interconnected web helps to explain why the New History transformed into relativism, because, just as Nietzsche's criticism of modernity lets us articulate some of the problems modernity was trying to overcome, so Beard's relativistic questioning of the New History's faith in science lets us articulate some of the problems that it was trying to overcome.

The notion of an interconnected web makes the effort to pinpoint a single cause of the New History an exercise in futility. Nonetheless, one cause is suggested when Haskell links the growing awareness of interdependence that coincided with the development of an international market with the rise of the professional social sciences and pragmatism. What Haskell does not point out, however, is the difference between this late nineteenth-century sense of interdependence and earlier versions, such as the medieval one. Whereas medieval interdependence assumed a closed cosmos, in which elements of the system turned back on themselves in resemblance, late nineteenth-century interdependence assumed an open context in which the elements of the system stretched to infinity. What today is called the decentering implied by this interdependence is neatly expressed when Henry Adams asserts that "all opinion founded on fact must be error, because the facts can never be complete, and their relation must always be infinite."[27] An open-ended sense of interdependence tends to question transcendental explanations of the world, for they will never be able to account for continual changes within the system. Instead, the causes for social action are more often sought within society's highly complex interconnections. As a result, so argues Haskell, specialized disciplines were developed to study that complexity. Those trained in these disciplines in turn became the new sources of authority in a culture of professionalism.

In urging New Historians to align themselves with the social sciences, Robinson recognized that histories written from the transcendental perspective of moral philosophy were no longer adequate responses to the highly complex, interdependent world of the late nineteenth century. But his interdisciplinary approach was also a response to a problem presented by the rise of so many specialized disciplines to study that world. Recognizing the potential of the new disciplines to fragment knowledge, Robinson saw history as the discipline that could draw from them all. To the objection that if, as he urged, each discipline would adopt a historical model of knowledge, there would be no need for the discipline of history, Robinson replied that the task of historians is to unite these separate histories. The New History would serve as a synthesis of various disciplines in order to arrive at a scientific explanation of how the present came to be.[28]

A succinct way to show why the faith in a scientific history eroded is to look at the most celebrated product of the New History, Beard's *Economic Interpretation of the Constitution of the United States* (1913). Beard wrote this widely debated book while a colleague of Robinson's at Columbia. Together the two had edited a two-volume textbook on *The Development of Modern Europe*. Appearing at a time when the Constitution was frequently evoked to protect vested interests, Beard's book intervened into current political debates by arguing that the founding fathers were an economic elite who fashioned a document that served their special interests. The superiority of his argument, Beard declared, grew out of a method that used economics to distinguish between "remote and proximate causes."[29] Beard takes the notion of remote and proximate causes from the law where in the late nineteenth century it was combined with the doctrine of "objective causation" to determine the award of damages in torts. The courts could take money from A to give damages to B only if it could objectively be proved that A caused an injury to B. Borrowing from current science the notion of "chains of causation," the courts felt that they could trace the line of causation from A to B by distinguishing between remote and proximate causes. Only proximate causes, they concluded, counted as evidence.

But the very legal notion to which Beard appeals had already been attacked by a lawyer named Nicholas St. John Green. Green is important for our story because along with Holmes he was a member of the Metaphysical Club that gave rise to pragmatism in the 1870s. Relying on pragmatic assumptions, Green refuted the doctrine of objective causation. As Green pointed out, what the courts accepted as scientific proof was actually based on two metaphors, that of a chain and that of the distinction between remote and proximate. Appealing to the notion of an interconnected world (which, I should point out, relies on another metaphor) he argued, "To every event there are certain antecedents . . . It is not any one of this set of antecedents taken by itself which is the cause. Not one by itself would produce the effect. The true cause is the whole set of antecedents taken together."[30] Green, in other words, anticipates Beard's relativist argument about the impossibility of singling out a cause for World War I. As Beard's earlier reliance on proximate and remote causes illustrates, the very interconnectedness to which the New History responded undercuts its claim to scientific authority.

A highly complex, interconnected world posed to Beard a dilemma familiar to new historicists who try to explain, as most historians do, why things happened, not only describe what happened. If everything is interconnected, it seems arbitrary to single out some causes at the expense of others. Indeed, Beard even toyed with the possibility of writing histories without causes, thus anticipating the practice of "thick description." But if Beard faced the new historicism's problem of arbitrary connectedness, he did so in different historical circumstances.

One way to characterize the difference between Beard, the New Historian, and Beard, the relativist, would be to say that he moved from Peirce's scientifically-based pragmatism to James's, which challenged the tendency to lapse into scientific foundationalism. Indeed, James's "The Will to Believe" provides important insights into Beard's "Written History as an Act of Faith." What needs to be emphasized, however, is that Beard's faith included a faith in science and its contribution to progress. In one of his last defenses of relativism, Beard evoked Peirce in calling for a "consensus of competence."[31] What also needs to be emphasized is Beard's faith that scientific progress found its proper sphere in the United States. In *The Rise of American Civilization* Beard and his wife proclaimed that "it was science, not paper declarations relating to the idea of progress, that at last made patent the practical methods by which democracy could raise the standard of living for the great masses of the people."[32]

Beard's faith in American exceptionalism, though somewhat shaken by events in the thirties, remained intact and helped him avoid the "bottomless pit" of relativism feared by the German historian Meinecke.[33] In the late thirties, especially with the signing of the Hitler-Stalin pact, there were good reasons for maintaining that faith. For instance, René Wellek, a recent immigrant, chided Van Wyck Brooks for attacking modern writers and for uncritically celebrating America's literary past. "We may and should deplore Mr. Brooks's bludgeoning attacks on modern writers and his far too crude distinctions between primary and secondary literature." Nonetheless, Wellek adds, "But in his emotional, quite untheoretical way, Mr. Brooks gives voice to a genuine need of our time: A return to the sources of the American national tradition which fortunately is also the hope of all humanity."[34]

If Europe faced a crisis in historicism in the 1930s and 1940s, America's dramatic confrontation with it was yet to come, and the period after World War II saw the celebration of American progressive reform by the consensus historians. For instance, in 1970 Fischer, whom I quoted in the second chapter, could continue his description of historicism with:

> German historicism is dead, or dying, but the same ethical version of the genetic fallacy still appears in other forms . . . American historians such as Daniel Boorstin came close to arguing in the 1950s that *Die Amerikanische Geschichte ist das Weltgericht*, and they were not alone in that assumption. Something of the fallacy of ethical historicism appears in the absurd and dangerous idea that America's rise to power and prosperity is a measure of its moral excellence—that the history of the Republic can be seen, in short, as a system of morality. How many of us have not, at some time, silently slipped into this error?[35]

To read this passage in the 1990s is to remind us of the important influence that events in the 1960s, 1970s, and 1980s have had on the outlook of cultural critics in the United States. Liberal scholars occupying today's literature departments may admit to having slipped into the error Fischer describes, but having experienced the civil rights movement, the women's liberation movement, Watergate, Vietnam, and the Reagan era, they do so only with a bad conscience. If the belief in American exceptionalism helped to delay America's confrontation with a crisis in historicism, the recent experience of what David W. Noble has cleverly called *The End of American History*[36] has forced members of this generation to face it more squarely. In turn that confrontation was a precondition for the "theoretical" revolt that rocked the study of literature in the United States in the seventies and eighties. Faced with its own crisis in historicism, a generation of critics suddenly found important uses for poststructuralism, which, if my argument is correct, needs to be seen as a response to a crisis in European historicism. To use James's image, poststructuralism along with the entire continental tradition that it engages passed from "cold-storage to do work in the world" (162). New interpretations were developed for Nietzsche, Marx, Freud, and Heidegger. Figures like Gramsci and Bakhtin were discovered, and their work entered literary debates simultaneously with that of Derrida, Foucault, and Lacan. In addition, ideological criticism was rediscovered, and the politics of interpretation became a new subfield in literary studies.

One reason for the sudden explosion of ideological criticism in the United States is that the belated crisis in historicism transformed descriptions of American exceptionalism into ones of an American ideology. It is probably no accident that the most persuasive account of that ideology came from someone intimately familiar with United States culture, yet born outside of its political boundaries. In *The American Jeremiad* Sacvan Bercovitch eloquently argues that most criticism of the United States within the United States has appealed to an ideal notion of America as a reference point for its criticism. Inequities, exclusions, and unfair practices have often been criticized, but they have been criticized by pointing out how little the reality of the United States lives up to the ideal construct known as America. Such criticism has often proved quite effective in producing reforms, but ultimately it ends up confirming what Bercovitch has called the symbol of America.[37]

A different way to confirm the American ideology is to claim to be offering a new brand of cultural criticism by drawing on continental thought while unwittingly remaining within a native tradition. And this, I would argue, is precisely what many new historicists have done, for many poststructuralist "innovations" are actually part of a native tradition. For instance, some new historicists point to poststructuralism's questioning of disciplinary boundaries as enabling their more expansive move to a cultural poetics. But, as we have seen, Robinson's New History also called for an interdisciplinary approach. His crossing of disciplinary boundaries even evoked complaints similar to ones leveled against today's new historicists. When the chairman of Columbia's history department retired in 1915 he wrote that Robinson and a fellow New Historian had so departed from traditional history that what they did amounted "almost to a secession and to the creation of a new department." In their courses, he complained, they teach "everything except history, as their colleagues understand it. Neither is expert in any one of the subjects as discursively treated, and the departments of economics and sociology have been disturbed by the trespass."[38]

Some economics departments today might be disturbed by new historicists' fascination with economics and the marketplace, a fascination that was anticipated by people like Beard. And, just as Beard relied on Marx for his analysis without buying into his particular brand of socialism, so many new historicists have rediscovered marxist analysis as a tool of criticism without accepting it as a model for a political program.

As we saw in the second chapter, the non-marxist use of the marxist emphasis on offering a total understanding of a culture has caused problems for new historicists because it infinitely expands the field of evidence available without providing a master narrative to structure that field. But this was also a problem faced by the progressive historians. Indeed, Cohen's marxist condemnation that the new historicism is committed to "arbitrary connectedness" gains an added resonance when we juxtapose it to Beard's argument that it is impossible to write a causal history "unless we arbitrarily decide to cut the web and begin at some place that pleases us." Becker even recognized that this relativist argument came into tension with the desire to construct new histories. "Relativity," he admitted, "becomes a convenient weapon for destructive criticism, but useless for constructing a system of knowledge."[39] For the relativists, the construction of histories could not be based on a firm scientific or rational foundation, but on an act of faith.

Clearly, then, poststructuralists were not the first to note that histories are constructed from a present point of view and carry with them implications for present political debates. Indeed, such arguments are a vital part of pragmatic historiography. For instance, in the early years of this century Becker referred to historical thinking as a "social instrument, helpful in getting the world's work more efficiently done."[40] If poststructuralism offers something "new" for present-day historians, it is not the reminder that we constantly rewrite the past. Instead, it offers a challenge to the pragmatic desire for efficient newness. Before turning to how poststructuralism challenges the usefulness of a model of efficiency, however, I want to examine the "Against Theory" argument in terms of the dilemma of presentism that constantly plagues pragmatic historiography.

· IV ·

Statements about the past would seem to cause special problems for pragmatism. As we have seen, James's conflation of a statement's usability and truth can combat charges of relativism because of his insistence on verification. Nonetheless, verification for James is future-oriented. What does he do, then, with statements about the past? Do not statements about the past raise special epistemological dilemmas precisely because they are about an experience that no longer exists?

Pragmatists were not unaware of the dilemma. Nonetheless, except for one chapter in a late work by Dewey, its philosophers did not extensively treat questions of historical knowledge. Even Beard, whose desire to construct usable pasts profitted from the conflation of usability and truth, noted the lack and lamented it. Recently, however, that version of neo-pragmatism represented by the "Against Theory" position has relied on pragmatic assumptions to make the special epistemological questions concerning historical knowledge disappear by arguing that they are inconsequential for practice. To see how pragmatism could give rise to such an argument and why it is inadequate to face the challenge posed by poststructuralism, we can turn to earlier pragmatic attempts to answer, however briefly, the questions involved.

Recognizing a possible problem raised by statements about the past, Peirce argued that, "as for that part of the Past that lies beyond memory, the Pragmaticist doctrine is that the meaning of its being believed to be in connection with the Past consists in the acceptance as truth of the conception that we ought to conduct ourselves according to it (like the meaning of any other belief). Thus, a belief that Christopher Columbus discovered America really refers to the future. . . ."[41] James confronts the particular problem of historical truth in the midst of his discussion of the role of discourse. "All human thinking," James writes, "gets discursified; we exchange ideas; we lend and borrow verifications, get them from one another by means of social intercourse. All truth thus gets verbally built out, stored up, and made available for everyone" (166). This verbal store is especially important for ideas about history, because they "admit of no direct or face-to-face verification. . . . The stream of time can be remounted only verbally, or verified indirectly by the present prolongations or effects of what the past harbored. Yet if they agree with these verbalities and effects, we can know that our ideas of the past are true" (167). By recognizing how ideas get embodied in discourse, James can solve the problem that historical knowledge poses to pragmatism's face toward the future. Statements about the past are not true because they correspond to what really happened in the past, but because they will do work in the future by finding agreement with verbalities that continue to exist in the present or those aspects of the past that have not disappeared. Nonetheless, knowledge of the past still seems to cause difficulties for the pragmatic notion of truth.

A theory, James writes, "must mediate between all previous truths and certain new experiences" by deranging "common sense and previous belief as little as possible" (167). But what happens to our commonsensical beliefs about the past when we place them next to James's chiasmatic claim that it is the same to say that something is useful because it is true as to say that it is true because it is useful? Since past experience no longer exists to verify statements about it, can it really be that a usable past is necessarily a true past, with the measure of its truth being its ability to do work in the present? If so, its truth would seem to be more a matter of persuasion than demonstration, of construction rather than discovery. A true past would be one that convinced those in the present that its version is correct, not one that necessarily tells us what the past was really like. And if this is so, how can we still claim to be talking about the past?

But it is precisely at this point that James's stress on the need to find agreement can be evoked to make this apparent dilemma disappear. People will only be convinced that an account of the past is true if they are persuaded that it is verified by past experience. Any account that cannot bring about that act of persuasion is of no use, and therefore not true. Clearly, the best way to persuade people that an account of the past is true is to rely on accepted standards of what it means to verify statements about the past. To be sure, those standards may change, but not by imposing a set of principles that will guarantee validity. They will change only when people are persuaded that different principles are more useful, that is, true. Changes in the criteria for truth cannot be externally imposed upon a discipline because they are always internally developed by it.

What I have just offered is my account of the "Against Theory" argument, at least as it pertains to questions of reconstructing the past. It derives its force from pragmatically asking what the experiential payoff is in worrying over the fact that our accounts of the past are constructs. One answer is that to do so is to fail to convince people that such an account is about history. Like all disciplines, history is defined by its object of study; that is, the past. To say that one's account is not about the past, but merely a present construct, is to remove it from the discipline of history and make it something else. Since to remain a historian means that one has to believe that one is offering an account of the past, the only practical consequences of saying that one's account is merely a construct is to remove one from the practice of history into the practice of metahistory, which is the study of what historians do. That study can be a valuable one, but it does not alter the fact that historians still have to persuade people that their accounts are, after all, about history. Thus the dilemma historians have to face concerning the special nature of historical knowledge seems to be a false, id est, inconsequential, dilemma.

This argument serves to remind us that we do not solve the problem of the constructed nature of historical knowledge merely by being aware of it. It also serves to mark a historical moment when pragmatic assumptions have begun to lose their power to do critical work in the world. Progressive historians conceived of their histories as tools, part of the arsenal of a professionally trained community of experts needed to engineer the good society. Agreeing with pragmatic attacks on rationalism and a correspondence definition of truth, neopragmatists adhering to the "Against Theory" argument continue to grant authority to communities of the competent. Knowledge, for them, is produced within a set of institutional and disciplinary constraints. Influenced, however, not only by Foucauldian analysis of such disciplinary knowledge, but also by historical events, they can no longer share Peirce's faith in the disinterestedness of such knowledge. It no longer represents the "public" interest or the interests of the "whole community." Instead, it represents more local interests, the interests of the particular community that produces it. Furthermore, this knowledge, produced within particular disciplinary boundaries, provides no position outside of those boundaries from which to control the direction of disciplinary change, not to speak of the direction of social change at large. Historical analysis no longer helps in the project of doing the world's work, it merely does the work of the particular discipline of history, extending its practices and its specifically constituted knowledge.

Some have charged that such an argument gives an inadequate account of change. In the words of Stanley Fish, one complaint is that because an interpretive community is identified by a set of shared assumptions it would be "enclosed in the armor of its own totalizing assumptions." Thus it is "impervious to change and acts only to perpetuate itself and its interests: in this view, the business of an interpretive community and of the theory that privileges it is the legitimation of the status quo." Fish, however, has responded by arguing that an interpretive community is not a static object but an "engine of change." It is an "engine of change because its assumptions are not a mechanism for shutting out the world but for organizing it, for seeing phenomena as already related to interests and goals that make the community what it is. The community, in other words, is always engaged in doing work, the work of transforming the landscape into material for its own project; but that project is then itself transformed by the very work it does." But why, we might ask, would not this process lead to a vicious circularity in which the community organized the world so as continually to reconfirm its own assumptions rather than to be transformed in the process of organization? "The answer lies in the nature of an interpretive community which is at once homogeneous with respect to some general sense of purpose and purview, and heterogeneous with respect to the variety of practices it can accommodate."[42]

Change not only occurs, it is inevitable because the contingency of a historical world necessitates continual adjustments and accommodations. But the very contingency that makes change inevitable undercuts any attempt to control its direction. For instance, Fish dismisses as "antifoundational theory hope" the belief that it is emancipatory to expose the historical contingency of beliefs and institutions that are commonly held to be a result of nature not convention. This activity could be emancipatory only if it were possible to escape the contingency that will in turn render any new beliefs and institutions prone to similar "deconstruction." But because the first premise of antifoundational thought is that we cannot escape historical contingency, we will never be free of the constraints of conventional beliefs and institutions. If such change is inevitable, it occurs within temporal continuity not discontinuity. There can be no breaks with present practices only extensions of them.

Fish's argument that we can have only extensions of present practices starts to reveal the inadequacy of his position, especially his response to the complaint that his account of change helps to legitimate the status quo. To be sure, he shows why the notion of interpretive communities does not necessarily lead to a vicious circularity that rules out changes in beliefs. Nonetheless, he fails to address the argument that in modern pluralistic societies what remains constant is a sense of the inevitability of change. As Walter Benjamin noted, this sense of change, which he associates with life in capitalist culture, makes the desire for novelty recurrent in both senses of the word. "Fashion," Benjamin muses, "is the eternal return of the new."[43] The new (as in the new historicism) becomes the latest fashion. We have change, but nothing really changes. As Benjamin knew, the sameness resulting from a sense of inevitable change can have important political consequences.

For instance, Fish argues that there is no need for a theory of change because every mechanism of social stabilization has transformative possibilities built into it. For Fish change just happens. There is no struggle involved in it. But there are varieties of change. For instance, Fish's argument does not address the interests of those who suffer under existing conditions, which, to be sure, are always changing but do not seem to change their suffering. One of the strengths of the tradition of pragmatic progressivism in the United States was that it not only assumed the inevitability of change but promised to influence the direction of change in the name of the public interest. At a time when it is increasingly difficult to ignore the fact that in United States history the "public" interest has been served by excluding segments of the population from that promise, we need more than a renewal of a pragmatic tradition, especially one turned against itself.

For those whose heterogeneous voice in a pluralistic community of interpretation is swallowed up by a homogeneity claiming to represent the whole, the extension of existing practices is not enough. And yet it is precisely in Fish's argument about how practices are extended that we can see how deeply his sense of temporality is lodged within pragmatism's sense of a continuous stream of time. To extend means to stretch or draw out. Spatially it means to elongate, temporally to prolong. In both cases it implies a substantialist continuity from one point to another. To be sure, it need not imply a notion of teleological progress. For instance, for Fish the changes in beliefs and institutions that occur are not "better" than the ones they replace. They are merely "different."[44] Nonetheless, Fish does not give up the notion of progress altogether. Indeed, he shares striking similarities with an old-fashioned *Historismus* that posed a challenge to the philosophy of history's sense of teleology.

Intent on saving historical specificity, Ranke wrote, "Should one want to suppose, in opposition to the view offered here, that progress resides in the higher potentiality of each age in the life of man, that each generation completely surpasses the preceding one, and that the latter is inevitably the most privileged, the previous ones being only the bearers of those that succeed them, this would be an injustice on God's part. Such, as it were, mediated generations would have no meaning in and of themselves; they would only have meaning as a stage preparing the way for the following generations and would not stand in an immediate relation to the divine. I maintain, however, that each era is immediate before God, and its worth does not at all depend on what follows from it, but on its own existence, its own self." "Before God," Ranke insists, "all generations of mankind possess equal rights."[45] From God's atemporal point of view, then, there is no progress. Human beings, however, do not share God's point of view. As a result, the very notion that seems to deny progress turns out to legitimate the direction history has unfolded as a working out of God's will. So long as each generation is "immediate before God," we are discouraged from imagining alternatives within history. Not only what was, but also what is, has God's sanction.

Fish does not share Ranke's theology. Nonetheless, he too smuggles back a notion of progress. From some omniscient perspective current beliefs and institutions might not be better than previous ones. But since such a perspective does not exist, current beliefs and institutions must be better for their particular moment in time, otherwise they would not have replaced ones that now seem outdated. Like Ranke, Fish implies that a period's beliefs and institutions are appropriate to it, and if they are not they will automatically change. Unlike Ranke, however, Fish has a tendency to deny historical difference. We can see this tendency in his response to the new historicism, a response that perfectly illustrates how his account of change rules out the possibility of substantive change.

Whereas Ranke had a clear sense that he proposed a new method of historiography, Fish denies the very possibility of a "new" historicism. We may, Fish argues, come up with new historical truths, but they will not result from a new "way of doing history, but merely another move in the practice of history as it has always been done."[46] We need to look closely at Fish's use of "always." On the one hand, it might imply that the practice of history has always already been with us; on the other, that once the practice of history arose it has always been done a certain way. If the first (which I doubt, because it is such a historically naive position), he can offer no account of how the practice of history came into being in the first place. If the second, he implies a homogeneous continuity to the practice of history that most historians of the practice of history would deny.

The frequency that at crucial moments "always" creeps into Fish's discourse suggests that despite his appeal to historical contingency he actually has little respect for historical difference. That lack of respect helps to account for Fish's attempt, by definition, to rule out the possibility of a new historicism. Ranke's historicism posed a challenge to philosophers who would subordinate history to the logic of their systems. Fish and others embracing the "Against Theory" position, while claiming to operate historically, actually conduct their argument about historical studies epistemologically. Thus they perpetuate the tradition of those who would subsume history under a *logos*.[47]

It is important, therefore, to recognize that the logic Fish draws upon to make universal statements about how history has always been practiced grows out of a very particular historical situation. For instance, even if we were to agree that Fish's description of interpretive communities and change holds for modern pluralistic societies, need we grant that it holds for other societies? Were interpretive communities in the medieval era simultaneously homogeneous and heterogeneous, or does that description make most sense in a country whose pluralistic ideal is *E Pluribus Unum*? Is the notion of interpretive communities itself universal or does it have its own history traceable through Josiah Royce to Peirce's notion of "communities of the competent?" And if, as I have implied, Fish's account of change does not hold for all time, how can Fish account for the historical change that gave rise to his account of change?

Clearly, Fish does not speak for all who advocate renewing the pragmatic tradition. Steven Mailloux, for instance, urges that "more needs to be done to ensure that rhetorical pragmatism realizes the radical potential that Cornel West suggests for neo-pragmatism in general."[48] Against such calls, a strength of Fish's position is its reminder that precisely such guarantees are impossible in a historically contingent world. I will not be so naive as to suggest that I can offer an alternative that can ensure its own radical potential. Nonetheless, I do want to suggest that the particular sense of temporal continuity that helped pragmatism become a progressive force in the early decades of the twentieth century minimizes the possibility of it's fulfilling today the radical potential that West envisions for it. In a country where Ronald Reagan was hired to do television commercials for a company declaring "progress" to be its most important business, one challenge facing a new historicism is how to imagine a possibility for substantive change without lapsing into a sense of progressive temporal continuity that more often than not serves to produce the sameness of the new.[49] It is to the poststructuralist challenge to the pragmatic sense of temporality that I now want to turn. If, as we have seen, much of what new historicists attribute to poststructuralism is part of a native pragmatic tradition, the poststructuralist sense of temporality is at odds with that tradition. Lacking the faith in a progressive American exceptionalism that helped Beard avoid the bottomless pit of relativism, today's new historicists need to face this poststructuralist challenge squarely. At the same time, the pragmatic emphasis on usability points to some of the limits of the poststructuralist response.

· V ·

In the essay in which he urged the emancipatory use of history, Holmes declared that continuity with the past, which is "only necessary not a duty," limits "the possibilities of our imagination, and settles the terms in which we shall be compelled to think" (444). A year before he coined the phrase "a usable past," Van Wyck Brooks, although clearly influenced by pragmatists, declared that their concern with adaptation so confined them to the perspective of the present that they could imagine no alternatives to it.[50] Brooks's later work, which celebrated his own continuity with an American tradition he once criticized, seems to confirm Holmes's point. It is possible, however, that Brooks's own failure of the imagination grew out of his pragmatic insistence that a usable past must be one that establishes continuities. Insofar as the new historicism's imagination is limited by the unacknowledged continuities it maintains with the tradition of pragmatic progressivism, poststructuralism places pressure on it by challenging pragmatism's sense of temporality. We can get a sense of that challenge by briefly comparing pragmatism's and Nietzsche's responses to late nineteenth-century historicism and rationalism.

Like pragmatists, Nietzsche questioned rationalism's essentialism and its correspondence theory of truth. He also questioned conservative historicism's backward-looking traditionalism and argued for present uses of history. Unlike pragmatism, however, he does not conflate usefulness with truth. For William James an idea is true, if it agrees with reality, insofar as agreement covers "any process of conduction from a present idea to a future terminus, provided only it run prosperously" (162). For Nietzsche the will to truth implies a will to power. Truth is possible, therefore, only through an act of repression. Thus, whereas James measures true ideas in terms of their ability to lead to consistency and stability, away from eccentricity and contradiction, Nietzsche emphasizes the distortions and violations required in order to bring about such consistent stability. James claims that "surely in this field of truth it is the pragmatists and not the rationalists who are the more genuine defenders of the universe's rationality" (176). Nietzsche calls into question the sovereignty of reason.

In questioning the sovereignty of reason, Nietzsche implicitly questions the mode of political governance implied by a pragmatic definition of truth. We can see how by turning to the way that recent thinkers have used pragmatism to appeal to Aristotelian *phronesis* to describe the open-textured rules that enable the play of political debate in a community. *Phronesis* creates the conditions for unconstrained communication necessary for the proper mode of democratic governance. Used by someone like Habermas, *phronesis* recalls the legal realists' effort to find an immanent rationality through a process of balancing the particular interests of an always-changing historical situation. Like James, the realists could argue that their emphasis on process better speaks for rationality than rationalists' appeal to a set of fixed rules. But we should not forget that Aristotle maintained an important distinction between "cosmos," which is a divine order of rationality that people must find, and "taxis," which is an order that people construct.

For Aristotle, the *doxa*, or public opinion produced by *phronesis*, was inevitably fallible. Its fallibility was evident when it was confronted with the cosmic order governing human actions. Recognizing the fallibility of laws produced by *phronesis*, Aristotle posited the need for a system of equity to provide for a more just system of governance. Equity could correct errors resulting from a strict application of human-made law. The disappearance of equity in modern democratic states reminds us of a dilemma faced with the rise of modernity and the demise of the notion of a closed cosmos. With the collapse of the distinction between "cosmos" and "taxis" in the modern era, humans began to confront the possibility that order would not exist without explicit human intervention. As a result, efforts were launched to correct the inevitable fallibility resulting from *phronesis* by appealing to human reason. Such efforts to found political governance in rationality fall prey to the same problems faced by modern efforts to establish philosophical systems on a purely rational foundation. Reason, in Blumenberg's phrase, gets overextended.[51]

One of pragmatism's strengths is that it questions Cartesian attempts to base all thinking on a foundation of rationality. Nonetheless, its version of antifoundationalism can be seen as the latest, and certainly one of the most effective, of modernity's attempts to guarantee the rule of reason. Rationality is not guided by a set of timeless principles, but is perpetually reconstructed through a process of open-ended negotiation and exchange best accomplished within democratic institutional structures. The effectiveness of the pragmatic solution is testified to by the work it has done and continues to do in the world. Nietzsche's version of antifoundationalism, however, poses a challenge to it.

Like Aristotle, Nietzsche insists upon the fallibility of the *doxa*. Unlike Aristotle, Nietzsche offers no cosmic order to correct its fallibility. This is because, like pragmatists, he lives in a world in which previous realities can be rendered unreal. But his sense of that world's temporality is at odds with the pragmatists' sense of progressive temporality. Pragmatists use the progressive movement of history through time as a way to verify an idea's truth. In contrast, Nietzsche sees history as generated by acts of repression that call into question the very possibility of progressive temporality. In arguing that the new can only be brought about by an active forgetting that releases the burden of history, Nietzsche both responded to and contributed to a crisis in historicism and thus became one of the most important "fathers" of poststructuralism. The challenge his thought poses to the project of a new historicism is perhaps most economically expressed in Paul de Man's appropriation of him.

According to de Man, "the reconciliation of memory with action is the dream of all historians."[52] Through a rigorous study of the past, the historian hopes to contribute to a new future. For de Man, however, the dream of reconciling memory with action will always remain a dream, for action depends not on memory but forgetting. De Man explores the implications of this Nietzschean notion for efforts to write new literary histories in "Literary History and Literary Modernity." Following Nietzsche, de Man defines modernity as "the form of a desire to wipe out whatever came earlier, in the hope of reaching at last a point that could be called a true present, a point of origin that marks a new departure." This need of the modern to wipe out the past in order to establish the legitimately new would make the notion of a *new* history inevitably contradictory, since the modern would be in direct opposition to history. Opposition, however, is not the correct word to describe the relationship between the two. "Modernity and history relate to each other in a curiously contradictory way that goes beyond antithesis or opposition." Modernity is not only opposed to history, it depends on history for its very articulation, and vice versa. "If history is not to become sheer regression or paralysis, it depends on modernity for its duration and renewal; but modernity cannot assert itself without being at once swallowed up and reintegrated into a regressive historical process. Nietzsche offers no real escape out of a predicament in which we readily recognize the mood of our own modernity. Modernity and history seem condemned to being linked together in a self-destroying union that threatens the survival of both."[53]

In this essay, de Man is not arguing, as some have assumed, that history does not exist. History is indeed generated. But it is generated by a structure of blindness and insight that undermines the very possibility of progressive, linear time. Modernity, or a new history, is not a movement toward progressive enlightenment but is "swallowed up and reintegrated into a regressive historical process." If, according to James, a true idea must agree with reality, and agreement is a process of leading from "a present idea to a future terminus, provided only it run prosperously," for de Man there are no fully true ideas.

Of major importance for those intent on attempting to reconcile memory with action, the poststructuralist challenge to the pragmatic definition of truth is most marked concerning statements about the past. We can pose the poststructuralist challenge in pragmatic language. James speaks of truth in terms of its "cash value in experiential terms." Our only obligation to seek the truth is because "it pays for our ideas to be validated." Poststructuralism forces us to measure the cost this pragmatic notion of truth has for our sense of history. The answer comes into focus when we look at what a notion of truth celebrating consistency, stability, and freedom from clash and contradiction implies for statements about the past. As James admits, such statements can be verified only indirectly by agreeing with the effects of the past prolonged into the present or through consistency with existing verbalizations. Whereas statements about the present are tested against the fullness of present experience, those about the past are tested against a partial experience of the past, that which survives. This partiality is evident in Robinson's New History. There is no doubt about the sincerity of Robinson's desire to write more inclusive histories. But working within a pragmatic framework of progressive continuity and consistency, he felt that the study of the past could produce truth usable for the present only if it rejected "the anomalous and seeming accidental" (NH 15). In stressing the need for historical accounts to help those in the present adapt to their environment, he reduced the immense richness and diversity of the past to a set of serviceable truths, ones that transformed past conflicts and contradiction into a process of consistent and progressive reform.[54]

Poststructuralism questions the usability of such usable truths by asking whose interests they serve. In contrast to Robinson, for instance, Foucault, evoking Nietzsche, insists on a historiography that "will cultivate the details and accidents accompanying every beginning."[55] His strategy is not, as we have seen, without problems of its own, for too often the disruptive force of the accidental can be domesticated by placing it within a more inclusive but, nevertheless, consistent narrative. Recognizing the need to resist such domestication, Derrida works to produce narratives that are themselves subject to chance. "This is," he writes, "the only chance—but it is only chance—for them to be history."[56] Only a history allowing the play of chance will provide a chance for a new history.

The poststructuralist emphasis on the accidental and chance serves as a countermemory to the pragmatic stress on adaptation and accommodation. Nonetheless, it is precisely at this moment that pragmatism's stress on usefulness poses a return challenge to poststructuralism. What, after all, are the practical possibilities of basing a practice on chance? On the one hand, it would seem impossible since chance is by definition something that we cannot control. On the other, it would seem inevitable since, if Derridean arguments about "differance" or Foucauldian ones about the accidental nature of history are correct, chance will always disrupt our attempts to achieve consistency. To put it quite simply, if we place our hopes for bringing about a new order on chance, chances are not very good that it will come about.

Indeed, at the time that pragmatism was taking shape many progressives cited the current economic and social system's reliance on chance as a cause of its repressions. Willing to grant the inevitability of chance in questions of life and death, Basil March, one of William Dean Howells's fictional characters, goes on:

> But what I object to is this economic chance world in which we live and which we men seem to have created. It ought to be law as inflexible in human affairs as the order to the day and night in the physical world, that if a man will work he shall both rest and eat, and shall not be harassed with some question as to how his repose and his provision shall come. Nothing less ideal than this satisfies the reason. But in our state of things no one is secure of this. No one is sure of finding work; no one is sure of not losing it. I may have my work taken away from me at any moment by the caprice, the mood, the indigestion, of a man who has not the qualification for knowing whether I do it well or ill.[57]

As *A Hazard of New Fortunes*, the title of the book in which March appears indicates, the power of capitalism might rest precisely in its ability to allow for the play of hazardousness and speculation. Ironically, then, the poststructuralist emphasis on the need to allow for chance might, by chance, not challenge the economic and social status quo, but help to maintain it. For how would poststructuralism find a basis on which to distinguish between "real" chance and the humanly created chance that exists in the "economic chance world" that Howells describes? Indeed, apologists for capitalism often attribute its inequalities and inequities to the inevitability of chance rather than any inherent logic to the system.

To many, the hazards of that system no longer seem as great as they were at the time that Howells wrote. Much of the credit for this sense of improvement should go to pragmatic progressives who worked to minimize the social costs of chance. Peirce, for instance, was fully aware of the inevitability of chance. Appealing to the model of insurance companies, he urged active intervention based on science, statistics, and measure to produce a more secure social system by controlling chance. Progressive slogans, for instance, likened their programs to ethically operated games of chance. Theodore Roosevelt promised a "square deal." His cousin a "new deal." Recognizing that people's chances for a square deal are minimized if they are born as members of particular groups, affirmative action programs continue in this tradition. When someone like Fish argues against the possibility of engineering social change, what he misunderstands is that the progressive claim was not an absolutist claim. Working with an awareness that we inhabit a world of chance, pragmatic progressives were concerned with probabilities not absolutes. In a world of chance, programs cannot guarantee change that holds for every case, but they can work to minimize the risk of unfair practices.[58] For Peirce life in a universe of chance meant that we needed to think in terms of the entire community, not individuals. In an essay entitled "The Doctrine of Chance," he wrote, "Logicality inexorably requires that our interests shall not be limited. They must not stop at our own fate, but must embrace the whole community. This community, again, must not be limited, but must extend to all races of beings with whom we can come into immediate or mediate intellectual relation. . . . Logic is rooted in the social principle."[59]

Such a vision may not be inherent within logic, but it is still a socially constructed vision with uses today. A problem, however, comes in the notion of a community based on an "immediate or mediate intellectual relation," for there is a risk, called to attention by poststructuralism, that our intellect will not establish a relation to those who do not fit into what is considered rational logic. Historical memory can help us to see what present constructions of logic have excluded. But it is precisely on the point of memory that the Nietzschean aspect of poststructuralism reveals its limits for such a historical enterprise. So long as action depends on forgetting, not memory, poststructuralism can expose past exclusions but also be used apologetically to argue that they are necessary to get on with the work of the world. Such a vision certainly challenges a sense of progressive temporality, but it also seems to guarantee that all attempts at a new history will, in de Man's words, be "swallowed up and reintegrated into a regressive historical process." We have temporal breaks, only to confirm the eternal return of the same.

I ended the last chapter by turning to Blumenberg's notion of reoccupation to suggest an alternative to the poststructuralist emphasis on discontinuity and historicism's on continuity. I want to end this one by proposing an alternative to the tradition of pragmatic progressivism, which does not so much deconstruct Peirce's desire for an inclusive community as use memory to construct an even more inclusive one. To move toward that alternative we can turn to a measure of discontent with the pragmatic sense of history registered by a non-American trained in the pragmatic tradition. Pragmatism, George Santayana complained, results in a strange "reduction of yesterday to tomorrow."[60] Perhaps it is no accident that this complaint comes from Santayana, who at the urging of Josiah Royce had written his dissertation on the German philosopher Hermann Lotze. Lotze, in turn, helped to shape Walter Benjamin's notion of community and is quoted by him at the start of the second section in his "Theses on the Philosophy of History." More than even poststructuralists, Benjamin, who also had engaged Nietzsche's challenge to *Historismus*, undermines the premises of progressive historiography. He does so by proposing a mode of historiography based on a "constructive principle," not a destructive one.[61]

· VI ·

Lotze was important to Benjamin because he wrestled with a dilemma posed by a progressive sense of time. If history inevitably progresses, why are not present generations envious of future ones? Kant himself had suggested that it would be strange to think that each generation worked for the betterment of future ones without being able to participate in the happiness they made possible. Nonetheless, lodged within a progressive philosophy of history, he concluded that it must be so. Lotze, though certainly no radical, recognized a class dimension to the problem. It was, he admitted, the masses who most bore the burden of such toil and who least benefitted from the gains. His answer was to revise the sense of the human community. Peirce, we have seen, used logic to argue that our interests must embrace the whole community. But for him that community was a synchronic one. In contrast, Lotze insisted that a sense of common humanity implies a belief "in which the past is not simply *not* there but in which rather all the things the course of historical time irrevocably separates from one another exist side by side in a timeless community."[62] This enlarged sense of the human community allows him to understand the phenomenon described in the sentence which Benjamin quoted. "One of the most remarkable characteristics of human nature is, alongside so much selfishness in specific instances, the freedom from envy which the present displays toward the future" ("Theses" 253). Working within a very different sense of temporality, Peirce asserted in a notebook that all it concerns us to know is how to conduct ourselves on future occasions.

Lotze, like the pragmatists, maintains a sense of progress, but his sense of reality is at odds with pragmatism's future-oriented definition of truth. "The premonition that we will not be lost for the future, that those who have come before us may well have departed from our earthly existence but not from all reality, and that, in however mysterious a manner, the progress of history also takes place for them, this belief alone allows us to speak as we do of a humanity and its history."[63] Benjamin maintains Lotze's sense of the redemption of the past but severs it from the notion of automatic progress. In doing so, he reveals the costs involved in adhering to a pragmatic definition of truth. Holmes insisted that "the law of fashion is a law of life" and demanded that we adjust our laws and beliefs to serve the needs of a changing world. History was useful in this process because it helped to clear away rubbish. Benjamin, in contrast, like Thomas Pynchon, is intent on redeeming what has come to be considered the waste of history. In his notes for "Die Passagen-Arbeit," Benjamin sketches a "small methodological proposal for a cultural-historical dialectic." For every epoch this dialectic distinguishes between that which from a certain point of view is "fruitful, future-oriented, living, and positive" and that which is "futile, backward, and dead." The contours of the positive, Benjamin argues, can be made clear only by placing them next to the negative. The negative, however, has a value other than serving as a background for the living and positive. Through a displacement of the angle of perception (Gesichtswinkels) Benjamin hopes to grant the negative a new positivity: "And so on into infinity until the entire past is restored to the present in a historical apocatastasis."[64]

Apocatastasis originally meant the recurrence of a specific planetary constellation and then in rhapsodic piestic treatises to mean the setting right again of all that through Adam has fallen into sin, death, hell, and eternal damnation. Clearly Benjamin's notion of apocatastasis, his attempt to restore the energies contained in obsolete things that are no longer fashionable, puts him at odds with the pragmatic emphasis on usable truths. For him, "a chronicler who recites events without distinguishing between major and minor ones acts in accordance with the following truth: nothing that has ever happened should be regarded as lost for history" ("Theses" 254). If this sounds backward-looking, Benjamin turns it into a challenge for the future. In the present much is lost for history, and the partiality of our present perspective causes us to select those aspects of the past that we find usable and to exclude others. For Benjamin, however, the task of the historian is to strive to create conditions in which a new angle of vision will allow what now appears futile, backward, and dead to take on new life. For him "only a redeemed mankind receives the fullness of its past—which is to say, only for a redeemed mankind has its past become citable in all moments" ("Theses" 254). The present selects a pragmatically usable past at the cost of its own redemption, for it risks having aspects of itself, which will one day be part of the past, fall into neglect. As E. P. Thompson puts it in another context, "In the end we also will be dead, and our own lives will lie inert within the finished process, our intentions assimilated within a past event which we never intended. What we may hope is that the men and women of the future will reach back to us, will affirm and renew our meanings, and make our history intelligible within their own present tense."[65]

Of course, Benjamin was not specifically attacking the pragmatic notion of a usable past. A more familiar object of attack is Historismus. Like historical relativists, he challenges Historismus' claim to recover the past as it really was. That aspect of Benjamin's argument is well known and deservedly popular with today's reconstructionists. According to Benjamin, the goal of *Historismus* was to have historians "blot out everything they know about the past" in order to "relive an era" ("Theses" 256). What resulted instead was monological views of an age in which the historian empathized with the victors. "Empathy for the victor," he goes on, "invariably benefits the rulers. . . . Whoever has emerged victorious participates to this day in the triumphal procession in which the present rulers step over those who are lying prostrate" ("Theses" 256). As impressive as Benjamin's attack on *Historismus* is, H. D. Kittsteiner has recently speculated that "the attacks against [*Historismus*] . . . could well turn out to be a sideshow; the critique of the philosophy of history and its idea of progress might then emerge as the actual theme."⁶⁶

Indeed, for my purposes, more important is Benjamin's less-cited attack on the way in which Social Democrats took over the philosophy of history's idea of inevitable progress. This idea "did not adhere to reality but made dogmatic claims. Progress as pictured in the minds of Social Democrats was, first of all, the progress of mankind itself (and not just advances in men's ability and knowledge). Secondly, it was something boundless, in keeping with the infinite perfectibility of mankind. Thirdly, progress was regarded as irresistible, something that automatically pursued a straight or spiral course" ("Theses" 260). The conception of progress questioned by Benjamin is not the modest one defended by Blumenberg as a legitimate contribution of modernity. Instead, it is one that cannot be sundered from the concept of "progression through a homogeneous, empty time" ("Theses" 261). Benjamin advocates a "notion of a present which is not a transition but in which time stands still and has come to a stop" ("Theses" 262). That notion of a present is created by a historian who "stops telling the sequence of events like the beads of a rosary" and instead "grasps the constellation which his own era has formed with a definite earlier one." In that constellation the historian recognizes a "cessation of happening, or, put differently, a revolutionary chance in the fight for the oppressed past" ("Theses" 263). Only by arresting the flow of progressive time in which power by definition wins will the triumphal procession of the rulers have a chance to be broken. For Benjamin that moment of cessation occurs through a "tiger's leap into the past." Thus "to Robespierre ancient Rome was a past charged with the time of the now which he blasted out of the continuum of history. The French Revolution viewed itself as Rome incarnate" ("Theses" 261).

Benjamin's example is a direct quotation from Marx's *The Eighteenth Brumaire of Louis Bonaparte.* The constellation that he creates between the present he was writing in and this marxist past indicates the extent to which, in Kittsteiner's words, he not only tried to understand marxism, but to change it. Benjamin is not interested so much in telling us how marxism really was, but in putting it to present uses.

Early in *The Eighteenth Brumaire* Marx articulates a central idea of marxism. "Human beings make their own history, but they do not make it just as they please; they do not make it under circumstances chosen by themselves, but under circumstances directly encountered, given and transmitted [überlieferten] from the past." At stake, as Blumenberg noted in citing this passage, is how we imagine the transmission of the past. For Marx the question becomes how to imagine breaks with the triumphal procession of the victors. As Marx puts it, "The tradition of all the dead generations weighs like a nightmare on the brain of the living." The problem is that just when people "seem engaged in revolutionising themselves and things [sich und die Dinge umzuwälzen], in creating something that has never yet existed, precisely in such periods of revolutionary crisis they anxiously conjure up the spirits of the past to their service and borrow from them names, battle cries and costumes in order to present the new scene of world history in this time-honored disguise and this borrowed language." This turn to the past confirms Marx's famous opening that history repeats itself, the first time as tragedy, the second as farce. Faulting the revolution of 1848 for conjuring up the services of the dead, he proclaims, "The social revolution of the nineteenth century cannot draw its poetry from the past, but only from the future."[67]

Marx criticizes this turn to the past because, as Benjamin puts it, it "takes place in an arena where the ruling class gives command" ("Theses" 261). Indeed, this remains a problem with Greenblatt's version of the new historicism, which otherwise shares much with Benjamin's project. Like Benjamin, Greenblatt provides a new angle of vision that forces us to reconsider those aspects of a past era that have been neglected by official histories. Nonetheless, he constructs his constellation between past and present within an arena in which the ruling class—or at least a powerful hegemonic rule—gives command. Thus he simultaneously grants attention to the previously excluded and fits it into a historical logic in which its defeat was inevitable. In contrast, Benjamin urges an act of construction that is a dialectical "leap in the open air of history . . . which is how Marx understood the revolution" ("Theses" 261).

There is, however, a danger with this leap in the open air of history when it draws its poetry from the future not the past. That danger is apparent in the doctrine of social realism, in which poetry, literature, and art are limited to the task of doing work in the world by mirroring an already existing image of what the future should be. When the future can already be imagined in nameable five-year plans and representable goals, we are no longer in the open air of history but another teleological version of it in which a different sort of moral philosophy tries to control its direction. Benjamin works against the grain of this teleological tendency within marxism by imagining a way in which we can draw on the poetry of the past to make a dialectical leap into the open air of history. For Benjamin, as we have seen, the use of the past for the present is the challenge it poses to it, the challenge to create a society in which the sufferings of the past can be redeemed.

Terry Eagleton has clarified Benjamin's sense of redemption in terms of narrative. On the one hand, the past can never be redeemed. History unfolds in a temporal order that is irreversible. Those who died remain dead. Injustices in the past cannot be undone. This is, as Eagleton puts it, the story of the past. On the other hand, the historian can *imaginatively* redeem the past by constructing a plot out of the inevitable story of the past. In such a plot history is "'textualized,' its chronology modernistically disrupted, its linear segments stacked spatially together, the fertilizing shades of the unjustly quelled summoned from their graves to gather protectively around the frail, struggling band of the living. The liberation struggle extends backwards to nurture and embrace these dead, for the oppressed understand that not even they will be safe from the enemy if he wins. Only by moving backwards in revolutionary nostalgia can one move forward in reality."[68]

Eagleton helps explain away charges of mysticism in Benjamin's notion of redemption. For me, however, the notion of a plot requires yet another clarification. As important as Benjamin's alternative to a sense of temporal continuity is, his "Theses" do not completely transcend the historical situation in which they were written. At that time, it made perfect sense to identify a clear-cut enemy against whom to direct one's plot. As Benjamin puts it, "The Messiah comes not only as the redeemer, he comes as the subduer of Antichrist" ("Theses" 255). The corollary to Benjamin's identification of an Antichrist is to grant a particular class a privileged status in constructing the plot of history. "Not man or men but the struggling, oppressed class itself is the depository of historical knowledge. In Marx it appears as the last enslaved class, as the avenger that completes the task of liberation in the name of generations of the downtrodden" ("Theses" 260). One danger with leaving the task of redemption to one particular class is that its sense of redemption can involve a desire to make history come out even. This attempt to balance accounts between present and past suffering can cause the once-enslaved class to perpetuate the story of domination rather than to construct a plot creating a more equitable present. Indeed, the desire to turn history into a perfectly balanced economy can paradoxically intensify the endless play of repression. Thus, in our time, it seems important to remember that redemption involves not only acts of vengeance, but also atonement, the ability to give without receiving in return. It might even pay for such a nonpragmatic sense of history to be validated.

The way in which poetry from the past can help in constructing such a sense of history is a topic that we need to explore. As I noted at the end of the last chapter, my discussion of the history of historicism leaves untouched the crucial question of the role literature might play in the new histories that we attempt to construct. As Van Wyck Brooks knew, literature posed a challenge to pragmatism's sense of truth and time. What, after all, is pragmatism to do with a mode of social discourse whose immediate aim is neither to record the past as it really was nor to do empirically verifiable work in the world? As Ross Posnock has suggested, it has special problems dealing with the idle curiosity that seems so closely linked to the production of much literature.[69] Instead, it has a tendency, like advocates of social realism, to redefine the literary to fit its notion of the truth. But perhaps some of the most important work that works known as literary can do is to disrupt the sense of consistency that William, not Henry, James associated with truth or the privileged access to truth that marxism grants to one point of view. Perhaps a careful reading of poetry from the past can help us to supplement Benjamin's modernistic disruptions of chronology with a postmodern shifting of points of view that resists totalization.

To raise the question of literature's role in historiography is to point to the limits of many neopragmatic accounts of history. It is no accident that the rise of neopragmatism has been accompanied by increased questioning about the special status of literature. Indeed, those holding the "Against Theory" position rarely even entertain the possibility that the question of historicism in literary studies might raise special problems *and* special opportunities. In a typical piece, Howard Horwitz claims that arguments about history "are not finally epistemological but empirical, involving disputes about the contents of knowledge, about evidence and its significance."[70] Appropriately, Horwitz's main piece of evidence is testimony from the Iran-Contra scandal; works of literature are hardly mentioned. Citing Horwitz's description favorably, Fish reveals a latent positivism when he poses as a historical problem the attempt to "determine what happened in 1649."[71] If such a question is inadequate for many historians who try to explain *why* things happened as well as describe *what* happened, it is especially inadequate for literary historians. Answering it might tell us that Milton published *The Tenure of Kings and Magistrates*, but it will not tell us much about "Lycidas," including its historicity. Horwitz's and Fish's assumption that the practice of history is merely concerned with recovering what happened neglects the difficulties involved in a historicism that takes into account texts making no claim to tell us what really happened. As we shall see in chapter 6, some historians, discounting the fictional nature of literary texts, deny their use as historical evidence altogether. To be sure, so long as the goal of historical inquiry is no more than to tell us what happened, literary texts would seem to have little to offer those interested in understanding history. But perhaps historicism, especially a historicism in literary studies, raises more questions than strictly empirical ones.

One such question might be a concern with the way in which we structure our accounts of what happened, how we link our sense of what happened at various moments in history with one another as well as with our present moment in history. If I understand Fish, however, he has no interest in this question. This is because he seems to consider only two possible ways of telling a story about the past. One is the "indeterminacy of discourse" that seems called for by the "New Historicist creed" of openness and nonexclusiveness. Fish identifies this indeterminacy with a "shifting mode" that for him can result only in vagueness. Since such discourse is impossible to sustain, the alternative for Fish seems to be to tell a "linear" story of what happened.[72] But certainly an experienced literary critic like Fish must know that a shifting mode of narration need not lead to either vagueness or indeterminacy. Shifting points of view can produce a variety of very different modes of narration (including linear ones) that interact with one another. Granted, even such mixed modes are not all-inclusive. They also have their exclusions. Nonetheless, they have a greater potential than what we have come to call monological ones of suggesting a dynamic field of play between different voices. It is precisely this sense of difference that is missing in the work of a new historicist who is also responsible for articulating the "Against Theory" position—Walter Benn Michaels. Before turning to the question of what role literary works from the past might play in our attempts to construct new histories, I want to examine Michaels's concrete practice in depth.

CHAPTER 5

Walter Benn Michaels and Cultural Poetics: Where's the Difference?

· I ·

WALTER BENN MICHAELS's *The Gold Standard and the Logic of Naturalism*[1] is a collection of essays that, with the exception of one on Hawthorne and Stowe, are on American writers of fiction at the turn of the century. All concern, in one way or another, the relation between fictional texts and the logic of the market in capitalist America. Three on Frank Norris (especially *McTeague, Vandover and the Brute*, and *The Octopus*), two on Theodore Dreiser (*Sister Carrie* and *The Financier*), and the one on Hawthorne and Stowe have been previously published. The collection adds a final essay on Edith Wharton's *The House of Mirth* that includes references to Stephen Crane's "The Five White Mice." It begins with an introduction interweaving an analysis of Charlotte Perkins Gilman's *The Yellow Wallpaper* and remarks outlining the assumptions that link the various essays. Michaels's collection is the second book in the University of California Press series, The New Historicism: Studies in Cultural Poetics, edited by Stephen Greenblatt. Whereas Michaels has a less vested interest in the currency of those labels than Greenblatt, a brief sketch of Michaels's professional biography can be read symptomatically to identify strands of thought that weave together to produce at least that brand of the new historicism identified with the journal *Representations*.

As a graduate student at the University of California, Santa Barbara, in the early 1970s, Michaels wrote a dissertation on Henry James and had a keen interest in the question of literary modernism. Hugh Kenner, then at Santa Barbara, lists him in his acknowledgments to *The Pound Era*. Taking his first job at the Johns Hopkins University not long after Kenner moved there, Michaels met Stanley Fish, also in his first year. Fish's and Michaels's compatible interests caused them, for a while, to be identified as reader response critics and more recently neo-pragmatists. At Hopkins Michaels also met (and married) Frances Ferguson, who had completed a dissertation on Wordsworth at Yale and had firsthand contact with the various versions of deconstruction in New Haven. Michaels himself already had exposure to French theory, partially through the influence of Herbert N. Schneidau at Santa Barbara and Joseph Riddel, whom Michaels had met during a brief stay at SUNY Buffalo.

In the 1970s Yale, Hopkins, Buffalo, and Cornell were recognized as the clearing houses for French thought in this country, and in 1977 the newly established *Glyph* was recognized as a journal in which deconstructive ideas were disseminated. Michaels helped establish *Glyph* and served on its editorial board, a position he retained even after he moved to the University of California, Berkeley. The last issue of *Glyph* in its original form appeared in 1981. In 1982 the first issue of *Representations* appeared. It was established by a group at Berkeley including Michaels, Ferguson, and Greenblatt, who also in 1982 identified the rise of a "new historicism" in the special issue of *Genre* that he edited.[2]

Representations' ascent, as it were, out of the ashes of *Glyph* makes it easy to mark the transformation of deconstruction into the new historicism. Too easy. The last issue of *Glyph*, edited by Michaels, included essays by, among others, Jane Tompkins, Fish, Riddel, Greenblatt, Ferguson, and Michaels. It would be very difficult to distinguish this issue from a typical issue of *Representations*. If *Representations* has self-consciously avoided printing the theoretical essays that gave *Glyph* its reputation, the "practical" essays in *Glyph* are not that much different from those in *Representations*, other than perhaps an increase in the amount of historical specificity and the increased use of nonliterary texts. To compare *Glyph* to *Representations* not only emphasizes the deconstructive roots of Michaels's strain of the new historicism, it also challenges the notion that deconstruction is inevitably ahistorical. Michaels makes precisely this point in the final footnote to his introduction. "It is often said that the 'new historicism' opposes deconstruction, in the sense that deconstructive critics are 'against' history and new historicists are 'for' it. Neither of these descriptions seems to me to have much content. In any event, the deconstructive interest in the problematic of materiality in signification is not intrinsically ahistorical . . ." (28, n. 43). Of course, there is always the possibility that Michaels's "new historical" analysis is not as historical as he claims, but that remains to be seen.

Of the essays collected in Michaels's book, the first to be written, "*Sister Carrie's* Popular Economy," did not, Michaels tells us, develop "out of any particular interest in the cultural history of the period" (17). When he wrote it he had "been working mainly on epistemological questions in literary theory" (17), but not exclusively. He was also teaching courses on American literature and, as we shall see, reading turn-of-the-century American philosophy. A look at two of Michaels's early essays can help explain how questions about epistemology turned to questions about literary naturalism and economics.

Michaels's work on epistemology was influenced by the deconstructive description of writing, which he summarizes in his introduction. "For writing to be writing, it can neither transcend the marks it is made of nor be reduced to those marks. Writing is, in this sense, intrinsically different from itself, neither material nor ideal" (21). In the 1970s this description of writing as a structure of "internal difference" (21) unleashed a massive amount of writing about writing. All literary works could be read as repeating the gesture of striving for the presence of meaning that its marks on a page suggested but which, by the very structure of writing, could not embody. As such, all works became comments on their existence as writing and all inevitably deconstructed themselves. In the first issue of *Glyph* Michaels exemplified this strategy of reading in "*Walden's* False Bottoms."[3]

But in another essay published in 1977, Michaels had already expressed his dissatisfaction with such readings. In "The Interpreter's Self: Peirce on the Cartesian 'Subject'"[4] Michaels used Charles Sanders Peirce to intervene in the debate over objective and subjective interpretation. For Michaels, Peirce's account of interpretation in which the interpreting subject was also a product of an act of interpretation not only turned the debate about objectivity and subjectivity into a false problem, it also suggested that the deconstruction of the subject so fashionable in French theory at the time had been anticipated by Peirce in late nineteenth-century America. But Peirce's pragmatic deconstruction of the subject was different from the structuralists' and poststructuralists' proclamation of the death of the subject. For Peirce, the subject did not disappear into an abyss of indeterminacy but was subsumed in concrete "communities of interpretation," a phrase generally attributed to Stanley Fish but used by Josiah Royce, who in turn adopted it to elaborate on Peirce's account of interpretation. For Michaels the problem with deconstruction, as it was being practiced, was that it was "in principle, infinitely repeatable" (Peirce 396). As one subject was deconstructed, another, implied by the very act of deconstruction, presented itself for further deconstructing. Or put another way, to deconstruct the ground of a philosophical system required the positing of a ground from which to perform the act of deconstruction, a positing that in turn demanded further deconstructing, and so on. Peirce halts this endless repetition, not by providing a ground of epistemological certainty, but by exposing the deluded effort of trying to locate a solid foundation outside the concrete activity of interpretation in which we are always already involved, and which constitutes us as subjects.

The Peirce essay raised two important possibilities. The first involved the relationship between pragmatism and deconstruction. Perhaps it was not simply a case of pragmatism being right and deconstruction wrong. Perhaps, as Fish was to argue,[5] deconstruction was properly understood as a version of pragmatism. What was mistaken was the practice of deconstruction guided by the desire to make general statements about the nature of language, a practice that guaranteed the production of an infinite number of essays all making the same point. Instead of seeking a ground for practice in a general theory of language, the proper practice of deconstruction would be the sort of radical empiricism of Michael Fried that has a ground in practice itself,[6] since, as Peirce and Derrida in their different ways had shown, practice did not need to proceed from a secure base/ ground/foundation but was generated by a continual positing of a fictional foundation. As I argued last chapter, this attempt to absorb deconstruction into pragmatism is flawed because it ignores the deconstructive challenge to pragmatism's sense of temporality. Nonetheless, the radical empiricism of a pragmatic "deconstruction" suggested to Michaels another possibility. If, indeed, Peirce anticipated the deconstruction of the subject, was there something about the concrete social practices of turn-of-the-century America that enabled his antifoundational thought?

Although the Peirce essay suggested these possibilities, Michaels did not pursue them immediately because he originally had other uses for Peirce. As he outlines at the end of the essay, he hoped to draw "some important consequences for our understanding of literary theory" (Peirce 399) by tracing the unacknowledged influence of Peirce on T. S. Eliot through Royce. But while he was working on this project, he was also teaching the literary naturalists who wrote at the same time as Peirce and Royce. When his reading of *Sister Carrie* turned him to the economic history of the time, a new argument materialized and the projected "American Epistemologies: Literary Theory and Pragmatism" never did. What Michaels saw was a homology between Peirce's and Royce's account of the subject, the naturalists' concerns with artistic representation, and dramatic changes occurring in economic production, distribution, and consumption in America after the Civil War. Furthermore, this homology had the structure of "internal difference" deconstructionists used to describe writing.

Just as writing is "intrinsically different from itself, neither material nor ideal," so the commodity as defined by Marx is "a thing whose identity involves something more than its physical qualities" (21). This is because the exchange value of a commodity, while impossible without an object's use-value, is not something perceptible by the senses. Money has the same structure of internal difference, because it "cannot be reduced to the thing it is made of and still remain the thing it is." So too the corporation, which cannot "be reduced to the men and women who are its shareholders" (21). This structural homology points the way "toward a still more general formulation": "the relation of bodies to souls, the problem of persons" (21). Michaels illustrates his point by citing Carrie's longing to be equal to the feeling that Ames sees "written upon her countenance." This longing Michaels argues,

marks what Dreiser appears to think of as a constitutive discrepancy within the self. The desire to live up to the look on your face (to become what is written on your face) is the desire to be equal to oneself (to transform that writing into marks). It is, in the logic of the gold standard, the desire to make yourself equal to your face value, to become gold. But really to achieve that equality is to efface both writing as writing and money as money; it is to become not Carrie but Hurstwood, a corpse in a New York flophouse. This is why the discrepancy is constitutive—when the self becomes equal to its body, as Dreiser sees it, it dies (22).

For Michaels, the discourse of naturalism is "above all obsessed with manifestations of internal difference or, what comes to the same thing, personhood. Continually imagining the possibility of identity without difference, it is provoked by its own images into ever more powerful imaginations of identity by way of difference" (22). Each of the essays goes on to describe a concrete manifestation of this logic.

But they do more than describe. At the end of his Peirce essay, Michaels admits that description inevitably slides into evaluation. By showing how capitalist practices conform to a structure of internal difference, he suggests important affinities between poststructuralism and capitalism. He especially counters the notion that the poststructuralist deconstruction of the autonomous subject is an attack on bourgeois capitalism. To be sure, it is commonplace to associate capitalism with self-sufficient individualism. But despite bourgeois ideology, the effect of capitalism has been to destabilize the subject. As Michaels notes, "It is a curious and not insignificant irony that the critics who have recently been most active in attending to the deconstruction of the self have characteristically seen themselves as heralding the death of a certain bourgeois mystification when in fact they are merely arriving at an account of self that was already implicit in the writings of Adam Smith and David Ricardo" (51).

If poststructuralism's oft-proclaimed opposition to capitalism is an illusion, at least in conforming to a capitalist logic it avoids the fate of what Philip Fisher, on the dust jacket of Michaels's book, calls "exhausted oppositional criticism" and what Michaels terms "the genteel or Progressive tradition in American cultural history" (14, n. 16). This tradition's opposition to capitalism is based on what deconstruction taught us to call a nostalgia for presence. In Michaels's formulation that nostalgia tries to escape the structure of internal difference at the heart of the capitalist economy. Its alternatives to America's culture of consumption, Michaels implies, are similar to the utopian visions of the period's fiction, which nostalgically yearn for a world of stable values in a closed, self-sufficient economy. In *The House of Mirth*, for instance, Lawrence Seldon imagines "personal freedom" as "a republic of the spirit" in which he would achieve freedom from "money, from poverty, from ease and anxiety, from all the material accidents" (225–26). There is also Howells's vision at the end of *The Rise of Silas Lapham* in which his hero returns to a precapitalist, agrarian setting where he can redeem the value of his solid character that had been threatened by the world of market speculation. The lesson that the logic of naturalism seems to offer to those holding such visions is embodied in Hurstwood's corpse: to efface the structure of difference is to die.

According to Michaels, oppositional critics try to efface the structure of internal difference in their method as well as their utopian visions. Their opposition, according to Michaels, depends upon finding a position outside the culture they would criticize. "Transcending your origins in order to evaluate them," Michaels asserts, "has been the opening move in cultural criticism at least since Jeremiah" (18). Without a doubt this has been a common move by American critics, who, within the tradition that allowed a notion of American exceptionalism to develop, repeat the gesture of those who sought the new space of "a world elsewhere" in order to transcend their origins and criticize the Old World. Michaels makes the almost equally common move of denying this possibility. But he has another point to make.

It is wrong, Michaels argues, even "to think of the culture you live in as the object of your affections: you don't like it or dislike it, you exist in it, and the things you like and dislike exist in it too" (18). Thus it is a mistake to try, as critics do, to assess whether an author like Dreiser liked or disliked capitalism, since to do so depends on "imagining a Dreiser outside capitalism who could then be said to have attitudes toward it" (19). But if "it is easy (and essential) to stop worrying about whether Dreiser liked or disliked capitalism," the effort to bracket the question of his attitude can be "only partially successful" (20). "The minute you begin to think about what Dreiser did like and dislike, it becomes, of course impossible to keep capitalism out—not only because capitalism provides the objects of fear and desire but because it provides the subjects as well" (20). Michaels uses this observation to support his brand of radical empiricism and its accompanying distrust of generalized concepts. "Dreiser didn't so much approve or disapprove of capitalism; he desired pretty women in little tan jackets with mother-of-pearl buttons, and he feared becoming a bum on the streets of New York" (19).

Michaels's call to look at a writer's concrete practices rather than to worry whether he liked or disliked capitalism is welcome, since it is not at all clear that a writer's general attitude corresponds to the effects of his practice. Indeed, Michaels is at his best in showing how those who are said to dislike the capitalist economy are in complicity with it. Nonetheless, ultimately his argument is flawed, and as a result, so is his account of oppositional criticism.

We can start to understand the flaw in his logic by returning to Derrida's essay that deals with the nostalgia for lost presence. At the end of "Structure, Sign, and Play in the Discourse of the Human Sciences" Derrida confronts us with two interpretations of interpretation, one that yearns for a lost center that will eventually put a halt to play and the other that in a Nietzschean affirmation celebrates the loss of the center and embraces endless free play.[7] He then confronts us with a choice between these two interpretations, that is, if choice is a category we can still entertain. Too often, this passage is read as if Derrida is implying that, in effect, there is no choice, that we must side with Nietzschean affirmation. In the terms Michaels has set up, this would mean embracing an economic system generated by the structure of internal difference that produces endless desire rather than a system based on intrinsic values that would erase the structure of internal difference. But, paradoxically as it might seem, this is counter to the logic of Derrida's essay. To embrace the Nietzschean alternative is actually to risk halting the play of play because it effaces the difference between the two interpretations of interpretation. The Nietzschean alternative depends upon and cannot do without the nostalgic desire for presence. Similarly, the capitalist economic system depends upon the nostalgic desire to escape from its system of internal difference, since it is that nostalgia for presence that helps to generate the structure of difference in the first place.

Michaels, who is much more familiar with deconstruction than I, knows this, and his description of the logic of naturalism expresses the play of difference that Derrida maintains between the two interpretations of interpretation. "Continually imagining the possibility of identity without difference, it is provoked by its own images into ever more powerful imaginations of identity by way of difference" (22). Nonetheless, his inability to sustain that play is illustrated by his treatment of a death other than Hurstwood's—that of Lily Bart in *The House of Mirth.* Arguing against those critics who see Lily's accidental death/suicide as her only way to escape the cruelty of the market world that exploits her, Michaels argues that instead it adheres to the logic of the market. He does so by showing that for the society she inhabits Lily's value lies in her being interesting. She remains interesting by, like a commodity, maintaining a structure of internal difference. For example, according to Michaels, "Seldon's speculative interest in Lily depends simultaneously on his realization that everything she does is an act (not an accident) and on his inability to know exactly what act it is" (233). But that is not all. Lily, viewed by others as a commodity, sees herself as a commodity. Thus, for Lily to remain interesting to herself "the relation between what she does and what she means to do must be as mysterious to her as it is to Seldon" (233). So when, at the end of the book, Lily for the first time (in Wharton's language) "seemed to have broken through the merciful veil which intervenes between intention and action, and to see exactly what she would do in all the long days to come," she takes a drug whose action was "incalculable" (quoted, 233). If that risky gamble leads to her death, it at least makes her interesting again. This reading does more than restore us temporarily to the world of Poe, in which the most interesting subject is the death of a beautiful woman. Without Michaels being aware of it, it balances his reading of Hurstwood's suicide, implying that ultimately there is little difference between attempts to escape the logic of capitalism (Hurstwood's) and actions that adhere to its logic (Lily's). Both end in premature death.

We could draw numerous lessons from the juxtaposition of these two deaths, but to stay within Michaels's logic we can say that the nostalgia for presence is and must be a structural element of a truly radical structure of difference. In other words, utopian images of "the republic of the spirit" or autonomous self-sufficiency should not be rejected as merely false nostalgias that do not deal with an inevitable market logic: they are an essential part of that logic. Indeed, people's powerful yearning for them helps to sustain desire. Thus it is not as curious as it seems that structuralists and poststructuralists proclaim the deconstruction of the self "as heralding the death of a certain bourgeois mystification" (51). The notion of the autonomous self *is* mystified by the bourgeoisie, which is not to say that capitalism produces such subjects. What I am suggesting is a point sometimes developed by Michaels but not rigorously maintained, a point closer to that made by Sacvan Bercovitch in *The American Jeremiad*: The power of America's middle class ideology draws from its ability to thrive on resistance.

Not surprisingly, we can point to other affinities between deconstruction and the American jeremiad.[8] According to Bercovitch the jeremiad has been so successful in America's middle class culture because it has offered a way to deal with crisis and change, not by resolving contradictions (most notably that caused by the structure of internal difference resulting from the disparity between society's actual material practices and its stated sacred mission), but by endlessly deferring any resolution of those contradictions. Similarly, deconstruction's displacement of dialectics by "differance" offers a reading strategy that endlessly defers the resolution of contradictions and justifies it as in the nature of our situation within language. Like the jeremiad, it is able to use the rhetoric of crisis to release productive energies, if on a more local level, as it produces numerous new readings of literary and nonliterary texts and a group of scholars dedicated to redefining the mission of literary studies.

My comparison between the American jeremiad and deconstruction is not intended to reassure oppositional critics. After all, it is extremely difficult for someone within a system that is generated by resistance to imagine alternatives to it. Nonetheless, Marx's analysis of consumer capitalism, at first glance, seems to offer no more promise of an alternative. This is indicated by the extent to which Michaels relies on *Capital* for his description, not evaluation, of that system. From Marx Michaels lifts not only his definition of a commodity but also the observation that capitalism produces the subjects as well as objects of consumption. Especially the latter creates a circular logic that seems impossible to break. To put this in terms of desire, all alternatives to consumer capitalism appear impotent, because none seem capable of sustaining desire in the subjects it has produced. In producing subjects that only it can "satisfy"—not by satiating them but by producing ever more desire—consumer capitalism reproduces itself.

But Marx does see an alternative, which directly counters Michaels's notion that it is wrong to like or dislike the culture one lives in. Before looking at Marx's alternative I want to dwell for a moment on the new twist Michaels gives to a familiar conservative slogan from the 1960s: "America, love it or leave it." Michaels's updated version is: "Don't like it or dislike it, because you can't leave it." The logic behind Michaels's version seems so simplistic that he himself seems not to believe it. In a footnote he asserts "distaste for consumer culture transcends what passes for politics in academia" (15, n. 16), implying that people on both the right and the left do like and dislike the culture they live in. So to make sure that I do not misrepresent him, let me quote Michaels again, this time in full.

> Although transcending your origins in order to evaluate them has been the opening move in cultural criticism at least since Jeremiah, it is surely a mistake to take this move at face value: not so much because you can't really transcend your culture but because, if you could, you wouldn't have any terms of evaluation left—except, perhaps, theological ones. It thus seems wrong to think of the culture you live in as the object of your affections: you don't like it or dislike it, you exist in it, and the things you like and dislike exist in it too (18).

The most obvious reason why it is not wrong to think of the culture you live in as the object of your affections is that a culture does not treat all people equally. Marx explained unequal treatment in terms of class, and he found hope for an alternative, not through people transcending their origins, but in those most exploited becoming increasingly conscious of their position within capitalism. Is it wrong for exploited people to dislike the culture they live in, especially when their dislike can be based, as it often is, on the terms of evaluation offered by most capitalist democracies: notions of equity and equal opportunity? Although Michaels at one time does refer to "lower-class [sic] women" (19), class does not exist as the structure of analysis for him. This neglect is all the more striking because class, which depends on its members' self-conscious awareness of their common interest, is another example of something whose identity is more than its physical qualities. Of course class is in part a product of "the market," but the very possibility of its existence plays havoc with Michaels's image of culture. For the most part, Michaels succumbs to the ideology of the bourgeois juridical system that treats all subjects equally under the law of capitalism. Thus we find him not only ignoring class, but also paying little attention to questions of gender and race.

More than groups, however, are affected differently by capitalism. Different regions of a country and sectors of the economy are also. Nonetheless, Michaels operates as if, at some moment he does not designate, the country as a whole suddenly transformed into a unified system of consumer capitalism. To be sure, after the Civil War transformations were rapid, and they affected all walks of life. But they were not uniform. Their uneven development produced a culture in which different stages of capitalism overlapped and even came into contact with residual elements of noncapitalist modes of production. Because there was not one uniform logic of capitalism but many different competing logics, it might be safer to speak of cultures rather than a single culture. Or if we want to retain the notion of a single American culture (which I think we should, in order to distinguish it from the different way in which consumer capitalism manifested itself in other countries) we would be wise to return to Ernst Bloch's concept of the nonsynchronicity of the synchronic.[9]

As Bloch notes, the different regions of a country and different sectors of the economy constitute different subjects. Indeed, many subjects produced within American culture were not inscribed by a single structure of internal difference unique to consumer capitalism but by a variety of structures of internal difference from various stages of capitalism. Similarly, if, as Michaels implies, a fundamental transformation occurred in American culture at the end of the nineteenth century, many of the people living at that time would have been born in a different culture. For instance, many of the period's most important thinkers were born in small communities and then encountered urban life.[10] Constituted by a different set of values, they certainly could use those values to evaluate whether they liked or disliked the new culture they found, even if exposure to new terms of evaluation would give them a different perspective on the culture from which they came. Thus it was not even necessary for writers to have lived in non-American cultures (as Norris and Wharton did) to have terms by which to evaluate the culture they lived in. American culture at the end of the nineteenth century was not homogeneous. Nor were subjects within that culture constituted by a homogeneous set of values. Instead, various subjects experienced competing sets of values. To be sure, the values and desires unique to consumer capitalism tended to dominate, but they were not monolithic.

Paradoxically, then, Michaels's emphasis on *a* structure of internal difference results in a tendency to produce eternal sameness. This tendency is not surprising since, as many have noted, a contradiction within consumer capitalism is that it produces an endless recurrence of novelty, a sameness of difference rendering legitimate newness difficult to imagine. By conducting his analysis within an overriding logic of capitalism, the very critic who distrusts transcendental categories ends by adopting the Market as one, much in the way that mechanical deconstructionists treat Writing, Play, or "Differance." In doing so, Michaels falls prey to an error similar to the one E. P. Thompson accuses Marx of making. In *Capital*, Thompson argues, Marx reifies the notion of capital itself.[11] Michaels, in turn, reifies the notion of culture within capitalism. Since Thompson's charge came in response to Althusser's structuralist reading of *Capital*, it is not surprising to find that in the last analysis Michaels is closer to structuralism than deconstruction. His use of the system of capitalism is similar to Saussure's use of the system of language. Both are generated by a structure of difference, but in their pure synchronicity both become logical, not historical, categories. In reifying the market Michaels constructs homologies that efface the very difference that supposedly generates them.

The error Michaels makes in subsuming all under a single logic explains why his notion of oppositional criticism is flawed. As we have seen, Michaels believes that oppositional criticism depends upon a transcendental move that places the critic outside the society he would criticize. In defining oppositional criticism this way, he stays firmly lodged within the tradition of American transcendentalism that he examined in his *Walden* essay. Thoreau did indeed seek a position outside culture from which he could achieve a critical perspective on it. The thrust of Michaels's essay is to deconstruct the possibility of achieving such a ground. But not all oppositional criticism adheres to the tradition of American transcendentalism. The entire tradition growing out of Marx (its roots are in Hegel) relies on an immanent critique. Rather than attempt the impossible move of transcending one's origins, it relies on the structures of internal difference within a culture for its critique. This is especially true of the way cultural critics have learned to use literature, which re-presents (with a difference) those structures of internal difference. Althusser articulates such a position very concisely. Rejecting the view that Balzac's art somehow allowed him to transcend his conservative beliefs in order to generate telling social criticism, Althusser argues, "On the contrary, *only because he retained them could he produce his work*, only because he stuck to his political ideology could he produce *in it* this internal 'distance' which gives us a critical 'view' of it." Statements like Althusser's indicate that Michaels's opposition to oppositional criticism leaves untouched an entire tradition of cultural analysis. But merely asserting that tradition does not make it correct. For instance, in the last chapter I will question the mimetic relation between literature and ideology that even Althusser maintains. For Althusser a literary text does not, as it can for Lukács, reveal underlying laws of history that provide correctives to ideologically incorrect false consciousness. Nonetheless, he does assume that it can make us "*see . . . the ideology* from which it is born, in which it bathes, from which it detaches itself as art, and to which it *alludes.*"[12] By revealing not a truth but the very ideology that helped to produce it, literature for Althusser provides knowledge in the service of critical reason. If I share Michaels's discomfort with the persistent efforts to make literature subservient to critical reason, I do not want to lapse into his error of making it subservient to a prevailing cultural "logic."

Arguing against the genteel notion that literary texts offer us a critical perspective by transcending culture, Michaels asserts, "the only relation literature as such has to culture as such is that it is part of it" (27). This makes as much sense as to say that the only relation the liver has to the body is that it is part of it. Recognition that the literary is an institution very much within a culture should not cause us to leave it undifferentiated from other institutions. As I will argue next chapter, if literature is one social practice among many, it is a different practice with a different social function from, say, the law. The task of the cultural historian, especially one dealing with literary texts, is to define that particular social function and how it changes. Indeed, this is one reason why Greenblatt's work is more historical than Michaels's. Recognizing distinctions between artistic production and other kinds of production, Greenblatt adds "they are not intrinsic to the texts; rather they are made up and constantly redrawn by artists, audiences, and readers."[13]

Greenblatt does not, however, help us when it comes to the specificity of the situation in nineteenth-century capitalism. Here the work of Walter Benjamin is of use, for there are remarkable similarities between Benjamin's analysis of the Paris of Charles Baudelaire and Michaels's analysis of naturalism. Like Michaels, Benjamin demonstrates a homology between the production of works of art, commodities, fashion, and even gambling and photography, which play a role in Michaels's essay on Wharton. But there are important differences. One is Benjamin's neglect of corporations, which can be explained by his concern with Baudelaire's Paris, not naturalism's America. Other differences are methodological.

Broadly speaking, Benjamin's cultural analysis is materialistic; Michaels's is textual. Benjamin notes specific changes brought about in the material conditions of life and analyzes how those changes affected human consciousness. Michaels analyzes people writing on various cultural phenomena. Whereas Benjamin writes on photography, Michaels writes on Joseph Pennell, Alfred Stieglitz, and others writing on photography. This is not to imply that Michaels does not have his own point of view on the topic, but how he arrives at it is important. Starting by acknowledging a debate—over the notion of corporate personality, for instance—he often ends by focusing on one writer's point of view, a point of view that fits into the argument he wants to make about the structure of internal difference inhabiting the market economy. What gets lost, of course, is the alternative perspective that generated the debate in the first place. As those loose threads disappear from the argument, we have to wonder if an author not treated would also fit into the homologous structure Michaels discovers.

My point is not that Michaels necessarily falsely constructs his homologies (although, as we shall see, he can). Michaels tries to select his material to make a case for the practice of a particular writer. The appropriateness of his evidence has to be decided on an individual basis. Nonetheless, the particularity of the homologies he establishes suggests that they do not cover the culture in the way that his use of phrases like the "logic of naturalism" implies.[14] On the one hand, Michaels seems to be making an argument about structures that embrace the entire culture. On the other, he seems merely to be offering a set of individual essays in which each describes the particular logic of a particular writer. What is lacking, other than the argument about a common structure of internal difference (a structure deconstructionists can find anywhere), is any sustained effort to link those various readings. That lack suggests that perhaps Michaels cannot produce the cohesion he implies. If so, it highlights the major difference between his analysis and Benjamin's.

Michaels is almost exclusively concerned with establishing resemblances, of fitting as many cultural phenomena as possible into a structure of internal difference. In contrast, the most characteristic gesture of Benjamin's criticism is, according to Jonathan Arac, to "draw distinctions where the ordinary reader, teacher, or student would stop, content with having found similarity (precisely what then makes the new differentiations possible)."[15] I want to emphasize three different ways in which those differentiations are made.

Unlike Michaels, Benjamin often compares the cultural moment he is analyzing with other moments in history. This is especially the case with cultural phenomena that seem similar. If Baudelaire uses allegory, Benjamin compares his allegory to that of seventeenth-century writers, always staying alert to differences. These historical comparisons are crucial because they remind us that alternatives exist even when we are tempted to see only a recurrence of the same. Thus, whereas Benjamin's model would seem to be synchronic, he includes an important diachronic element. This diachronic element has an effect similar to Foucault's project in *The Order of Things*. Caught within one *episteme*, we tend to think that no knowledge is possible except within its particular structural formation. But to describe historical changes in the space in which knowledge is produced is to hold open the possibility for a new structural formation.

This diachronic element is virtually absent in Michaels's analysis, and yet his use of a structure of internal difference cries out for it. To take just one example, desiring subjects, which Michaels claims are produced by consumer capitalism, clearly precede the particular economic structure he describes. There is, for instance, Rousseau's statement, quoted by Paul de Man, "If all my dreams had turned into reality, I would still remain unsatisfied: I would have kept on dreaming, imagining, desiring. In myself, I found an unexplainable void that nothing could have filled; a longing of the heart towards another kind of fulfillment of which I could not conceive but of which I nevertheless felt the attraction."[16] Or there is the figure of Faust, or the ambitious, overreacher in the Renaissance. And of course the notion that a person is defined by something more than its body is not a new one in Western thought.

If a structure of internal difference constitutes subjects in a variety of periods, to discover such subjects in late nineteenth-century America is not to establish a necessary connection between them and consumer capitalism. What Michaels needs to do, therefore, is create a historical account for their continued existence. He could do so by adopting the radical (but not universal) poststructuralist position that the only hope for radical social change would come in the effacement of the human subject. Since he seems to resist such an argument, his analysis implies something much closer to de Man's implication that the continuity of desiring subjects plays havoc with efforts, such as Marx's, to link them to a particular historical moment. It would seem, however, that Michaels would have to deny this position, since his stress on the market implies the opposite and because it is the historical specificity of his analysis that allows him to distinguish it from de Manian deconstruction. Nonetheless, when we come across phrases such as "the natural ontology of bodies and souls" (201), we cannot help but suspect that there is an unstated ideological reason for his opposition to oppositional criticism. If, as it sometimes seems, Michaels really believes in a natural ontology of bodies and souls, he falls victim to the most persistent move made by apologists for capitalism: the implication that it works because it, more than any other economic system, corresponds with the nature of human nature—in this case, an inevitable structure of internal difference that creates desiring subjects. I should add that even the move to discover a natural ontology of the desiring subject need not legitimate capitalism. It merely indicates that any system that hopes to compete with capitalism must account for the structure of internal difference. Thus, another possibility for analysis presents itself, one that we can term Benjaminian, in which we could show significant historical differences within subjects constituted by a similar structure of internal difference.

The confusion that results from Michaels's contradictory move of asserting the historical specificity of a certain type of subject and a "natural ontology of bodies and souls" points to the importance of another aspect of Benjamin's analysis. Influenced perhaps by Heidegger as well as Marx, Benjamin links changes in material conditions to an altered sense of temporality. Relating the action of pressing a button to produce a photograph (an action that Michaels discusses in his essay on Wharton) to a number of innovations in the nineteenth century, Benjamin notices one thing in common: "One movement of the hand triggers a process of many steps."[17] Combined with the individual's experience of the crowd in the city, these innovations served to isolate each moment from every other and to produce the sense of "starting all over again" epitomized by gambling. Once again, this attention to temporality is virtually absent in Michaels, as his model of analysis remains predominantly spatial, a model with serious consequences for his understanding both of history and narrative.

The final difference I want to stress brings us directly back to the question of the function of literature in consumer culture. In describing their respective homologies between literary works and other cultural phenomena both Michaels and Benjamin counter bourgeois aesthetics by emphasizing the exchange value of works of art. But whereas Michaels's statements about the role of literature pay attention to only their exchange value, Benjamin creates a dialectical tension by also paying attention to their use-value. To be sure, Michaels's neglect of a work's use-value makes perfect sense, since according to bourgeois aesthetics works of art have no social function. Their only purpose, Kant tells us, is to be without a purpose, merely to be themselves. By denying art a use-value bourgeois aesthetics could claim that it resisted commodification. Part of the power of Michaels's argument, like Benjamin's before him, is to insist that art is indeed commodified. But its very existence as a commodity confirms that it does have a use-value, since, as Michaels notes, a commodity by definition must be an object of utility, even though its exchange value cannot be reduced to that utilitarian function. Paradoxically, then, it is possible that in bourgeois society art's use-value is linked to its lack of social function. In that case, its existence as a commodity would result from its resistance to commodification.

Confronted by the contradiction expressed by this particular internal difference within works of art produced within bourgeois society, Michaels ignores it by simply dismissing as genteel and wrong any notion that art resists the market. In contrast, Benjamin works within this contradiction, knowing that, according to logic similar to Michaels's, such a prevalent attitude about art is not transcendental but produced by the very culture it would claim to transcend. And use-value—we should remember in this day when it is fashionable to argue that a work's meaning is the pure product of interpretive communities that can produce endlessly novel readings—use-value is intricately related to a product's intrinsic qualities, its material existence.[18]

Since the material existence of each work is different, it is hard to gen-
eralize about a particular function of literature. Nonetheless, a few generalizations can be made, one being that any investigation into the function
of literature has to pay close attention to that particularity. It is to Michaels's credit that he compels us to return to the specificity of individual
works and the specificity of cultural practices in which they were produced. His practice is so much more challenging than his general statements about culture that it is little wonder that he achieved renown by
coauthoring an essay "Against Theory."

But the very dazzle of Michaels's readings creates problems for his
argument as a whole. What is fascinating about them is their ability to
bring together details from a variety of seemingly random social practices
and to establish connections between them. As such they satisfy modernist aesthetic tastes that value a poet's ability to fuse diverse material. But
placed together the essays call attention to a problem raised by Pound's
Cantos. Relying on the modernist technique of montage, Pound hoped
that the bits and pieces he juxtaposed would ultimately cohere. But they
did not. Neither do the essays Michaels places next to one another under
the same cover. To be sure, individual essays all manifest a structure of
internal difference, but they do so differently. This leaves spaces between
individual essays that create an internal "distance" within Michaels's own
collection.

In this regard, the overall structure of the essays is revealing. Except
for the introductory one, they are organized according to the history of
their publication, not with any effort to correspond to the history they
presumably represent. Indeed, from one essay to another some important
shifts occur. For instance, in the *Sister Carrie* essay Michaels argues that
Howells's realism views art, like character, "as a kind of still point, a re-
positing of values that resisted the fluctuations and inequalities of industrial capitalism" (46). As a result, Howells distrusts sentimental fiction,
which operates by the logic of the popular economy. Based on a "relationship of life to art" that introduces "a discrepancy between the two terms,"
sentimental fiction, like the theater for Carrie, has the economic function
of producing desire for "hitherto unimagined possibilities" (45). In his
essay on Hawthorne and Stowe, Michaels's argument about *Uncle Tom's
Cabin*, the most famous sentimental novel, is quite different. Stowe, we
learn, fears slavery because it was "an emblem of the market economy"
(109). This is because the possibility of an autonomous self with inalien-
able rights is undercut by "the notion of a market in human attributes"
(111). Stowe's sentimentality, in other words, like Howells's realism,
imagines the possibility of an autonomous self resisting the market. What
defines sentimental fiction in one essay defines realism in another. To
be sure, in the final twist of his argument Michaels demonstrates how
Stowe's notion of freedom "was itself a product of the economy epitomized

for her in the slave trade" (111). But, then, would not this also be the case for Howells's sense of autonomy? And if so, what happens to the distinction Michaels needs in his *Sister Carrie* essay between realistic and sentimental fiction?

But the problem is larger than a shift in generic definitions from essay to essay. Taken together the essays do not confirm Michaels's argument about the reign of one logic of naturalism at this period of American history. For example, in "The Phenomenology of Contract" Michaels establishes a homology between freedom of contract and naturalism, as expressed in Norris's *McTeague*. In "Corporate Fiction" he establishes one between corporate personality and naturalism, as expressed in Norris's *The Octopus*. But, as we shall see, corporate personality and freedom of contract are not themselves homologous. Quite the contrary. The doctrine of corporate personality, which has a history going back to Roman law and can be linked to notions of the corporate body of the Church, asserts that the identity of a corporation is more than the sum of its individual membership. As such it came into conflict with the doctrine of freedom of contract that depended on a vision of autonomous individuals capable of entering into a contractual relationship with one another. Advocates of laissez-faire capitalism opposed the doctrine of corporate personality because it threatened free contractual relations between individuals. Thus, rather than one all-embracing structure of capitalism at the turn of the century in the United States, we have at least two competing versions: that of corporate capitalism and that of laissez-faire capitalism. What happens, then, when we bring Michaels's two essays together? Can Norris's naturalism be homologous with both corporate capitalism and laissez-faire capitalism?[19]

Finally, however, Michaels's method raises a problem even larger than the failure of the individual essays to cohere as a group. The historical argument of individual essays is itself often flawed. By suturing together different cultural phenomena without using their similarities to explore further cultural differences, Michaels might satisfy aesthetic tastes trained to expect unity (*ars* originally meant "fitting together"), but only by neglecting the messiness of history. To read a Michaels essay against the grain is to expose it to the ragged edges of history that he tries to weave together into a unified structure. What follows is the start of such a reading of the essay "Corporate Fiction."

· II ·

What is the connection between the legal fiction of corporate personality and the identity of real people? This is the question Michaels poses in "Corporate Fiction," and he sets about to answer it by interweaving analyses of Royce's philosophy of the community, Arthur Machen's legal discussion of corporate personality, and Norris's narrative about a corporate giant, *The Octopus*.

For Michaels the corporation is one more example of something whose identity involves more than its physical qualities. "What else," he asks, "is the corporation, which cannot be reduced to the men and women who are its shareholders" (22)? Those opposed to corporations at the turn of the century would have argued that it was quite a bit more than an example of a structure of internal difference. Corporate monopolies, they lamented, were destroying the principles of freedom on which the country's economic system was based. For the courts to grant a corporation the rights accorded to people was to create a monster with whom ordinary businessmen could not compete.

In part, this is the image of corporations in *The Octopus*. Nonetheless, Michaels points out what appears to be a contradiction in Norris's portrayal of the "Pacific and Southwestern Railroad Company." On the one hand, Norris imagines the company as a machinelike body, driven by a mechanical force. On the other, he portrays it as an intangible entity lacking a body that can be touched. Eventually Michaels argues that this seeming contradiction is not a contradiction at all but results from the structure of internal difference that constitutes the ontology of corporations. Indeed, the corporation's monstrosity results from its structure of internal difference. Because its identity involves something more than its physical qualities, it, like an alien in a horror picture, has a life, but no tangible body that can be killed, contained, or punished. Furthermore, as is often the case in horror pictures, the real shock comes in recognizing that the alien "other" is actually you. According to Michaels, the monstrosity of the corporation is the monstrosity of personhood that is also constituted by a structure of internal difference. It is futile to appeal to natural persons to oppose the rise of the artificial personality of corporations, because their very artificiality exposes the fictional nature of natural personhood.

At the start, however, Michaels is content to argue that the insatiable greed of corporations cannot be accounted for unless a corporation is considered intangible. Since a physical body can contain only so much, something with a body will, at least temporarily, be satiated. A corporation's intangibility allows it to consume forever and never be full. But the situation is complicated. If a corporation's intangibility accounts for its inhuman greed, it also allows Royce to use it as a model for world reform. Writing in 1914, Royce proposed establishing an international insurance company made up of the nations of the world. By creating a community interest against destruction, the corporation itself could never be destroyed, since its identity could not be reduced to any particular territory. Its power, for Royce, lay in "its essentially intangible soul" (189).

Royce complicates our sense of the corporation by celebrating its potential to transcend the interests of particular individuals and individual nations, but even he was not unequivocal about the ontology of the corporation. "Interestingly enough," Michaels notes, "what unease Royce felt about the ontology of the corporation surfaces most explicitly in his only novel, *The Feud at Oakfield Creek*, written in 1886 (just after [his] history of California) and based, like *The Octopus*, on the land dispute at Mussel Slough" (191). In Royce's novel, the dispute between settlers and a corporation (transformed from the powerful Southern Pacific Railroad Company to a small land-improvement company) is reduced to a feud between two old friends. The two quarrel when the son of the chief stockholder in the company (Alonzo Eldon) jilts the daughter of the other (Alf Escott), and Escott sides with the settlers against the corporation. Because Alonzo claims to want the dispute to be resolved, his daughter-in-law (Margaret) sees no reason why he cannot, since he virtually controls the company, which is, she says, "something about as big as your own thumb" (264/195).[20] Eldon, however, insists that he cannot act alone because the corporation represents the "capital of innocent shareholders." The corporation, not he, owns the property in dispute, and (in a sentence important for Michaels's argument) "a man isn't a corporation." If so, Margaret responds, buy back the corporation. But even this will not work because the shareholders do not want their money, they want to beat the settlers in court. Thus, according to Michaels, the irrational pride of the "'miserable little monster' of a corporation is doubled by Margaret's 'powerful, capricious monster of a father-in-law.' Where the novel's plot requires miracles, its cast of characters requires monsters, and what's most monstrous is finally the difficulty of saying exactly why and in what way a man isn't a corporation" (196).

In order to answer those questions, Michaels turns to legal history and asserts that Alonzo's declaration that a man is not a corporation coincides with the development of "the theory of the existence of the corporation as an entity distinct and separate from its shareholders" (196). A man is not a corporation because by a legal fiction "the corporation is another man" (198). The legal identification of corporate personality helps to explain Royce's reduction of a conflict between the settlers and a corporation to a conflict between two men. This transformation is possible, not because a corporation is merely a front for a powerful man like Alonzo, but "because the corporation is a new kind of man" (198). To identify that new kind of man Michaels draws on Machen's theory of corporate personality.

Michaels starts by summarizing Machen's challenge to the orthodox legal doctrine that "a corporation is a fictitious, artificial person, composed of natural persons, created by the state, existing only in contemplation of law, invisible, soulless, immortal" (257/198). Machen considers this definition contradictory. The contradiction most intriguing to Michaels—one that will eventually cause him to distort Machen's argument—is the notion that a corporation is both artificial and fictional. This is impossible, Machen argues, because something that is artificial is not fictional (that is, imaginary) but real. After all, an artificial lake, although man-made, is real. Machen uses the distinction between artificial and fictional to argue that a corporation is indeed a real entity distinct from the sum of the members who compose it, but that it is not a real, but fictitious, person.

This definition returns Michaels momentarily to anticorporate literature. Anticorporate writers also thought of a corporation not as a person but a thing, a thing that threatened people. These writers' sense of the corporate threat to people is similar to what Michaels's student, Mark Seltzer, has called naturalism's "discourse of force," which imagines a world of nonhuman forces competing with men, who "properly understood, already have been reduced to the things ('brutes,' 'machines') they are said to be competing with" (201). In addition to equating bodies with machines, the discourse of force surprisingly "undoes the opposition between the body/machine and the soul, between something that is *all* body and something that is no body at all" (201). An anticorporate thinker can characterize "the corporation as simultaneously 'intangible' (no body) and 'a machine' (all body) not because he is inconsistent but because these two conditions are more like one another than either is like the alternative, a soul in a body" (201). In other words, naturalism's discourse of force that reduces all, including people, to materiality is the mirror image of the pure idealism that we find in the philosophy of Royce. The reversibility of material and ideal finds concise expression in *The Octopus* when the shepherd Vanamee converts the "novel's central image of materiality" (wheat) "into an emblem of the immaterial" (189), by insisting that, "long, long before any physical change has occurred" (155/189), a grain of wheat feels a premonition of life.

By effacing the structure of internal difference constitutive of the definition of humanity as a soul in a body, naturalism seems to solve the problem of insatiability presented by the corporation. "Insofar as men are really souls, they don't desire at all. . . . And insofar as men are really bodies, they don't desire either; nothing can stop natural 'forces,' not because they are insatiable but—just the opposite—because they are 'indifferent'" (201). But in doing so, the "double reduction to ideal and to material" (201) effaces "a natural ontology of bodies and souls" (201) and renders human agency problematic. As Michaels puts it, "Reduced to the 'forces' they really are, human agents are not agents at all. To recall Machen's terms, they are more like rivers than persons. His claim that corporations are 'entities' appears now as simply a version of the more fundamental naturalist claim that 'persons' too are really entities and hence that natural persons are as fictitious as corporate ones" (201–2).

Nonetheless, Machen's radical separation of two different elements of corporate identity—corporations are real entities, but fictitious persons—raises a question that has a bearing on our understanding of human agency. Why, after all, do we have a desire to personify corporations? "If common sense tells us that corporate entities are real and corporate persons are not, why don't we just treat corporations as things and forgo the fiction of personality" (203). Michaels finds Machen's answer to that question unsatisfactory and, goes on, in a complicated argument that we will look at in depth, to extend Machen's logic for him. In doing so Michaels deconstructs the ground of Machen's argument.

According to Michaels, Machen explains our tendency to personify corporations by opposing "nature to figuration, conceiving the actual fact of corporate entity as the ground for the legal fiction of corporate personality" (205). For Michaels to discover an opposition between nature and figure is to return him to a familiar world, the one he inhabited in Thoreau's *Walden*. In "Corporate Fiction" he repeats the move he made in 1977 by showing that an act of figuration can serve as the ground for nature just as easily as vice versa. The difference between figure and nature blurs in Machen because the very condition for a corporation to be considered an entity involves an act of figuration. Whereas both a river and a corporation are real entities, according to Machen, "the bond of union in the case of a corporation is less material" (261/204). Without an immaterial act of figuration, a corporation would not be an entity that could be personified. Furthermore, it is an immaterial act of figuration that constitutes the differences between persons and things.

> The transformation of thing into person involves, as it were, the addition of a certain immateriality. Conceiving this immateriality as fictional, corporate theorists repeat the naturalist gesture of imagining persons as personified things. But, unlike rivers, the corporate entity requires the fiction of immateriality even to qualify as a thing. Without the 'less material' 'bond of union' that identifies the individual members of a corporation, there would be no body. Unless the individual members belonged to the same body, there would be no corporation. Hence the corporation comes to seem the embodiment of figurality that makes personhood possible, rather than appearing as a figurative extension of the idea of personhood (204–5).

In short, the ontology of the corporation inevitably resists the effacement of a structure of internal difference. "The scandal of the corporation, then, isn't that it's a new kind of man; the scandal is that it's the old kind. If what seemed monstrous to Royce in *The Feud at Oakfield Creek* was the discovery that Alonzo Eldon's declaration—'a man isn't a corporation'—was only true because the corporation was *another* man, what seems monstrous now is the discovery that for a man to be a man he must also be a corporation—a man *is* a corporation" (206). Michaels then turns back to

Norris to show how "the corporate moment, the moment when the nonidentity of material and ideal constitutes the identity of the person, is disseminated throughout *The Octopus*" (206). Thus he can conclude, "Here is perhaps the deepest complicity between naturalism and the corporation. In naturalism, no persons are natural. In naturalism, personality is always corporate and all fictions, like souls metaphorized in bodies, are corporate fictions" (213).

If we have not been completely swept away by the virtuosity of Michaels's performance, we could question his argument in a variety of ways. One would be to remind him that opposition to the combination of corporate and consumer capitalism has not always been linked to appeals to the notion of natural persons. A much more powerful opposition has appealed to the notion of a natural ecological web of interconnectedness, a web that consumer capitalism threatens. It would certainly be possible to agree with Michaels that naturalism "deconstructs" the notion of natural personhood, but to perform such a deconstruction is not to prove a complicity between naturalism and the corporation, especially the business corporation. Rather than rest content with an apparent similarity, we should also explore differences.

We can do so by introducing the physical reality of waste into Michaels's description of insatiable consumption. Michaels argues that Norris's novel about production is better seen as one about consumption. But he ignores the way in which a consumer society *produces* waste. This production of waste, clearly a major, if almost insoluable, problem for present-day consumer capitalism, threatens to limit insatiable consumption much more than a notion of natural persons. In showing how natural forces control economies generated by corporate persons as well as individuals, naturalism could be said to dramatize this limitation of corporate capitalism rather than be in complicity with it. Indeed, it is precisely this aspect of naturalism that finds its most articulate expression in Thomas Pynchon, our contemporary chronicler of W.A.S.T.E.

Another way to complicate Michaels's argument is to look at his use of sources. Relying on a received critical tradition, he assumes that Royce's novel, like *The Octopus*, takes events at Mussel Slough as its source. Thus he develops an elaborate reading to explain discrepancies, such as the change of setting from the San Joachin Valley to Contra Costa County and the metamorphosis of a huge railroad company into a small land improvement company.

But Mussel Slough was not Royce's only source. Another was a feud in Contra Costa County between a rich San Francisco lawyer holding title and settlers claiming to live on public land. When the lawyer tried to eject the settlers, bloody fighting broke out until it reached a climax in 1882, the year Royce sets his novel.[21] The existence of this obvious source would seem to undermine Michaels's entire reading. The reduction of a corporation to a man could be explained by the simple fact that there was no corporation to be reduced. This is not to deny that Royce drew on events at Mussel Slough. He clearly did. But Michaels's assumption that there was one source is symptomatic of the problems with his method that simplifies the relationship between literature and history by trying to fit all into a unified logic.

A more subtle homogenizing move involves Michaels's failure to respect the different meanings that key terms such as "corporate," "fiction," and "person" have in different disciplines. For instance, in everyday use a "person" means a human being. This is not the case in either theology or law. In theology a "person" can refer to any member of the holy trinity. Similarly, in law "person" need not refer to a human being. Even the most fervent advocates of corporate personality, who argued that corporations are living organisms with a will, never claimed that such a person was a human being. As a result, the logic of Michaels's entire argument is flawed. He cannot, for instance, move so smoothly from Alonzo's "a man isn't a corporation" to the assertion that a corporation is a man.

By ignoring the specificity of the different meanings of words in particular historical contexts, Michaels is able to stitch together an argument that makes dazzling connections between seemingly unrelated elements of a culture. But in doing so he risks confirming Leo Spitzer's warning that the "(in itself commendable) tendency toward breaking down departmental barriers" can too easily turn literary history into the "gay sporting ground of incompetence." This is not to argue that no verbal slippage from field to field takes place. John Dewey, for instance, justifies his entrance into the discussions of corporate personality because they have been confused by drawing on assumptions from nonlegal fields, such as philosophy and religion.[22] Such slippage is one reason why attempts to enforce rigid disciplinary boundaries are doomed to failure. Michaels, however, does not use verbal slippage to problematize the slippery boundaries between disciplines. He uses it to erase them by creating a structural unity that denies difference by paying attention only to similarities. If stitched together by the similarity of a few key words, the unity of his essays comes undone when we pay close attention to the concrete historical uses of those words. Such a close rhetorical reading exposes the loose threads of his seemingly seamless argument and opens us to aspects of the period's concrete history that Michaels's logic closes off.

· III ·

The most obvious place to look for loose threads is in Michaels's transitions from one figure to another. It is in these transitional moments that we become most aware of his imposing his own logic on the logic he claims merely to discover within the writers of the period. It is in these moments of failed translation that we can most readily detect a double voice, an internal distance, within the essay.

The first transition I want to look at is from the analysis of *The Feud at Oakfield Creek* to legal history. Michaels argues that the quarrel between Margaret and Alonzo is a "quarrel between two different legal theories of the corporation: the theory of the corporation as one mode among others of organizing a 'group of natural persons' and the theory of the corporation as not simply a group but a 'group' 'which is recognized and treated by the law as something distinct from its members'" (197). This dispute, he claims, "had already been decisively answered" by the case of *Button v. Hoffmann* (1884), when the sole owner of a corporation brought suit to recover corporate property to compensate for personal property that had unlawfully been taken from the corporation. The Wisconsin court disagreed, arguing that "the owner of all the capital stock of a corporation does not own its property . . . and does not himself become the corporation, as a natural person, to own its property and do its business in his own name. While the corporation exists he is a mere stockholder of it, and nothing else." Michaels then adds, "The man is not the company and the company is not the man because the company is, 'by a fiction of law,' another man" (198).

In this transition Michaels abandons Royce's voice to let that of legal history speak. The problem is not only his identification of legal persons with men, but that both legal history and Royce's relation to it are more complicated than Michaels allows. There was a debate over the theory of business corporations (a theoretical debate with important practical consequences). But it was not simply a debate between two theories, nor did *Button v. Hoffmann* decisively resolve the debate in 1884.

The orthodox legal doctrine of corporations in America was established by John Marshall in the famous *Dartmouth College* case of 1819. Dartmouth College's involvement in such an important corporate decision serves to remind us that businesses are not the only corporations. (The oldest still existing corporation in the United States is Harvard College.) Corporate law has its roots in Roman and canon law, and the use of the corporate form for commercial purposes is fairly recent, having been primarily developed in seventeenth- and eighteenth-century Britain. Marshall's *Dartmouth College* decision draws on common law tradition to define a corporation as "an artificial being, invisible, intangible, and existing only in contemplation of law. Being the mere creature of law, it possesses only those properties which the charter of its creation confers upon it, either expressly or as incidental to its very existence."[23] Marshall's definition grants the corporation the status of an entity distinct from the people who comprise it, but asserts that this entity has existence only in contemplation of the law. Depending on the state for its charter, it is recognized by a fiction of law to have a personality but remains an artificial creation of the state. Its real basis remains that of the contracting individuals who comprise it. Thus, the artificial entity theory maintains the individualistic basis of the legal system.

If Marshall's artificial entity theory was orthodox legal doctrine, the rapid rise of corporations after the Civil War posed a challenge to it. Before 1850 corporations were usually created by special charters of incorporation enacted by state legislatures. These special charters came under attack because they encouraged legislative bribery, political favoritism, and monopoly. As a result, between 1850 and 1870 new laws were passed making the corporate form universally available. Free incorporation made it easy to forget that business corporations owed their existence to the law. Instead, they increasingly were regarded as a natural mode of doing business, and various theories of the corporation competed to replace Marshall's artificial entity theory. Legal historians find one expressed in the Supreme Court case of *Santa Clara County v. Southern Pacific Railroad Co.* (1886), which extended the equal protection clause of the Fourteenth Amendment to corporations. Since this case involves the corporation that Norris drew upon for *The Octopus*, one wonders why Michaels cites the relatively obscure case that he does rather than this important one.

Before *Santa Clara* the Court had narrowly construed the equal protection clause as limited to protecting rights of recently freed slaves. *Santa Clara* expanded the meaning of the clause to questions other than race. Because it interpreted the clause to include corporations, *Santa Clara* has often been cited as the case in which the Supreme Court treated corporations like individual people. Thus it has been said to illustrate the rise of the natural, as opposed to artificial, entity theory. According to the natural entity theory, corporations are not artificial creations of the state but exist prior to the state. Furthermore, this entity has a real personality and should be treated by the law as one, a person being defined here as a subject of rights. By including corporations under the Fourteenth Amendment *Santa Clara* certainly seems to subscribe to the natural entity theory.

Recent scholarship, however, has disputed this reading. Most likely, *Santa Clara* can be understood as merely extending Marshall's artificial entity theory. We can see why by looking at a related case decided in Circuit Court that, like *Santa Clara*, involved a county's taxation of the railroad. In *San Mateo v. Southern Pacific Railroad Co.* (1882), Supreme Court Justice Field makes explicit the logic behind *Santa Clara*. He writes: "Private corporations are, it is true, artificial persons, but with the exception of a sole corporation, with which we are not concerned, they

consist of aggregations of individuals united for some legitimate business."
Therefore, "it would be a most singular result, if a constitutional provision
intended for the protection of every person against partial and discriminating legislation by the States, should cease to exert such protection the
moment the person becomes a member of a corporation." He goes on,
"The Courts will always look beyond the name of the artificial being to
the individuals whom it represents."[24] In other words, corporations were
originally granted Fourteenth Amendment protection in order to guarantee the rights of their individual members, not to guarantee the rights of
an intangible entity.

Santa Clara appeals to Marshall's orthodoxy, but it also indicates the
rise of a new concept of the corporation. In this model the corporation is
a contractual agreement between individuals, very similar to a partner-
ship. Like the natural entity theory, this theory asserted corporate existence prior to the state. Like orthodox thought, it considered the corporate form to be an aggregate of individuals; any personality it had was an
artificial creation of the law. In short, this model adheres to laissez-faire
doctrine of individual rights and free contract.

How the laissez-faire doctrine of Santa Clara was later construed to
declare that corporations should be treated as personalities with natural
rights is a fascinating story in American legal history, a story that helps to
explain how the courts moved to legitimate a curious mixture of laissez-
faire and corporate capitalism. In supposing the courts to have clearly
adopted the natural entity theory as early as 1884, Michaels greatly simplifies that story. For example, if Button v. Hoffmann treats corporations
as legal entities distinct from their members, it does not necessarily recognize their real existence to be such. As we have seen, long before Button
v. Hoffmann orthodox legal doctrine treated corporations as having fictitious personalities under the law. Button v. Hoffmann merely makes clear
the implications when the corporate personality is granted property
rights, for even in the extreme case in which a company has a sole stockholder the corporate personality, not the man, has rights to the company's
property. If this violates commonsensical notions, it makes perfect legal
sense. What is at issue is not the real makeup of the corporation but its
legal identity. Until that legal identity is dissolved, the corporate personality has property rights.

In other words, Michaels's "leading decision" makes perfect legal sense
even under Marshall's artificial entity theory. Furthermore, even if it had
been decided by natural entity theory, it would not have made a corporation into a new kind of a man. When, around 1900, the natural entity
model began to govern decisions in the Supreme Court, no one claimed
that corporations were individual human beings, artificial or natural. The
corporate personality could not, for instance, marry or be given in marriage. And in Hale v. Henkel (1906) when the Supreme Court granted

corporations Fourth Amendment protections, it denied them Fifth Amendment ones, something it could not, under the Constitution, do to human beings. Finally, even as late as 1911 the natural entity theory had not completely triumphed. If it had, Machen would not have had to argue against lawyers hanging on to Marshall's orthodoxy and Machen himself would not have hung onto aspects of the aggregate theory.

Michaels's confused sense of corporate legal history tempts him to manufacture inaccurate conflicts in the works he treats. For instance, to prove that Eldon's notion of the corporation coincides with the "new" entity theory expressed in *Button v. Hoffmann*, he subtly misrepresents Eldon's meaning. We can see that misrepresentation by restoring the quotation to its context. Eldon says, "But I take it, at any rate, that it's plain a man isn't a corporation. There are more interests than mine over there; there's more capital invested than mine" (258). Eldon is not arguing that a corporation is an entity more than the sum of its individual members; he is merely insisting that his corporation involves more interests than those of a single man. Artificial and natural entity theorists of the period would have agreed.

Another problem with Michaels's argument is his claim that Royce is the "great philosopher of American corporate life" (188). To be sure, his insurance company proposal for peace indicates the influence of the business corporation on his thought, and in the corporate form he did see a *potential* corrective to the self-interest of individuals and individual nations. In *California* he welcomes the mining industry's transformation from "lonely pan washing" (C 312) to large-scale operations because these "more complex forms" gave men what they needed, "namely something to give a sense of mutual duties and of common risks" (C 313). But Royce adhered to an aggregate, not natural entity, model for business corporations. In his history, for instance, he uses the corporate form interchangeably with partnerships, such as when he describes the vast mining corporations as forming "the necessary partnerships" (C 313) for the development of group loyalty. Royce, like many socialists at the time, welcomed corporate organization as a possible way to combat individualism. But his sense of the business corporation remained one of contracting individuals. To argue that Royce would "identify the business corporation with the Christian corporate entity" (194) is to distort Royce's complex relationship to corporate capitalism. For instance, by 1908 in the *Philosophy of Loyalty*, when searching for abuses committed *in the name of individualism*, he cited "the recent history of misdeeds and unwise management of corporations in this country" (230). Furthermore, Royce's belief, derived from his German training, that "it is the State, the Social Order, that is divine. We are all but dust, save as this social order gives us life" (C 501) would be inimical to the manner in which corporations conduct business in the United States.[25]

· IV ·

Michaels's monological understanding of corporate history also leads to a misreading of Machen's 1911 essay on corporate personality. Machen's essay is important for those interested in corporate history because it expresses a particular way of synthesizing laissez-faire and corporate notions to argue against state interference into the "free" and "natural" workings of the market. As we have seen, he is most clearly against Marshall's artificial entity theory. The reasons why are quite clear. To assert that a corporation is an artificial entity created by the state is to recognize that any rights the corporation has derive from the state. Such a theory invites governmental interference. Marshall minimized it by establishing in *Dartmouth College* that charters of incorporation were contracts and thus protected by the impairment of contracts clause of the Constitution. But when free incorporation laws replaced acts of incorporation, this safeguard against governmental interference eroded, and, as we have seen, corporate apologists turned to different theories. In granting corporations the status of real entities but fictional personalities, Machen tries to synthesize the two most important theories.

With natural entity theorists, Machen asserts that corporations have an identity prior to the state distinct from the sum of their individual membership, as illustrated by the fact that a corporation retains its identity even when its membership varies. Machen was not, however, willing to grant those real entities a real personality. Confronted with the fact that the law, nonetheless, treats corporations as having personalities while it denies them to partnerships, Machen turns to legal orthodoxy to argue that such personalities are merely fictional conveniences of the law. The corporation's personality is thus akin to the personality the law grants to Joe Doe and Richard Roe in ejectment cases. It helps the legal system solve problems; once those problems are solved, it has no more existence.

Machen denies corporations the status of real personality because to do so would, as Michaels argues, threaten the notion of individuals, and Machen, like aggregate theorists, remains a defender of the individual. A mere tool of the law, the fiction of corporate personality leaves the notion of human personality untouched. For instance, in legislative debates about "the justice or injustice" of a law the doctrine of corporate personality is "altogether irrelevant." "In order to determine whether a law is just or unjust, its effect upon *men*, and not corporate personalities, must be considered" ("CP" 358).

But if the law grants a corporation a personality, albeit a fictional one, how can it take away what it has given? For Machen the answer lies in the very nature of fictionality. If something that is artificial is nonetheless real, something that is fictional is merely imaginary. Since real personality is something that exists prior to the state, the only personality the state can give to anything, including corporations, is a fictional personality, which is "like any other imaginary gift, of no value" ("CP" 361). Because corporate personality is imaginary, the law can grant it any qualities it wants to, including granting it some rights but not others, as the Supreme Court had already done in 1906.[26] Seeming inconsistencies like this can occur, Machen argues, because judges realize that the ultimate effect of their decrees, although expressed in terms of the corporate personality, must be "the determination of rights and liabilities of actual human beings" ("CP" 352). Corporate personality is nothing but a useful fiction, and "infinite harm has come from assuming that [it] will solve all problems in the law of corporations" ("CP" 357).

If Machen argues that the fictionality of corporate personality does not affect the personality of individuals, Michaels argues that it does. It is time, therefore, to return to that moment in the essay when Michaels's voice enters to extend Machen's logic in a direction Machen did not choose to follow.

Michaels's voice most clearly takes over in his summary of Machen's explanation of why the law personifies corporations. As we have seen, Machen claims that it does so out of convenience. He also argues that "the human mind is so constituted that it is difficult not to personify a compact hierarchy like the Roman Catholic Church. We instinctively speak of that organization as a person; and the law finds it difficult or impossible to refrain from doing the same" ("CP" 349).[27] Michaels, however, is not convinced.

Neither the appeal to convenience nor the appeal to nature is entirely satisfactory, however, for reasons having to do not so much with the distinction between (real) corporate entity and (fictitious) corporate personality as with the retroactive questions raised by such appeals about the nature of the corporate entity in the first place. For if a corporation created by the state is real and not imaginary, in the same way that "an artificial lake is not an imaginary lake," and if that corporation is endowed by the state with many of the powers of persons, why isn't it a real, albeit artificial, person? The answer to this is presumably that we find it more difficult to conceive of artificial persons than of artificial entities; indeed, our very notion of a person seems to require that it not be artificial. But why then is it more "natural" to personify a corporation than it is to personify another artificial entity like an artificial lake or river? If real persons are "men of flesh and blood, of like passions with ourselves," why is it natural to think of corporations as real persons (203–4)?

Michaels's answer to that question, as we have seen, is that a corporation's "material identity as a thing is thinkable only in terms of the immateriality that constitutes its identity as a person" (205). But as the "presumably" in the paragraph I quoted suggests, this answer results more from Michaels's logic than from Machen's. Michaels's mistake is his failure to understand how Machen uses the distinction between artificial and fictional. Michaels is misled when Machen, drawing on this distinction, refutes the orthodox doctrine that a corporation is a "fictitious, artificial person . . . created by the state" ("CP" 257). To point out the contradictions in this doctrine Machen argues that a "corporation cannot possibly be both an artificial person and an imaginary or fictitious person" ("CP" 257), because an artificial entity is not imaginary but real. Thus, if indeed the state creates a corporation, "it is real, and therefore cannot be a purely fictitious body having no existence except in the legal imagination" ("CP" 257).

But the notion that the state creates corporations is, for Machen, only a hypothetical possibility used to demolish the opposition by exposing the flaws in its logic. His own view is quite different. For him a corporation is not an artificial entity created by the state, as Michaels believes, but a natural entity preexisting the law. "A corporation exists as an objectively real entity, which any well-developed child or normal man must perceive: the law merely recognizes and gives legal effect to the existence of this entity. To confound legal recognition of existing facts with creation of facts is an error,—nonetheless serious because the law sometimes, ostrich-like, closes its eyes to facts and assumes that they have no existence" ("CP" 261). The last thing that Machen would want would be to succumb to the "utter futility, and worse," ("CP" 360) of thinking of a corporation as deriving its existence from the state.

Unfortunately, Michaels is so intent on finding structures of internal difference everywhere that he assumes that Machen accepts the very argument that he is at pains to discredit. As the passage that I quoted indicates, Michaels thinks that Machen considers corporations artificial, but real, entities "created by the state." Clearly missing the historical significance of Machen's argument, Michaels inappropriately asks, "Why then is it more 'natural' to personify a corporation than it is to personify another artificial entity like an artificial lake or river" (204)? But since Machen does not consider corporations artificial entities, this question is inappropriate. Indeed, Machen does not, as Michaels claims, even consider it more natural to personify corporations, whose bond of union is immaterial, than entities whose bond is material. In fact, in making his case for the naturalness of personifying corporations Machen asserts, "It is as natural to personify a body of men united in a form like that of an ordinary company as it is to personify a ship" ("CP" 266). When Machen raises the question about which entities it is more natural to personify, he is not concerned with distinctions between materiality and immateriality—that is Michaels's concern because it can lead to a discussion of bodies and souls.

Instead, he compares different kinds of associations. "There are some associations which it is more *natural* to personify than others; there are none that it is *impossible* to personify" ("CP" 349).

To be sure, Machen's argument about personification eventually leads to inconsistencies that I need not go into here. But it does not produce, despite itself, a "dazzling legitimation of corporate personality" (212). Instead, it serves to highlight contradictions that our legal system still has as a result of maintaining a curious mixture of natural rights doctrine and corporate theory. Those contradictions do question people's revered sense of the individual subject. But our detailed look at Machen and Royce provides a very different view of what was going on.

Most obviously we cannot use Machen, as Michaels does, to represent "corporate theorists" (204) in general. Nor can we treat the period from 1884 to 1911 as homogeneous in terms of corporate theory. *Button v. Hoffmann* did not decisively establish a new view of corporations that ruled throughout the period. Instead, a variety of different corporate theories competed without any one gaining complete ascendancy, although clearly some were more successful than others. This complexity undercuts any effort to establish a synchronic system that could produce a single logic for the business corporation of the period. Michaels, however, prefers to work within a uniform logic of an undifferentiated Market, a logic that serves his need to show all works conforming to a single structure of internal difference. We can see the limitations of that logic for the historical analysis of literature in his transition from legal theory back to a discussion of the logic of naturalism in *The Octopus*.

Having announced that the scandal of the corporation is, not that it is a new kind of man, but that it's the old kind, that it embodies the "monstrosity of personhood, the impossible and irreducible combination of body and soul" (206), Michaels adds, "In *The Octopus*, the monster is the railroad, the 'leviathan' (130), the 'colossus' (42), the 'ironhearted monster of steel and steam' (228). But the corporate moment, the moment when the nonidentity of material and ideal constitutes the identity of the person, is disseminated throughout *The Octopus*" (206).

If my analysis of Machen is more accurate than Michaels's, there is no "corporate moment" to be disseminated. To take one example, twice in his last paragraph Michaels returns to the notion of "the artificial person behind the natural one" (213) that he claims to derive from the logic of corporate theorists. "The corporation, the 'artificial person,' incarnates (for better or for worse) this transcendence of the limits that make up 'natural' persons" (212). This point is essential for Michaels because it not only links naturalism with corporate theory, it also helps to explain the problem of insatiability with which he began his essay. The endless production of desire can be linked to the rise of corporate capitalism. His point is similar to one he makes in his *Sister Carrie* essay that the immortality of the corporation resists the drying up of desire that leads to Hurstwood's death. Indeed, at the beginning of "Corporate Fiction" he cites the *Sister Carrie* essay as evidence for his claim that numerous scenes in *The Octopus* imagine death as a form of satiation. Furthermore, as his parenthetical phrase, "(for better or worse)," indicates, he implies that this is a situation that those within a corporate capitalist economy may as well get used to, for there is no alternative.

But, as I have shown, Machen presents a theory of the corporation as a fictional, not artificial, person. Not versed in the legal history of corporations, Michaels misrepresents Machen's distinction between artificial and fictional and goes on to conjure up a single corporate moment. Since history offers no inevitable logic of corporate identity, Michaels's analysis of *The Octopus* is severed from the history it claims to inhabit and becomes merely one more fascinating, but isolated, close reading. The problem with trying to construct seamless arguments is that refutation of one stage exposes the ragged edges of the whole. Thus rather than repeatedly returning to Michaels's misreading of Machen to demonstrate how his claim to offer a historical reading is false, I prefer to end by drawing out some of the implications of a reading strategy for which the temporality of prose fiction, indeed that of history itself, is the dissemination of a single structural moment.

· V ·

Michaels's identification of a corporate moment has an effect similar to the New Critics' stress on organic unity: the temporality of narrative is subsumed under a unifying spatial structure. This spatial emphasis might help to explain the affinities between Michaels and Fried, who was trained as a critic of the visual arts. What it clearly does in Michaels's hands is efface distinctions between voices that someone like Bakhtin claims is constitutive of the novel as a genre.[28] Just as in Michaels's version of history competing theories of corporate personality become one, so the various voices in a novel tend to be subordinated to an overall structural principle that is identified with the author's intention. For instance, in Michaels's world competing theories of materialism and idealism within *The Octopus* turn out to be the same. "Writing here is an emblem of the ideal and as such, given the reversibility of material and ideal, it can easily be made mechanical" (208). The ability to perform the priestly task of transforming material and ideal at will certainly makes it easier to establish a structure of internal difference at work throughout *The Octopus*, but it also might efface some of the book's important conflicts.

Another way in which Michaels effaces distinctions between voices is through an increased disregard for irony. According to Lukács irony is the most important trope expressing temporality in the novel. Although the New Critics eventually subordinated this temporal element to a vision of balanced harmony, their stress on paradox kept the ironic dimension of the genre alive. Michaels is far too sensitive a reader not to be alert to irony. For instance, in his essay on *Sister Carrie*, he challenges established readings by refusing to accept Ames as Dreiser's spokesman. But in his later essays, as he becomes more intent on fitting all into a structure of internal difference, irony, ironically, plays a lesser role in his analysis. An obvious example is his reading of Crane's "Five White Mice." Wanting to demonstrate a common pattern in the period, Michaels argues that Crane's story illustrates a psychologist's argument about "the gambler's overwhelming desire to substitute 'will' for 'chance,' to put 'law in place of lawlessness'" (224). He makes his point by citing a poker dice player's "faith in 'the five white mice' ('if one was going to believe in anything at all, one might as well choose the five white mice')" (224). Thus he concludes that in Crane's "'house of chance'" there is "no chance" (225). But Crane's language indicates that the choice of an object of faith is itself arbitrary. The attempt to escape chance locks the gambler into a universe of chance.

By ignoring distinctions between voices, Michaels neglects one of the most important ways in which historical difference gets inscribed within works of fiction. But the novel, a genre that arose with the rise of the middle class, also makes demands for a plot generated by individual characters. This demand does create problems for any representation of group reality. How deeply the novelization of history pervades our thought is indicated by Michaels's own personification of the Southern Pacific Railroad as the "central character" (195) in the Mussel Slough affair.

If there is a "logic" to naturalism, and especially the works of Norris, it is not that it expresses some inherent ontology of corporations or phenomenology of contract. Instead, it is related to the difficult effort to express the rising influence of all sorts of associations within American culture (including labor unions, ethnic groups, and professional organizations, as well as corporations) in a genre that demands individual characterization. The effort to reconcile group with individualistic explanations of social action was clearly not confined to literature. Peirce tried in his notion of scientific communities of the competent, which Royce drew upon in his attempt to subsume William James's individualistic pluralism under a theory of the Great Community. And, as we have seen, corporate legal theorists struggled to integrate a notion of groups into a legal system founded on the sacredness of individual rights. Nonetheless, if this conflict between group and individualistic narratives finds expression in a variety of disciplines, its expression within them is not necessarily the same. Indeed, the generic demands of the novel seem to guarantee that novelistic representation of corporations will lag behind the way in which other forms of discourse have been able to respond to the rise of corporations. Thus rather than conclude by saying that in naturalism all fictions are corporate fictions, we might be wiser to note that, so far, our literature has failed to produce any truly satisfactory corporate fiction.

The novel, however, is a genre quite used to failure,[29] and in our analysis of its relationship to America's corporate history we should not forget that, if the genre demands individualized characters, it also provides within itself the potential ironically to undercut its individualistically based narratives. If the genre generally fails in representing corporations, more often than not reducing them to monstrous characters or impersonal forces, its most interesting attempts—I am thinking of Melville's *The Confidence-Man* and Pynchon's *Gravity's Rainbow*—also stretch the novel to its generic limits. As many have argued, a productive way to explore the relationship between literature and history is to analyze those works that not only create an internal distance within themselves but also within their generic form.

In trying to describe the relationship between the economy of America at the turn of the century and changes in the genre of the novel that produced what we label naturalism, Michaels points the way for such an exploration. In "Corporate Fiction" he especially suggests how analysis of the form of the novel can prove fruitful in understanding a conflict that still exists in the American legal system between individualistic and group narratives of social explanation. But his work also poignantly illustrates that our modes of analysis affect our sense of present possibilities. Creating a sense that everything in American culture conformed to an inevitable logic of the market, Michaels denies a sense of alternative directions that history might have taken; for instance, the different ways in which the legal system might have defined corporations. Such alternatives serve to remind us that to deserve the adjective "new" any mode of analysis relating a variety of social practices and literature needs to pay attention to the differences within—and between—both. In the next chapter I will try to do just that.

CHAPTER 6.

Literature: Work or Play?

· I ·

The Gold Standard and the Logic of Naturalism cannot stand for all attempts to produce a cultural poetics. Nonetheless, it does return us to the problem of arbitrary connectedness. Why, Walter Cohen has asked, do new historicists juxtapose some social practices rather than others with particular literary texts? That question could be supplemented by the one asked by canon busters. Why choose certain literary texts rather than others? Indeed, Michaels, like Greenblatt, could be accused of privileging canonized works. But if he continues to select well-known literary texts, his claim that the only relationship that literature as such has to culture as such is that it is part of it raises an even more fundamental question of canonization for literary critics intent on producing cultural analysis. Why privilege the literary? If literature has no special relation to culture, why should literary texts play such an important role in the project of a cultural poetics? To be sure, some cultural critics urge us to abandon categories such as the literary and the aesthetic and to replace them by more inclusive ones, such as rhetoric or discourse.

If so far I have been concerned with general questions of historiography that the call for a new historicism raises, in this chapter I want to respond to questions raised about the privileged status granted to literature by attempting to describe a particular role the literary might play in our understanding of history. Before doing so, however, I need to review some of the reasons it is looked upon with suspicion, as well as some of the arguments that would privilege it.

· II ·

In questioning the status of literature the new historicism differentiates itself from both the New Criticism and older historicism that it hopes to displace. Old-fashioned literary historians always considered literature their object of study. They emphasized the importance of history because they felt that a work of literature could not be understood without an understanding of its historical context. In contrast, the New Critics argued that literary historians too often subordinated literature to history and as a result ignored what was uniquely literary about literature. The New Critics tried to discover what made a poem or story literature, not some other kind of writing. The belief that there is a distinct form of writing which is literary has been attacked by structuralists and poststructuralists. The new historicism has sustained the attack. Whereas New Critics emphasized the uniqueness of the discipline of literature, new historicists emphasize interdisciplinary analysis as a way to understand culture at large. In their "cultural studies" literary texts often seem to offer no more than an occasion to produce an interpretation of culture-at-large.

But if the questioning of the privileged status of the literary is a relatively novel phenomenon in the discipline of literary studies, we should not be surprised to find that it is not new in the discipline of history. I have already pointed out similarities between James Harvey Robinson's New History and the project of the new historicism. Especially important is their emphasis on interdisciplinarity. What I did not point out, however, is Robinson's suspicion of what he called the "literary" imagination in historical investigation. A brief comparison between the New History's distrust of the literary imagination in history with the New Criticism's distrust of history in the analysis of literature can give us a perspective on the role of literature in historical analysis not provided by purely theoretical debates about the status of the literary.

Robinson's desire to turn history into a science made him suspicious of the literary imagination. The historian, Robinson argued, "is at liberty to use his scientific imagination, which is quite different from a literary imagination." For him,

> the conscientious historian has come to realize that he cannot aspire to be a good story-teller for the simple reason that, if he tells no more than he has good reason for believing to be true, his tale is usually very fragmentary and vague. Fiction and drama are perfectly free to conceive and adjust detail so as to meet the demands of art, but the historian should always be conscious of the rigid limitations placed upon him.[1]

The "literary" historian is too prone to "yield to the temptations to ignore yawning chasms of nescience at whose brink heavy-footed History is forced to halt, although Literature is able to transcend them at a leap" (55).

Robinson's call for historians to abandon the literary imagination for the scientific was an important part of his attack on late nineteenth-century formalism that continued to subordinate the study of history to moral philosophy. For the formalists history revealed eternal values. Using the techniques of literature, they could structure their accounts of the past to tell a proper moral lesson. In attempting to align history with the social sciences rather than literature, Robinson hoped to break the hold moral philosophy had on the study of history.

A generation after the New History tried to free the study of history from the yoke of the literary imagination, the New Critics, concerned about the demise of moral values, countered Robinson's call by demanding that the study of literature free itself from subordination to history. As opposed as they were, the two agreed that the literary imagination and a scientifically-based history were at odds. Robinson's distrust of the literary imagination for historians grew out of an Aristotelian notion of literature. In the *Poetics* Aristotle argued that poetry differed from philosophy and history because it combined the concreteness of history with the universality of philosophy. As Hans Blumenberg has argued, the ability to represent universal truths depends upon a belief in a closed cosmos, in which nothing new or unfamiliar is allowed to become real.[2] To be sure, Aristotelian mimesis is not merely a passive act of imitation. Involving an act of *poeisis*, or making, it simultaneously produces that which it imitates by organizing the world in recognizable forms. Nonetheless, mimesis reveals a truth that does not change over time. As we have seen, however, the New History abandoned a belief in eternal truths for a modern sense of temporality in which the passage of time can render previous realities unreal. Insofar as the literary imagination attempts to shape the flow of history into a form that embodies universal truths, it is clearly incompatible with Robinson's sense of history. Histories subordinated to the literary imagination are opposed to a scientific understanding of history.

New Critics did not share the New History's modern sense of temporality. But in accepting its split between the scientific and literary imaginations, they also maintained an Aristotelian notion of literature. Nonetheless, whereas Robinson rejected the timeless universality that Aristotle attributed to literature, the New Critics embraced it and celebrated great works of literature as a humanistic bulwark against the course of history that had led to a fragmented modern world of science, technology, and commerce. If historians, like Robinson, no longer saw the past as a repository of eternal values, those values could still be found in a separate order of the aesthetic with a temporal logic of its own that resisted historical flux. If Robinson wanted to free history from the literary imagination because it would subordinate history to moral philosophy, the New Critics wanted to keep literature separate from history because history would obscure the universal truths dramatized in great works of literature.

A comparison between the New History and the New Criticism helps to explain the separation between studies of literature and history that the new historicism works to overcome. It is, however, a bit too symmetrical. Robinson may have distrusted the literary imagination for use in historical investigation, but he did not discount literary works as historical evidence. He gave courses in what today would be called intellectual history, and the Beards, like Vernon Parrington, made frequent use of literature in their histories. Nonetheless, the very popularity of their histories might have been a source of the New Critics' efforts to separate literary analysis from history. The Beards and Parrington analyzed literature as little more than a reflection of history or class conflict. Both complained about Hawthorne's and Henry James's lack of realism. Thus, even in their attention to literature, the New Historians invited a response from the New Critics (one passed on to today's new historicists) insisting that literature is more than a passive imitation of history. The notable exception was Carl Becker, who was himself a polished stylist. A devoted reader of James and Joyce's *Ulysses*, Becker produced an accomplished stylistic comparison of Jefferson's *Declaration of Independence* with Lincoln's public oratory.[3]

To mention Becker, however, is to call attention to another need to complicate my symmetrical history. The rise of historical relativism disrupts any simple binary opposition between the literary and scientific imagination. As we saw in chapter 4, the New History's efforts to align itself with the social sciences soon led to relativism. This move from science to relativism makes perfect sense from a New Critical perspective. If the study of history really severed itself from moral philosophy, relativism, for them, was inevitable. Indeed, the major target of New Critical attacks was not science, but relativism. As I have already pointed out, it is no accident that New Criticism arose in literature departments at the same time that relativism reigned in the study of history. One of the strongest arguments that the New Critics had against literary historians was that their historical relativism allowed aesthetic value to change over time. Such an attitude threatened to undercut the task of the humanities, which was increasingly defined in terms of moral values rather than the preservation of a rich heritage.[4] Condemning literary historians' relativism, Cleanth Brooks declared that "the Humanities are in their present plight largely because their teachers have more and more ceased to raise normative questions, have refrained from evaluation. In their anxiety to avoid meaningless 'emoting,' in their desire to be objective and scientific, the proponents of the Humanities have tended to give up any claim to making a peculiar and special contribution." If the humanities are to endure, he argues, "they must be themselves—and that means, among other things, frankly accepting the burden of making normative judgments."[5]

To be sure, relativism was also challenged within history departments. But the direction that challenge took increased the separation between literature and history by insisting on more rigorous scientific analysis. If Beard's and Parrington's mechanical use of literature in their histories caused an outcry from the New Critics, it also caused a reaction from historians intent on producing a science of history. For them literature was not objective historical evidence. Sharing Robinson's desire to write more inclusive histories, these new New Historians have drawn on the social sciences more than Robinson could have imagined. Relying on quantifiable, statistical evidence and eschewing narrative, they question literature's status as historical evidence. For instance, Lee Benson makes the general argument "that no set of systematic propositions have yet been developed to define the relationships between literature and life, and that historians, therefore, cannot now use literature as a valid and reliable indicator of public opinion." Benson makes it clear that "to say that historians have not yet systematically attempted to define those relationships, is not to say that they do not exist or that no possibility exists of establishing them."[6] Nonetheless, the new historicism needs to confront arguments like Benson's squarely, for if cultural historians are not allowed to use literary evidence until the connections between literature and life are empirically established, we might be in for a long wait.

As I mentioned in the first chapter, the new New Historians' attempt to produce scientific, quantitative histories has been challenged by both a new cultural history and those insisting upon the inevitability of narrative in any account of the past. This turn to textuality and narrative within historical studies has been welcomed by many literary critics, for it seems to confirm Linda Orr's argument that a "history of history" reveals the "revenge of literature."[7] Or, as Cathy Davidson writes in the preface to her book, "Metahistorians have suggested that every work of history is essentially an imaginative work, a narrative little different from a novel."[8] Clearly, such responses are one way to bridge the gap between literature and history, but they do so at the risk of resubordinating history to literature. If that is not too risky in literature departments, where people are always pleased to hear that another discipline is a subset of their own, it does raise problems for a cultural poetics that tries to reimagine the relationship between literature and history.

The force of such arguments too often depends upon maintaining the opposition between the scientific and literary imaginations accepted by both the New History and the New Criticism. For instance, Hayden White can argue against "scientific" historians who try to purge their histories of all fictional elements by concluding that, "In my view, we experience the 'fictionalization' of history as an 'explanation' for the same reason that we experience great fiction as an illumination of a world that we inhabit along with the author." Put slightly differently, "In point of fact [an interesting metaphor], history—the real world as it evolves in time—is made sense of in the same way that the poet or novelist tries to make sense of it, i.e., by endowing what originally appears to be problematic and mysterious with the aspect of a recognizable, because it is familiar, form.

It does not matter whether the world is conceived to be real or only imagined; the manner of making sense of it is the same."[9]

White is clearly correct to remind historians of similarities between works of history and literature. As he well knows, however, similarities do not necessarily create identities. No doubt, history writing does have fictional components, and, as White has carefully demonstrated, it is constituted by tropological discourse. But these formal characteristics would turn histories into works of literature only if they were the exclusive property of literary discourse, which they are not. For instance, fictionality is an important component of the scientific method. A hypothesis is, after all, a fictional construct that awaits testing by experimentation.[10] Furthermore, it was a strain of the empirical tradition that led to Vaihinger's philosophy of "Als ob"—as if—a poignant reminder of the extent to which empirical discourse is also a tropological one.

White does not make the mistake of identifying history with literature. But some of his followers do, because they perpetuate the false assumption that fictionality and tropes properly belong in the realm of literature, whereas scientific discourse avoids them. One step toward reconnecting history and literature is to escape the binary logic of such oppositions. A first step is to give up the attempt to define the peculiarity of literary and historical discourse in formalist terms. Instead, we need to focus on their different functions. For this task White offers little help insofar as his comparison between works of history and literature depends upon a questionable notion of the function of literature. Do poets and novelists necessarily try to make sense of the world "by endowing what originally appears to be problematic and mysterious with the aspect of a recognizable, because it is familiar, form?"

White, it seems, like Robinson, maintains an Aristotelian notion of the literary imagination. It gives the contingent world of history shape and form. White, however, disagrees with Aristotle on the status of such fictional forms. This disagreement grows out of a different sense of temporality. On the one hand, White shares Robinson's modern sense of reality in which the passage of time undermines the possibility of universal truths. What for Aristotle is a *revelation* of truth, for White and Robinson seems to be an *imposition* of form on reality. On the other hand, White's rhetorical formalism leads him to conclude that the historical and literary imaginations are structured by four basic tropes. Thus, whereas Robinson hopes that by relying on the scientific imagination historians can avoid such impositions, White feels that they are inevitable. Neither, however, entertains the possibility that literature might serve a non-Aristotelian function. It might, for instance, as the Russian formalists have argued, make strange or defamiliarize given ways of organizing the world. It might also have the capacity to help bring new forms into existence rather than relying on familiar ones.

Indeed, both scientific historians and White betray an ahistorical sense of literature's relation to history by assuming that it is a constant one. Benson, we recall, wants to develop a "set of systematic propositions . . . to define the relationship between literature and life." But developing such propositions would be possible only if the relationship did not change. Furthermore, his threatened exclusion of literary texts until those propositions are established depends upon an idealistic model, in which there could be a human activity that somehow is not part of the complex network of social practices and institutions that it is the historian's task to study. To be fair to Benson, I should emphasize that he merely rules out the use of literature as a "valid and reliable indicator of public opinion." Nonetheless, he seems to conceive of no other reason why historians would want to include literary texts in their analyses.

As different as White is from Benson, he too assumes a set role for the poet or novelist, as if that role may not be a historically changing one. In addition, his attempt to describe the nature of historical writing in formal terms is of little use for new historicists attempting to go beyond formalism. Literary critics relying on his work might think that they are breaking out of the narrowness of their own disciplinary training by turning to history, but what they end up confronting turns out to be another version of literature, in which, as the title of White's most recent collection of essays puts it, we have the "content of the form."[11] Rather than productively reconnecting the study of literature and history, this particular way of privileging the literary is a mirror image of the scientific attitude of someone like Benson who distrusts the literary imagination. As Luiz Costa Lima has argued, works of history or literary history (he is referring to Auerbach's) may "provoke an aesthetic response," but that response does not "make them literature, nor should it be concluded that literary criticism and history are literary genres! This is a necessary conclusion only for those who finally go on to believe that history is the accurate representation of what happened, exactly as it happened. If we go beyond this old, positivistic assumption, we will be better able to face the problematic frontiers between two *discourses*, that is, between two different forms of the appropriation and construction of reality: historiography and fictional discourses."[12]

Costa Lima himself continues to fall prey to the opposition between historiography and fiction; nonetheless, his insistence on facing the problematic frontiers between discourses brings us back to the work of Greenblatt, who is not content to conclude, as Michaels does, that the "only relationship literature as such has to culture as such is that it is part of it."[13]

Instead, as we have seen, Greenblatt insists on exploring problematic frontiers between various social practices. But even Greenblatt's sophisticated analysis has problems when confronted with the role played by literature in his cultural poetics. Because I devote the entire next chapter to Greenblatt's description of aesthetic practices, I will look at his ideas only briefly now. I do so because they so economically pose a dilemma faced by the new historicism's uses of literary texts.

· III ·

In *Renaissance Self-Fashioning* Greenblatt tries to justify why "the literary text remains the central object of [his] attention." It does "in part because . . . great art is an extraordinarily sensitive register of the complex struggles and harmonies of culture and in part because, by inclination and training, whatever interpretive powers I possess are released by the resonances of literature."[14] Greenblatt's two reasons are ones commonly cited by cultural historians, and yet they come into potential conflict. The first opens him to charges that he is privileging literature, especially great literature. The second implies that there is nothing special about literature: it remains an object of Greenblatt's attention merely because it offers him an occasion to do cultural analysis. To stick with one or the other of these reasons would allow Greenblatt to be more consistent, but his work remains interesting precisely because he chooses the difficult task of trying to work out the tensions that result from holding both. By drawing out the implications of his argument, we can focus on the issues that we need to pursue in trying to access a role that the literary can play in new historical analysis today.

Greenblatt's second reason for focusing on literature is similar to an argument that we can imagine Stanley Fish making. Literature remains important for new historicists because most are trained as literary critics. When they turn to literary texts they are not so much implying its privileged status as merely extending the practices in which they were trained. This explanation carries with it a certain disciplinary modesty. To acknowledge that one is merely extending the practices of one's discipline is to acknowledge the limitations and constraints that go with those disciplinary practices. But such disciplinary modesty comes into conflict with the new historicism's goal to give us access to the "complex network of institutions, practices, and beliefs that constitute the culture as a whole."[15] So long as the interpretive powers that the resonances of literature release speak about the culture as a whole, it seems that large claims are being made about literary texts.

To be sure, other discursive practices might release similar interpretive powers in those trained in other disciplines. For instance, social historians might argue that by inclination and training their interpretive powers are released by examining demographic tables. But if we look at cultural historians who have formed an alliance with new historicists trained as literary critics, it becomes clear that one thing drawing them together is their interest in literary texts and techniques. The central role that literature plays in a cultural poetics seems to be more than a matter of disciplinary training. The interpretive powers that the resonances of literature release, it would seem, must have something to do with Greenblatt's first reason for focusing on literature: it is a sensitive register of cultural complexity.

At first glance Greenblatt's description of great literature's relationship to cultural complexity seems to risk lapsing into a reflection model used by an older historicism. His choice of the metaphor of a register is, however, a self-conscious effort to break with a reflection model. To think of literature as a reflection of historical complexity is to imply that a work can somehow occupy a position outside of history to imitate it. In contrast, a register does not stand outside a culture's network of institutions, practices, and beliefs but is part of that network.

Greenblatt's metaphor of a register distinguishes him from those literary critics who claim to have returned to history by offering allegorical readings that reveal the historical as the neglected level of a text. That kind of historical criticism has produced essays on *The Scarlet Letter* as a story about Hawthorne's relation to the marketplace, on "History as the Suppressed Referent in Modernist Fiction," or *Macbeth* as a comment on the ascendancy of a Scottish king to the British throne. But, as Greenblatt knows, if literature relates to history by telling a story about it, even a complex story, we may as well go directly to historical accounts. In contrast, he avoids strictly allegorical readings. He does not analyze texts so "that we may see *through* them to underlying and prior historical principles."[16] Instead, he shows the complicated interplay between literature and a culture's various social practices, of which it is one. Unfortunately, his metaphor of a register finally does not help him in that task much more than the metaphor of text as reflection.

Conservative on this matter as I may be, I do not want to deny great literature's capacity to register historical complexity. The traditional argument that literary texts are valuable vehicles for introducing us to a past era's complexity seems to me worthy of defense. As both a critic and a teacher, I use literature in this way, even going so far as to offer my own allegorical readings. Nonetheless, literary works are clearly not alone in registering historical complexity. A well-written history can do the same.

As a result, if the task of the cultural critic is to open us to such complexity, we still need to ask why we should include literary texts at all. The answer that Greenblatt comes up with is to reprivilege literature. In the next chapter I will examine the complicated process by which Greenblatt does this when he develops the notion of a mimetic economy. For now I can evoke another notion popular with the new historicism, that of "cultural work" developed by Jane Tompkins and, among others, Philip Fisher. For them literature's important connection with history is not that it registers historical complexity but that it influences people by fixing community opinion.[17] Their emphasis on cultural work is clearly indebted to pragmatism, which stresses how ideas do work in the world. But even if we accept this pragmatic solution, a problem comes in measuring the amount of work done by a particular text. The easiest solution, one adopted by Tompkins and Fisher, has been to assume that popular fiction, because of its wide readership, accomplishes the most work. Thus, whereas the notion of cultural work privileges literature by assuming that is has had an important role in shaping community opinion, in the hands of Fisher and especially Tompkins it challenges the privileged status the profession has granted to works of complexity. Insofar as a text's work is measured by its popularity, a text's complexity might actually limit the amount of work that it can do. To the objection that an appeal to popularity risks having us privilege texts that are not true, proponents of popular fiction could respond by turning to William James's belief that it means exactly the same thing to say that a belief is useful because it is true and that it is true because it is useful. A popular work's acceptance in the marketplace would seem to be a verification of its truth and a sign of the amount of work that it has done.

Unfortunately, the relationship between literature and belief is not that simple. For instance, for both Fisher and Tompkins Uncle Tom's Cabin is a supreme example of literature's ability to accomplish cultural work. Appropriately, however, Benson uses Uncle Tom's Cabin as an example of his attack on historians' use of literature. According to this respected historian of the period,

> no credible evidence now exists to substantiate the alleged influence of Uncle Tom's Cabin. Actually, scattered, impressionistic evidence indicates that historians have tended to exaggerate greatly the book's role as a reflection of, or influence upon, public opinion. More to the point, and more significantly, I do not know of any systematic attempt to study the book's influence. Ringing assertion has substituted for credible demonstration.[18]

Again, Benson does not deny the possibility of influence. He merely notes that influence has not been established. But since Tompkins's argument is based on the assumption that popular fiction does have an influence, it is weakened by the fact that "ringing assertion has substituted for credible demonstration." Indeed, Tompkins would need to prove not only that popular fiction has influenced the course of history but also that it has had more influence than so-called nonpopular fiction. A wide readership does not necessarily correspond with influence.

Benson's phrase "a reflection of, or influence upon, public opinion" raises another problem. Is a work's popularity a sign that it has actively shaped many people's beliefs or that it confirms already existing beliefs? Wyndam Lewis is reported to have remarked that a bestseller is like a mirror; it never lies. He did not mean that it accurately reflects social complexity. Instead, he implies that it reflects back the way people already think. To be sure, such a reflection or, perhaps better, register can be useful for someone studying cultural history, but if Lewis is correct, the study of popular fiction would return us once again to a more passive notion of the role of literature in historical analysis. Indeed, if he is right, it is possible that the most active work is done by texts that, although not widely popular, challenge rather than register popular opinion.

And there are other possibilities to consider. It has been rumored that a private viewing of *Patton* influenced Richard Nixon's decision to bomb Cambodia, a decision that caused massive destruction and set off a wave of protests, including violent ones. Could not this single act of reception be said to have done more cultural work than numerous acts of reception? This is especially possible because there was by no means universal agreement on how to interpret the film. Many considered it an ironic comment on Patton's militaristic mind. *Patton* is a film, not a work of literature. Nonetheless, the conflict over how to interpret it reminds us that any argument about the amount of cultural work done by literature also needs to confront the question of *how* people read various works. Did, for instance, *Uncle Tom's Cabin* do the same work in the South and the North? Finally, as I pointed out in the second chapter, a theory of cultural work also needs to confront the problem of the work done when we read past texts in the present. Not to do so is to turn our literary histories into antiquarian studies. In contrast, one task of a new historicism is to ask how reading literature from the past can alter and shape beliefs of those reading it today. To ask this question may not keep us from privileging literature, but it might help us to find more convincing reasons for doing so.

To pay attention to the work done at the moment of reception as well as the moment of production is to complicate yet another use that new historicists have found for literary works—that of ideological unmasking. Assuming that a work's work has been completed in the past, a number of ideological critics place themselves in a privileged seat of judgment in which they expose literature's ideological complicity, a complicity that they either champion or decry depending on their attitude toward the particular culture. Just as I do not want to deny literature's ability to register historical complexity, so I do not want to deny literature's potential complicity with reigning ideologies. But exclusive attention to such complicity helps lead to arguments like Michaels's that the only relation literature as such has to culture as such is that it is part of it. After all, so long as we believe that in some way or another all social practices are part of the complex network that constitutes a culture as a whole, all social practices have at least a minimal complicity with the culture of which they are a part. Rather than rest content with exposing literature's ideological complicity, a more productive way to proceed is to continue our analysis by examining the ways in which reading works from the past can put at risk the privileged position of judgment that we occupy in the present, a position that is, after all, ideologically constituted. It is in examining the way in which literature (or the literary) can put at risk privileged ideologies, including our own, that *I* risk privileging literature. For me the way in which the play of literary texts can challenge fixed historical beliefs is at least as important as how they work to fix them.

· IV ·

My defense of literature begins by looking at the argument that there is no intrinsic difference between literary and nonliterary language. I basically agree with the argument, but not with the way that some use it to proclaim the death of literature or, in what seems a lapse into the essentialist thought they attack, to proclaim that the literary itself is an inherently elitist category.

The difficulty of demonstrating an inherent distinction between literary and nonliterary discourse is illustrated by the work of a critic whom I will refer to frequently in the rest of this chapter—Northrop Frye. In *Anatomy of Criticism*, Frye tries to explain the distinction by evoking the traditional division of studies into the trivium of grammar, rhetoric, and logic. Grammar, he defines, as "the act of ordering words"; logic as "the art of producing meaning." He goes on:

> What we have been calling assertive, descriptive, or factual writing tends to be, or attempts to be, a direct union of grammar and logic. An argument cannot be logically correct unless it is verbally correct, the right words chosen and the proper syntactical relations among them established. Nor does a verbal narrative communicate anything to a reader unless it has continuous significance. In assertive writing, therefore, there seems to be little place for any such middle term as rhetoric, and in fact we often find that among philosophers, scientists, jurists, critics, historians, and theologians, rhetoric is looked upon with some distrust.[19]

Rhetoric, however, is essential to literature. "If the direct union of grammar and logic is characteristic of non-literary verbal structures, literature may be described as the rhetorical organization of grammar and logic" (*Anatomy* 245). Having made this distinction, Frye eventually admits "that all structures in words are partly rhetorical, and hence literary, and that the notion of a scientific or philosophical verbal structure free of rhetorical elements is an illusion. If so, then our literary universe has expanded into a verbal universe, and no aesthetic principle of self-containment will work" (350).

Frye's expansion of a literary universe into a verbal one would seem to confirm the folly of trying to maintain a distinct category of literary texts. Stanley Fish, for instance, has persuasively argued that there is no ahistorically intrinsic quality of a distinctly literary language. Drawing on a spatial metaphor, he asserts that literature is "language around which we have drawn a frame, a frame that indicates a decision to regard with a particular self-consciousness the resources language has always possessed. . . . What characterizes literature is not formal properties, but an attitude—always within our power to assume—toward properties that belong by a constitutive right to language."[20]

But if Frye himself recognizes that, since all discourse is rhetorical, all can be read as if it were literature, we have to wonder why such an intelligent critic still insists on talking about a distinct category of literature.[21] He does, because he realizes that, although lines between disciplines blur, disciplinary distinctions are useful to maintain. There may be no intrinsically literary quality of language, but this does not mean that there is no such thing as literature. The frame we draw around language to call it literary may be invisible, but it is, nonetheless, real. Furthermore, the attitude that we can adopt toward language to call it literary is not an attitude which originates in an autonomous individual. Instead, it is an attitude that makes sense only because it has been socially defined. There is a socially defined sphere of activity called the literary.

To recognize literature as a socially defined sphere of action leads nowhere unless we go on to ask: What is its social function?[22] If literature is one social institution among others, it is also a different social institution with a different social function from others. To claim that literature has a particular social function different from other social practices is not to assume, as Benson does, that its function does not change over time. In fact, its changing function is what necessitates a *historical* analysis of literature as a social institution, since it is impossible to establish a timeless set of propositions about its function.[23]

Just because, for good historical reasons, present critical energy is focussed on the slippery boundaries between disciplines, there is no reason to abandon disciplinary categories altogether. Indeed, to do so would be to ignore our present historical situation. For instance, if, as Fish argues, the literary is an attitude we assume toward language to read it with a particular self-consciousness, it is possible that writers will produce works which tap the resources of language so as to reward such a reading. This is especially true since most of our "creative" writers still think of themselves as producing something called literature. What they are prone to emphasize, therefore, is the rhetorical dimension of language. It is even possible that works with a sophisticated use of rhetoric were partially responsible for our present definition of the literary, since people found that it paid to read them with a self-conscious regard for language.

Increasingly, works we call literary have become self-consciously reflexive about their own status as language. Often considered a sign of artistic self-indulgence and a retreat from the field of social reality, this reflexivity might be in keeping with what traditionally has been considered literature's representational function. If literature, as a social practice, very often represents other social practices, it makes sense that it might turn on itself and represent its own practices. With the communication/information revolution, Western modes of production are more and more concerned with the production of signs. We can expect its literature imaginatively to represent those practices.

In saying this, I should not be misunderstood as arguing that literary texts are the only ones that will do so, or that the literary is an absolute category. To repeat, no verbal structures are free of rhetorical elements. But once we abandon the effort to define literature formally, the rhetoricalness of all discourse implies neither the death nor (alternatively) the infinite expansion of the literary. On the contrary, the study of the rhetorical elements of all discourse would, it seems, be enhanced by close study of those works that we call literature, although such study does not turn all discourse into literature.[24] To be sure, this enhancement will not occur if we limit our study of literature to the discovery of its internal coherence. But not even Frye advocates such a limited role for the critic. In his "Tentative Conclusion" to *Anatomy of Criticism*, Frye risks a few comments on "the external relations of criticism as a whole with other disciplines" (342). He ends his book advocating that, because "metaphysics, theology, history, law" are all "verbal constructs" (354), literary criticism should play a central role in analyzing their rhetoric.

Frye's program for the literary critic exposes problems with one of the most widely circulated calls for the end of literary studies: Terry Eagleton's *Literary Theory*. Attacking the literary as ideologically discredited, Eagleton simultaneously calls for a return to rhetorical studies and the death of literature. Eagleton also dismisses Frye as a perpetuator of the bourgeois institution of literature when he describes him and the New Critics as examples of liberal humanists who tried to pull off a synthesis of technocratic rationality and spiritual wholeness. He then wonders, "But how many students of literature today read them?"[25] Presumably, once upon a time Eagleton did, and if he did, he must have read Frye's "Tentative Conclusion" that advocates a program of study very similar to the one Eagleton advocates in his "Conclusion: Political Criticism," the very conclusion that includes Eagleton's dismissal of Frye. Eagleton, it seems, either refuses to acknowledge what he learned in "Tentative Conclusion," or he has forgotten.

Forgetfulness, I should point out, is not a quality to be cultivated by historical critics. And yet, quite a few new historicists concerned about "privileging" literature seem prone to it. Using the increasing number of sophisticated analyses of nonliterary texts as proof that there is nothing special about literary texts, they too often seem to forget that most honed their analytical skills on works of literature or learned from those who did. Such critics are like those who, after reading James Joyce's *Finnegans Wake*, go back to *Dubliners* and demonstrate that all rhetorical principles in the *Wake* are at work in "The Sisters," the first story of Joyce's early collection. In a sense they are right. I know; I have made a similar argument.[26] But in making it we should not forget that we would not even notice some of those principles at work in "The Sisters" if we had not read the *Wake* or read those who had. In short, if part of the program of the new historicism is to make us aware of the rhetorical quality of all discursive practices, literary texts should remain an important object of study for them.

Such a defense of literature does not imply that literature is an ahistorical category. On the contrary, I am arguing that many attempts to deprivilege literature ignore history in that all they really dislodge is an ahistorical, essentialist view of literature and therefore avoid the more difficult problem of defining the particular social function of literature in today's society. As Frye admits, the very notion of "works of art" is a relatively modern one. "Nearly every work of art in the past had a social function in its own time, a function which was often not primarily an aesthetic function at all" (*Anatomy* 344). Nonetheless, these works are considered literature today, and it is our task to define their function for us. If Frye's expansion of literary criticism into the field of rhetorical analysis does not have the explicit political agenda that Eagleton's does, it does share Eagleton's goal of exposing the way in which discursive practices dominate. Recognizing the numerous intellectual activities moving in the direction of "conceptual rhetoric," Frye suggests, "Many of these movements were instigated by a desire to free the modern mind from the tyranny of emotional rhetoric, from the advertising and propaganda that try to pervert thought by a misuse of irony into conditioned reflex" (350).

No doubt, in our poststructuralist world we would state this somewhat differently. When Frye asserts the need for criticism to combat the "compulsions of habit, indoctrination, and prejudice" (348), we can point out that his liberal humanism is not free from doctrine. But it does not necessarily follow that we should dismiss Frye's goal to keep thinking from being no more than a conditioned reflex. As Eagleton admits, especially those interested in political criticism need to maintain the belief that discourse can be a "humanly transformative affair" (*Literary Theory* 206).

In the next two sections I will stress the transformative potential in the literary as it is defined at this particular moment. To do so is to advocate a particular role for histories calling themselves new—one that James Harvey Robinson emphasized in his collection. A new history should not only be a new version of the past, it should also be a version of the past that wrestles with the possibility of transforming our present into a new future. Robinson, however, distrusted "the literary" and entrusted the transformative power of his New History to the alliance it would forge with the social sciences. Perhaps the role of the new historicism in literary studies should not be to reinforce the prejudices of those historians who look at literature with suspicion, but to define a role that the literary can play in making history new.

· V ·

In claiming that the literary has a transformative potential, I will be accused of reverting to the old argument that literature transcends ideology. But this is not the case, just as it was not the case that to acknowledge the literary as a socially defined activity is to revert to an essentialist notion of literature. The need to examine the ideological function of the literary remains, especially in the Anglo-American world where for years it was rarely scrutinized. But it should not become our exclusive concern. The belated discovery by literary critics in this country that literature is ideological is similar to their belated discovery two decades ago that literature is after all made up of words. At that time numerous critics abandoned their studies of character, action, and plot and began to see all literature as commenting on its status as language. Today an equal number of critics are exposing the ways in which the category of the literary serves the ideology of capitalism. Both trends constitute necessary correctives to old-fashioned practices, but both can lead to simplifications. If all social practices are ideological, not all have the same ideological function. Our task is not to reject every activity that is ideological (which would leave us with no activity at all, including our own acts of rejection), but to define the particular ideological function of the literary. It may not be in necessary or total complicity with the status quo.

If a new historicism really wants to make history new, then in addition to exposing literature's ideological complicity with the dominant ideology (a term that makes sense only when it is concretely defined) it might also take an interest in considering whether and how the literary can resist particular ideologies. Granted, any such resistance would take place in a larger ideological context, but it is the local resistance to particular sets of beliefs that helps to make history new. Bourgeois critics may not have been completely wrong when they saw within the literary a capacity to resist dogma.

For bourgeois critics, literature's capacity to resist dogma is related to their belief that the function of art is to have no explicit social function. The primary purpose of a work of art is not to make statements about the world, but to be itself. As Frye puts it, literature's intention is "centripetally directed. It is directed towards putting words together, not towards aligning words with meaning." The word "intention," Frye writes,

> is analogical: it implies a relation between two things, usually a conception and an act. Some related terms show this duality even more clearly: to "aim at" something means that a target and a missile are being brought into alignment. Hence such terms properly belong only to discursive writing, where the correspondence of a verbal pattern with that of what it describes is of primary importance. But a poet's primary concern is to produce a work of art, and hence his intention can only be expressed by some kind of tautology (*Anatomy* 86).

Literature is able to resist dogma because what is properly literary about a work is not its statements about the world, but its "purposiveness without a purpose."[27]

In defining art as "purposiveness without a purpose" bourgeois critics associate it with play. This association seems to cause anxiety for a number of new historicists concerned with using literature to transform the world. To associate literature with play seems to deny its capacity to do cultural work. This is one reason why a critic like Tompkins champions those texts whose primary intention was to change readers' minds. Whereas for bourgeois critics literary texts are a special kind of rhetoric whose aim is aesthetic, Tompkins asserts that they, like all forms of rhetoric, aim at persuasion. To claim that literature performs important cultural work has the pragmatic function of reassuring members of a profession anxious about its marginalized status in contemporary society that what they study has social utility. Ironically, however, to do so is to succumb to the bourgeois demand for practicality. In attacking bourgeois aesthetics, Tompkins's populism validates middle class standards of taste. In our earnestness to reap a social payoff for our labor, we should neither overemphasize the transformative potential of what we do nor underestimate the transformative potential of play. Perhaps we need to cast off our Puritan and pragmatic heritage and recognize the social possibilities within play. Without a doubt, the work accomplished by play has severe limitations. But rather than make extravagant claims for the influence of popular texts or, as some poststructuralists do, enhance the importance of what we do by positing discourse as the basis of all social institutions, we might focus on the subversive possibilities of play without forgetting its limitations.

The subversive potential of the literary, along with its limitations, is most easily illustrated by returning to Fish's notion that the literary is an attitude that we adopt toward language. To do so is to invite the question: What are the social consequences of adopting a literary attitude toward language not labelled such by social convention? What, for instance, happens when a legal text is read as literature? This can occur in at least two ways. First, a legal text can appear in a work of literature, such as when Melville draws on excerpts from a legal deposition in "Benito Cereno." Second, we can read a legal decision as if it were a work of literature, something happening more and more as legal and literary scholars apply literary theory to legal texts.

There is, of course, no way to predict all of the ways in which all readers would respond to law read as literature, but we do have evidence that in our present institutional framework to do so is to undermine established ways of reading. For instance, the legal language in "Benito Cereno" has been read (if not by all) as undercutting its own claims to objective authority. This occurs because, in placing a legal deposition within a work of literature, Melville invites us to read it with what Fish calls "a particular self-consciousness" about its linguistic resources. As a result, we are able to see the extent to which its authority depends upon its rhetoric not necessarily an eternal logic of the law. Reading legal decisions as if they were literature produces a similar effect. The result has caused one legal scholar, worried that such readings provide no measure for correctness, to spout charges of nihilism.[28]

Such charges may be needlessly alarmist. We can read a case as if it were literature, but to do so is to deprive it of its social function as law. If the social function of the literary allows us to be content with pursuing the free play of its language into the realm of indeterminacy, the social function of the law demands a determinate interpretation. The courts have to decide a case one way or another. That is why we go to court in the first place. We can read a legal decision as literature, but no one will be sent to prison when we do so. Similarly, to place a legal decision or statute in a work of literature is to alter its status. When Harriet Beecher Stowe had a fictional judge pronounce the words of Judge Thomas Ruffin's North

Carolina slave case in *Dred, A Tale of the Dismal Swamp*, those words had no direct authority over a real slave's life.

As we have seen, it is precisely because reading a text as literature places it in a realm distant from immediate political effects that some politically motivated critics urge the abandonment of the categories of the literary and the aesthetic. For instance, for Jochen Schulte-Sasse "the individual work . . . turns into a testing ground without effect . . . because we tend to organize our 'habitual norms of conduct' along the lines of institutional demarcations; we defuse the impact of art's mimetic elements by differentiating our habitual norms of conduct parallel to the functional differentiation of society and never permit our aesthetic norms of conduct to penetrate other realms of our life."[29] If to stay in the sphere of the literary is to remain harmless, it seems that the literary is an inherently ideological activity in complicity with the status quo. Politically, it would seem necessary for those concerned about changing society to abandon such a realm. Eagleton, for instance, argues that the value judgments which help shape the category of literature "refer in the end not simply to private taste, but to the assumptions by which certain social groups exercise and maintain power over others." As a result, he cautions, "When I use the words 'literary' and 'literature' from here on in this book . . . I place them under an invisible crossing-out mark, to indicate that these terms will not really do but that we have no better ones at the moment" (*Literary Theory* 16). But the situation is not that simple.

If, as Eagleton argues, all discourse is inscribed within a set of power relations, it is naive, even when being polemical, to perpetuate the illusion that we will find some uncontaminated terms to replace the fallen ones of "literary" and "literature." What, after all, is to keep the term he offers to replace them, like "rhetoric," from also being ideologically contaminated? Rather than search for premature theoretical consistency by rejecting the concept of literature as inherently ideological, the new historicism would do better to use to its advantage the contradictory nature of "the literary" within bourgeois society. To be sure, the examples from law and literature would seem to confirm Schulte-Sasse's claim that individual works turn into testing grounds without effect. But although his argument is an important counter to those who would make too much of literature's ability to perform cultural work outside the realm of the aesthetic, he overexaggerates the stability of institutional demarcations when he says that they "*never* permit our aesthetic norms of conduct to penetrate other realms of our life" (my emphasis). As firmly entrenched as institutional boundaries may be, there is slippage between them. Schulte-Sasse himself seems aware of such slippage when he chooses the cautious "we *tend* to organize our 'habitual norms of conduct' along the lines of institutional demarcations" (my emphasis). But this tendency shortly transforms into a statement of absolutism. It may well be, however, that within the institutional boundaries established by bourgeois society the aesthetic is one realm in which such absolutist statements are contested. I will not go so far as to claim that "only through bourgeois aesthetics, bourgeois aesthetics will be conquered," but I do feel that the new historicism should learn to play with the possibilities available within the realm of bourgeois aesthetics to question bourgeois ideology rather than attempt to put a halt to that play.

One important contradiction within bourgeois society is that its stress on "freedom" is so pervasive that it constrains our ability to conceive of "real" alternatives to it. Insofar as literature promises a space of unconstrained freedom it partakes of the contradictions of this ideology. Indeed, the very need of bourgeois society to designate literature as a space in which the imagination has free play indicates that literature's freedom is defined by social practices and institutions in which the imagination is not free. Nonetheless, the freedom in this space, limited as it might be, is not totally illusory.

Both ideological and capable of contesting dominant ideologies, the literary in bourgeois society is similar to the legal system, which, on the one hand, serves the ruling order through its promise that rule by law provides justice and equality for all and, on the other, provides a realm in which its order can be contested, since for the appeal to justice through rule by law to be an effective ideological tool it cannot be merely illusory but at times actualized. The literary, however, is a social institution which provides more freedom, imaginary as it might be, than the legal system. As Raymond Williams argues, "However dominant a social system may be, the very meaning of its domination involves a limitation or selection of the activities it covers, so that by definition it cannot exhaust all social experience, which therefore always potentially contains space for alternative acts and alternative intentions which are not yet articulated as a social institution or even project."[30]

An activity less "covered" than the law, the literary occupies a space in which it is freer to play with alternatives, including alternative ways of reading. Granted, the alternative ways of reading have some of their most important effects when they escape the sphere of the literary, and play is by no means inherently subversive. Play can also release unforeseen reactionary ways of reading, and play for the sake of play has little immediate political effect, other than to provide escape (in both senses) from a sense of total constraint. Furthermore, the sphere of the literary does not operate by a principle of self-generation. Unless it is exposed to modes of analysis and discourse from other disciplines, it will stagnate. One of the strengths of the new historicism is that its transgression of too-rigidly established disciplinary boundaries has taught literary critics that their close readings need to pay closer attention to the political, economic, and social implications of discourse. Nonetheless, it would be unwise at this moment totally to abandon the sphere in which those new ways of reading have been given the freedom to develop.

I have warned against a form of disciplinary imperialism that would turn all disciplines into a subset of literature because they are all constituted by language. The way in which some literary critics have welcomed post-structuralism's linguistic turn has, with justice, been analyzed as a conservative move, an effort by people in the humanities faced with an increasingly marginalized social role to reassert themselves as the most sensitive interpreters of human experience. But others, also feeling the threat of marginalization, should not underestimate the important work such a linguistic turn has led to. At a time when philosophers are starting to recognize the importance of a rhetorical analysis of their discourse, when political scientists are using literary theory to explore the political implications of discursive practices, when psychologists are arguing that the unconscious is structured like a language, and when historians are paying increased attention to the literary aspects of histories that other historians tried to exclude, at such a time, it is an unfortunate irony that various critics, marching under the banner of the new historicism, reject the sphere of social activity known as the literary. After all, the most important contribution the new historicism makes to our new histories is not so much sophisticated historical research—much of it relies on work already done by historians—but sophisticated ways of reading.

In this section, I urged the new historicism to use to its advantage, rather than reject, the association of the literary with play. I argued that a transformative potential can be released when we adopt a certain way of reading—we call it literary—to nonliterary discourse. In the next section I will argue that we can achieve a critical perspective when texts that we call literary are read a certain way—a way which I will describe as historical.

In making my argument, I do not want to overexaggerate the power which reading and discourse have to change the world. I would do no more than lapse into a naive idealism if I were to argue that discourse alone could transform the course of history. Nonetheless, not to believe in the contributory power of discourse to influence the course of history is also to lapse into a form of idealism that assumes that discursive practices are not embedded within a complex set of interrelated social practices. To alter one realm of social practices is potentially to alter the entire interrelated network. Even so, it would also be naive to think that texts we call literary can do anything in and of themselves. It is clear that our culture allows us to read texts in many different ways. This, indeed, is one way of defining a "literary" way of reading. Any argument about the potential effect of literary texts is also an argument about *how* we should read those texts. Nonetheless, to argue that all texts can produce the same effects is once again to lapse into a form of idealism, for it denies the specific material reality of individual texts. The particular texts we read do matter. Texts do not produce effects in and of themselves, but different texts still have the potential to release different effects.

· VI ·

As I have emphasized, if the new historicism is to live up to its name, it needs to implicate itself actively in the present. Its new histories should not be merely different versions of the past, but constructions of the past which provide a new perspective on our historical present. The need for such new histories is particularly acute today because, despite the recent "politicization" of criticism, it has become increasingly difficult to imagine alternatives to our present situation. Indeed, that difficulty is in part a result of the success of our present political criticism. Having persuasively demonstrated that all social practices are always already embedded within a system of ideological constraints, we find it impossible to locate a ground from which to achieve a critical perspective on the present. "Antifoundationalist" thinkers dismiss as deluded attempts like Jürgen Habermas's to achieve such a perspective. Others reject theory itself as the misguided effort to step outside of present practices in order to control their direction.[31]

What I want to propose is that in contradictory bourgeois society, a form of discourse that by accepted convention is antifoundational—we call it literary—can provoke us to reflect on our historical situation, not by providing a foundation but through the activity of reading particular texts. It is by concentrating on what happens when we read texts that Frye proposes a way in which literature can contribute to transforming our beliefs. In so often evoking Frye I do not mean to accept his work uncritically. Instead, I am playing with the possibilities it suggests.

As if he were responding to certain versions of the antifoundationalist argument, Frye wrote over thirty years ago:

> The tendency to insist that man cannot be a spectator of his own life seems to me to be one of the lethal half-truths that arise in response to some kind of social malaise. Most ethical action is a mechanical reflex of habit: to get any principle of freedom in it we need some kind of theory of action, theory in the

sense of *theoria*, a withdrawn or detached vision of the means and ends of action which does not paralyze action, but makes it purposeful by enlightening its aims (*Anatomy* 348).

Frye urges a principle which will enlighten the aims of action. But clearly this principle cannot be solely the product of literature, for, as we have seen, Frye believes that literature has no aim other than to be itself. Instead, Frye's theory of action comes from the critical act of reading these works. Frye's efforts to unite criticism and theory and the important role that he grants aesthetics suggest unexpected similarities with the Frankfurt School's Critical Theory. If he remains lodged within bourgeois aesthetics, he has learned to use the notion of literature's purposiveness without a purpose to very different ends from Kant's development of disinterested taste. For Frye "the aesthetic or contemplative aspect of art" is not "the final resting place for either art or criticism." Instead, literature and criticism are "an ethical instrument, participating in the work of civilization" (349). As Fredric Jameson has persuasively demonstrated, in order to turn literature and criticism into an ethical instrument, Frye had to banish history. By restoring literature to its historical context, Jameson is able to transform Frye's ethical criticism into a political criticism.[32]

Jameson's strategy of arriving at a political criticism by reading through Frye seems a better one than Eagleton's polemical dismissal of him, for Jameson's notion of the political unconscious offers a way to historicize literature without lapsing into a reflection model. Nonetheless, Jameson's important and necessary corrective of Frye continues to adhere to a model in which works are read as historical allegories, the historical replacing the anagogical as the final level of meaning in his hermeneutical system. I have already explained why I find reading literature as historical allegory not quite enough. One of the problems with it is its almost exclusive focus on a text's moment of production. Any new historicism in which the adjective "new" signals more than the latest academic fad also needs to concentrate on a work's moment of reception; or more precisely put, on the relation between its moment of production and reception as a way of altering our perspective on the present. Such a relationship is Walter Benjamin's concern in a short essay entitled "Literaturgeschichte und Literaturwissenschaft."[33]

Only recently published in English translation, Benjamin's essay has not been part of the Benjamin boom in this country. Nonetheless, new historicists can find in it a perspective on their own concerns. Published in 1931, it appeared at almost exactly the moment that New Critics were debating literary historians. Like the New Critics, Benjamin attacked the contemporary practice of literary history. Rather than argue that criticism should replace historical analysis, however, he advocated a different brand of literary history, one that would turn the analysis of literature into a mode of cultural critique.

Benjamin starts by recognizing the tendency to analyze the history of individual disciplines. Noting how that desire can lead to histories which chart a separate, independent course beyond the total political and spiritual realm, he affirms the necessity not only to relate a cross section of the prevailing state of the discipline to its autonomous historical development, but also to the state of culture as a whole. He then offers a very brief summary of the history of literary historiography in Germany, remarking that despite its name the latter did not emerge from the realm of history but as a branch of aesthetic education, a kind of applied science of good taste. As a result, even the best works could not problematize "the true relationship between literature and history, to say nothing of that between history and literary history" ("Literaturgeschichte" 284). Indeed, during the nineteenth century the historical orientation was abandoned for a positivistic dependence on exact natural science. Such positivistic histories were characterized by "the false universalism of the cultural historical method" (285), which turned its research to the service of a cult celebrating literature's eternal values. For use in the bourgeois household, these histories inhabited what Benjamin calls the swamp, which is the home of "the hydra with its seven heads: creation, empathy, disengagement from time, imitation, simultaneous experience, illusion, and enjoyment of art" (286). Such literary histories have little to do with literary science because their function "exhausts itself in the task of giving to certain classes the illusion of participating in the cultural assets of the belles lettres" (288). For literary science to come into its own it must cast away its tendency to confine literature to a museum of great works.

Benjamin's program should sound familiar to today's new historicists. He calls for the analysis, not only of works by literati and poets, but also of anonymous writings—of calendar and colportage literature, for instance. He also calls for a sociology of the reading public, of writers' guilds, and of bookselling at various times. Chastising the materialist historian Franz Mehring for holding to the conviction that works of literature are "the most precious goods of the nation" (287), Benjamin advocates an insurgent rather than a conserving literary history. His attitude toward these goods is clearly stated in his more famous "Theses on the Philosophy of History":

> They are called cultural treasures, and a historical materialist views them with cautious detachment. For without exception the cultural treasures he surveys have an origin which he cannot contemplate without horror. They owe their existence not only to the efforts of the great minds and talents who have created them, but also to the anonymous toil of their contemporaries.

There is no document of civilization which is not at the same time a document of barbarism.[34]

Nonetheless, Benjamin does not demand that the category of the literary be abandoned. Just as we should not forget that these documents are tainted by barbarism, so we should not forget that they are the product of great minds and talents. Thus "in every era the attempt must be made anew to wrest tradition away from a conformism that is about to overpower it" (255). In terms of literature, this involves waging war with those critics who control the writing of its history. He compares these critics to "a company of mercenaries," who "marched with heavy steps into the beautiful, solid house of poetry, pretending to admire the treasures and splendours," but who "don't quite give a damn about the order and inventory of the house. They moved in because the house is so well situated, and from here a bridgehead or a railway line whose defense is important in a civil war can be fired upon" ("Literaturgeschichte" 287).

Those opposing these mercenaries would be foolish to blow up a house so strategically situated. Instead, they need to occupy it and, by paying careful attention to its order and inventory, to use it critically. Indeed, in his emphasis on how close attention to literary works can release a critical potential, Benjamin shares important affinities with the New Critics. For instance, he partially agrees with Walter Muschg that the current generation, having lost faith in the meaningfulness of wholistic representation, "wrestles with figures and problems which it views as mainly marked by gaps in [the] epoch of universal histories," but hastens to add: "It wrestles with figures and problems—this may be right. The truth is that it should above all wrestle with works" (290).

He is, however, completely at odds with the New Critics on the importance of a work's historicity. It is a work's historicity and a historical analysis of it that makes literature a critical tool. For Benjamin, "the art work's being in time and its being understood are only two sides of one and the same condition" (289). Whereas the New Critics battled against philological scholars whose work had become hopelessly positivistic, Benjamin (as Paul de Man has more recently)[35] called for a renewal of philology. It was philologists, like the Grimm brothers, who succeeded, as no generation since them has, in interweaving historical and critical observation. Antiphilological advocates of modernism level the tension between criticism and literary history because, in trying to serve the present, they patronize contemporary writings. In contrast, the Grimm brothers served their epoch by exploring works in the past adequate to the present. The extent to which Benjamin's essay is such a work for us is made clear in its concluding sentences. "It is not," he announces, "a question of presenting written works in the context of their time, but of bringing forth the time which recognizes them—that is our time—within the time that produced them. With that, literature becomes an organon of history (*Geschichte*), and to make it so, not the material for writing history (*Historie*), is the task of literary history" (290).

This passage invites commentary. The English speaker needs, for instance, to be alerted to the distinction Benjamin makes between *Geschichte* and *Historie*, a distinction which lets us read his "Theses on the Philosophy of History" as a response to Nietzsche's *The Use and Abuse of History*. The English translations make it sound as if the two are writing about precisely the same concept, but Nietzsche's title is *Vom Nutzen und Nachteil der Historie für das Leben* whereas Benjamin's is "Über den Begriff der Geschichte." *Historie* is passive and abstract, and for Nietzsche it is clearly associated with an academic exercise. In contrast, *Geschichte* evokes not only the German for story but also *geschehen*, the German for "to happen." Benjamin is at pains to keep the activity of *Geschichte* from lapsing into the passivity of *Historie*. To do this he writes against the grain of histories which create the impression that events from the past had an inevitable occurrence. Human beings, Benjamin reminds us, make history, if not under conditions of their own choosing. That goes for literary history as well. Literature does not become an organon of history by revealing a previously existing past, but because it thrusts readers into a position in which they are forced to recognize their responsibility for its making. Not an organon in and of itself, literature becomes one only when readers accept their tasks as historical subjects.

To emphasize that task is to highlight a text's moment of reception. But the moment of reception should not be emphasized at the expense of the moment of production. This is important to stress because Benjamin's passage can easily be misunderstood, as it is when Eagleton mistranslates the first sentence as, "It is not a question of representing works of literature in the context of their time, *but of bringing them to representation in the time in which they emerged*, which knows them—that is our time"[36] (my emphasis). Eagleton's mistranslation recalls the emphasis in the 1960s on making works from the past "relevant" to the present. The problem with the cry for relevancy is that it denies a work one of the most important ways in which it could be relevant to the present. Rather than using the text to place the past in a critical relation to the present, the cry for relevancy leads to a more secure confinement in the present by leveling the tension between past and present, between criticism and history. For Benjamin a work from the past can offer us a critical perspective precisely because it blasts the present out of what in the "Theses" he calls homogeneous, empty time. To historicize a text is to create a "constellation" between its moment of production and its moment of reception.

Of course, the question still arises: What is it about literary texts that lend them to creating such a perspective on the present? To answer that question we need to examine in much more detail the temporal mode of works of literature, something that I will do in more depth in the next chapter. For now I can suggest one possibility by looking at the traditional distinction made between historical and literary discourse. Once again Frye is helpful in formulating that distinction. Evoking Aristotle, Frye argues that the historian is concerned with "what happened," the poet with "what happens."[37] This difference is reflected in the convention by which we use the present tense when writing about actions in a work of literature: "Hamlet contemplates suicide," not "Hamlet contemplated suicide." In a literary text, events have not happened but are in a perpetual state of happening. To use Wolfgang Iser's phrase—which draws on the German *Darstellung*, meaning both representation and a performance—literary representation is not a mimetic but a performative act. It does not imitate something that already exists or existed but can stimulate the production of new ways of organizing the world.[38] The way in which it allows something new perpetually to happen is related to its reflexive aspect which, in calling attention to its rhetorical element, denies a perfect union between grammar and logic, thereby opening the language of the text to its moment of reception, that is, the constructive activity of the reader. When Benjamin argues that "the art work's being in time and its being understood are only two sides of one and the same condition," he does not mean, as traditional historical critics might, that the work's being in time is confined to the moment of its production. Instead, its being in time is a mode of temporality that has the potential to bring us perpetually into a new relation with the past that produced it, which in turn can give us a new perspective on our present.

To be sure, what I have called the performative element of a work of literature is not the exclusive property of works that are defined as literature at this moment. As I acknowledged earlier, this element inhabits all discourse, making it possible for all forms of writing to be read as if they were literature. But to concede this point is to return us to the point I already made: this aspect which we call literary adds an important component to our understanding of the histories we construct, an aspect that no movement calling itself a *new* history can afford to neglect. For in reminding us of the constructive aspect of the historian in creating his *Geschichte*, the literary suggests a space in which humankind constructs its *Geschichte*. Literary history becomes an organon for history when it creates the sense which Benjamin argued that Bertold Brecht created when he set a play in the past. Even though the outcome of the event is known beforehand, the effect of watching a Brecht play, according to Benjamin, is to realize that history happened one way but could have happened another. If to hold out for the potential of the literary (as a field of social practice) and literary works (as social texts) to create such a sense of history is to privilege either, I must admit that I am privileged to do so. In the next chapter I will elaborate upon both the limitations and possibilities raised by this particular way of privileging the literary as part of a response to Greenblatt's attempt to confine literature to a mimetic economy.

CHAPTER 7

Stephen Greenblatt and the Limits of Mimesis for Historical Criticism

The term "energy" doesn't even pretend to stand
for anything "objective." It is only a way of measuring the surface of phenomena so as to string their
changes on a simple formula.[1]
—(William James)

· I ·

STEPHEN GREENBLATT's status as both a spokesman for and representative figure of the new historicism is well-earned. In addition to making
strategic statements defining the differences between an older historicism
and his cultural poetics, he has produced much of the most interesting
analysis. Furthermore, he has continually revised his ideas in light of criticism and new evidence. For instance, in his latest book, *Shakespearean
Negotiations: The Circulation of Social Energy in Renaissance England*,
he explicitly responds to complaints that his work totalizes. When the
book's first essay appeared in *Glyph* in 1981 it indeed presented a totalized view of Renaissance society. Revised for the book, "Invisible Bullets"
now suggests more openness and contingency. Greenblatt's effort to avoid
totalization is registered in the very form of the book. Greenblatt organized *Renaissance Self-Fashioning* by triads, implying a dialectical structure that brought previously published essays together into a unified
whole. In his new book he offers "instead four chapters that may be read
as separate essays. I had thought at first to weave them together, for their
local concerns intersect and their general project is the same, but the
whole point is that they do not sketch a unified field."[2]

Such a strategy certainly forces those, myself included, who have accused Greenblatt of totalizing, to rethink their criticism. But he counters
charges of totalization only to raise the specter of Cohen's charge of "arbitrary connectedness."[3] Indeed, to assemble essays that do not sketch a
unified field is to raise the question that Michaels's collection of essays
forced us to ask: what, then, holds the various essays together? Presum-

ably, they share, as Greenblatt puts it, the "general project," of a cultural poetics that claims to link a "given representational mode" to the "complex network of institutions, practices, and beliefs that constitute the culture as a whole."[4] What provides that link for Michaels is the circulation of capital in turn-of-the-century America. For Greenblatt it is the "circulation of social energy" in Renaissance England. But what is social energy?

Greenblatt turns to the notion of social energy because he wants to know "how cultural objects, expressions, and practices—here, principally, plays by Shakespeare and the stage on which they first appeared—acquired compelling force" (5). This force is the ability of language to cause what George Puttenham described as "a stir to the mind." To designate that force "English literary theorists in the period" (5) drew on the Greek rhetorical tradition and called it *energia*. "This is," Greenblatt continues, "the origin in our language of the term 'energy,' a term I propose we use, provided we understand that its origins lie in rhetoric rather than physics and that its significance is social and historical" (6).

One reason that Greenblatt turns to the notion of social energy is that it helps to combat criticism leveled against him because of his earlier use of the Foucauldian notion of power. Like Michaels's capital, Foucault's power is everywhere. Not a centralized force located in the state, it is dispersed throughout a culture, inhabiting all social relations. Social energy helps Greenblatt to avoid such totalizing implications. "The circulation of social energy by and through the stage," he assures us, "was not part of a single coherent, totalizing system. Rather it was partial, fragmentary, conflictual; elements were crossed, torn apart, recombined, set against each other; particular social practices were magnified by the stage, others diminished, exalted, evacuated. What then is the social energy that is being circulated? Power, charisma, sexual excitement, collective dreams, wonder, desire, anxiety, religious awe, free-floating intensities of experience: in a sense the question is absurd, for everything produced by the society can circulate unless it is deliberately excluded from circulation" (19). Power is no longer an overarching category, but one of many bits of social energy in circulation.

Nonetheless, Greenblatt's use of social energy still raises problems. If, on the one hand, social energy is potentially everything produced by a society, on the other, it defies description, for earlier when he asks the question, "What is social energy?" Greenblatt is forced to admit, "The term implies something measurable, yet I cannot provide a convenient and reliable formula for isolating a single, stable quantum for examination. We identify *energia* only indirectly by its effects: it is manifested in the capacity of certain verbal, aural, and visual traces to produce, shape, and organize collective physical and mental experiences" (6). Social energy, then, is both something produced by society, like collective dreams, and something manifested in the ability of traces to produce collective experience. It helps to produce the very society that produces it.

Circulating within what Greenblatt aptly calls this mimetic economy, aesthetic forms of social energy seem to be somewhat unique. They are "usually characterized by a minimal adaptability—enough to enable them to survive at least some of the constant changes in social circumstances and cultural value that make ordinary utterances evanescent" (7). Greenblatt's goal is to "understand the negotiations through which works of art obtain and amplify such powerful energy" (7).

Since *energia* describes "the ability of language . . . to cause 'a stir to the mind'" (5, 6), the simplest explanation would seem to be that works of literature obtain and amplify it through a certain deployment of language. Greenblatt, however, is not content with that explanation, which would leave him within the boundaries of formalism. Thus later he speaks of the "network of practices that governs the circulation of social energy" (18), a network that presumably constitutes the culture as a whole. Aesthetic forms may have an adaptability not usually found in other forms of social energy, but they are still governed by this network of practices. At the same time, it is precisely social energy, including its aesthetic versions, that produces, shapes, and organizes the very network that governs its circulation. After all, our very ability to conceive of social practices interrelating as a "network" would seem to depend upon some such productive and organizational force. Given the adaptability of the aesthetic forms of social energy and their capacity to recirculate in various cultural situations, Greenblatt at times grants them an extremely important role in the production, or shall we say *poiesis* or making, of a culture. Indeed, the aesthetic has the potential to provide Greenblatt with precisely what was missing in Foucault: an engine of change. Or perhaps better, it can provide the energy for such an engine. And so, with his notion of a mimetic economy, Greenblatt caps his efforts to develop what he calls a "less passive conception of mimesis" (*Representing* viii). Ironically, however, when he grants aesthetic energy such productive power, Greenblatt marks the limits of mimesis for historical criticism.

In this chapter I want to identify those limits by examining how the role Greenblatt grants to literary texts affects and is affected by contradictions between Greenblatt's stated desire to avoid sketching a unified or totalized field and the general project that he sets for himself. As we have seen, he prefers to call that project a cultural poetics rather than a new historicism. Given the problems with the label "new historicism," Greenblatt might seem to make a wise choice. But if problems in the label the "new historicism" also suggest an unrealized promise, "cultural poetics" presents problems despite its promise. One comes from the word "culture."

On the one hand, "culture" can be opposed to "society" to designate a particular set of practices and institutions, those that are usually associated with the humanities. Thus the phrase "cultural politics" can refer to politics generated by such activities. On the other hand, culture can become a virtual synonym for society, such as when new historicists refer to the makeup of "culture-at-large." When Greenblatt speaks of a "cultural poetics," it is not always clear how he is using the adjective. Sometimes he seems to be designating cultural practices in a narrow sense, sometimes in a general sense. The slippage serves him well when he describes the role that art has in society-at-large.

The role Greenblatt grants to art brings us to the second word in his label. I will try to show that it is precisely Greenblatt's desire to produce a *poetics* of culture that conflicts with his attempt to avoid totalization. In calling his project a poetics Greenblatt indicates his debt to Aristotle. My thesis is that the Aristotelian aspects of his cultural poetics put him at odds with the sense of historical contingency that he espouses. Indeed, the project of Aristotle's *Poetics* is closer to that of a natural scientist or biologist than a historian, for in it Aristotle tries to analyze and describe a social practice as if it were a biological species. The most important concept in *The Poetics* is that of mimesis. I will argue that Greenblatt's attempt to relate aesthetic practices to other social practices within a mimetic economy risks confining us to a bounded sense of reality that closes off possibilities within history. But before turning to my argument, I need to look at a concrete example of Greenblatt's work. Containing some of Greenblatt's most dazzling moves, the last essay of *Shakespearean Negotiations* is a good place to start.

· II ·

His most ambitious attempt to demonstrate the theater's participation in the circulation of social energy, "Martial Law in the Land of Cockaigne," interweaves readings of a sermon delivered by the Protestant divine Hugh Latimer, a historical account of a shipwrecked voyage on the way to Virginia, and *The Tempest*. In his typically sensitive readings of social events, Greenblatt argues that Latimer's sermon is staged to produce "salutary anxiety." Speculating that astute management of insecurity was a way of making spectators of such staged events more obedient subjects, Greenblatt examines *The Tempest* and proposes that the techniques of arousing and manipulating anxiety are "crucial elements of the representational technology of the Elizabethan and Jacobean theatre" (133).

It is, however, not enough for Greenblatt to establish the theatrical representation of a social practice. He adds:

But the strategy of salutary anxiety is not simply reflected in a secondhand way by the work of art, because the practice itself is already implicated in the artistic traditions and institutions out of which this particular representation, *The Tempest*, has emerged. Latimer may have been indifferent or hostile to the drama and to literature in general, but his tale of the Cambridge prisoner seems shaped by literary conventions, earlier tales of wronged innocence and royal pardons. And if the practice he exemplifies helps to empower theatrical representations, fictive representations have themselves helped to empower his practice (147).

In a footnote Greenblatt explains the intent of this passage. "I am trying to resist here the proposition that Latimer's story is the actual practice that is then represented in works of art, and hence that in it we encounter the basis in reality of theatrical fictions" (195). Greenblatt needs to resist this proposition for two related reasons. First, he needs to assert that social practices are themselves mediated, "always embedded," as he puts it elsewhere, "in systems of public significance" (RSF 5). Second, he needs to avoid the notion that the theater does no more than reflect or record a social reality with a prior existence. The most common metaphor for art as a reflection of reality is the mirror. In his introduction, however, Greenblatt offers a suggestive reading of Hamlet's famous comment that the purpose of acting is to hold a mirror up to nature. Noting that "both optics and mirror lore in the period suggested that something was actively passing back and forth in the production of mirror images" (8), Greenblatt urges us to remember that Hamlet's metaphor involves the pressure of the age and body of its time, not just the form. "Accurate representation," Greenblatt argues, "depended upon material emanation and exchange" (8).

Art, however, is not only interested in *accurate* representation. Another reason why Greenblatt needs to resist the notion that art passively imitates reality is that he wants to stress how it can disfigure what it represents. This aspect of artistic representation is crucial to Greenblatt's sense of the Renaissance's mimetic economy because without it the circulation of social energy that he describes might well appear to be a circular one in which everything turned back on itself in resemblance. Such a closed economy, however, is more appropriate to the medieval era. The economy Greenblatt describes is generated as much by difference as by resemblance, and that generation of difference opens it to endless, but not circular, circulation. Greenblatt indicates this production of difference by following the passage just quoted with an example of that favorite new historicist figure—chiasmus.

"This complex circulation between the social dimension of an aesthetic strategy and the aesthetic dimension of a social strategy," he tells us, "is difficult to grasp because the strategy in question has an extraordinarily long and tangled history, one whose aesthetic roots go back at least as far as Aristotle's *Poetics*" (147). Chiasmus is the perfect figure to express Greenblatt's notion of a mimetic economy, since its balanced structure mimes the very circulation that he writes about. The notion of both artistic autonomy and a preexisting historical reality are destabilized.

With this particular chiasmatic formulation, then, Greenblatt extends his efforts to go beyond a reflection model of art that had in turn limited various other attempts to connect literature and history. Those efforts began in *Renaissance Self-Fashioning* with the metaphor of art as a register rather than as a reflection. They continued with his introduction to a collection of essays on the Renaissance originally published in *Representations*. In that introduction he states that unifying these seemingly diverse essays is the assumption that "the work of art is not the passive surface on which this historical experience leaves its stamp but one of the creative agents in the fashioning and refashioning of experience" (*Representing* viii). This image of the reciprocal causality between art and historical experience leads directly to the mimetic economy of *Shakespearean Negotiations* in which the theater is part of the circulation of social energy.

Most of Greenblatt's energy is devoted to detailing the synchronic aspects of this circulation. But it also has a diachronic element. If the synchronic promises "insight into the half-hidden cultural transactions through which great works of art are empowered" (4), the diachronic explains how "the literary traces of the dead" have the capacity to "convey lost life" (3) to the present. As is to be expected, the synchronic and diachronic elements are related. Shakespearean plays have the power to speak to us, not because they contain an "untranslatable essence" (3), but because the "social energy initially encoded in those works" (6) enables a continual transformation and refashioning of them as they are recirculated in the flow of social energy at various moments of reproduction. The relation between past and present is itself one of negotiation and exchange that is necessitated and enabled by the synchronic production of difference.

As we saw, Greenblatt denies that theatrical representation of social practices was one of identity. "Rather it was partial, fragmentary, conflictual; elements were crossed, torn apart, recombined, set against each other; particular social practices were magnified by the stage, others diminished, exalted, evacuated" (19). The difference generated by theatrical representation implies that although the circulation of social energy is bounded, it is not closed. It generates a spiral rather than a circle. This production of difference makes possible social change. Represented in the theater, social practices are transformed and refashioned and then recirculated into the nontheatrical world as the aesthetic dimension of a social strategy, a recirculation that involves another transformation and refashioning, and so on. Social practices and theatrical representation are continually altered as they chiasmatically relate to one another. The difference inherent in the act of representation can thus act as an engine of social change. The spiral it generates allows works from the past to "convey lost life," if in a disfigured state.

Greenblatt's essay on *The Tempest* provides a concrete example of the mimetic economy at work diachronically. By linking the play to the production of salutary anxiety, Greenblatt's synchronic analysis adds an interesting twist to the commonplace new historical connection between it and imperialism. But he does not stop there. Concerned with how Shakespeare's plays acquired compelling force, he needs to explain why they still speak to us today. Trying to do so with *The Tempest*, he faces a dilemma. After all, when Greenblatt was a graduate student its compelling force was not linked to imperialism but to its celebration of the imaginative powers of art as embodied in the figure of Prospero. Faced with the historical fact that *The Tempest* has been read and performed as a supreme example of the autonomy of art, Greenblatt makes one of his shrewdest moves.

The Tempest encodes, not one, but two versions of a mimetic economy. One is Greenblatt's bounded one, taking place in a world of scarcity where aesthetic exchanges, while not identical with other kinds of exchanges, are not different in kind. The other describes the privileged view of art against which some new historicists have reacted. In this mimetic economy aesthetic exchanges somehow escape the laws of scarcity and produce a world of "pure plentitude" in which "things can be imitated, staged, reproduced without any loss or expense; indeed, what is borrowed seems enhanced by the borrowing, for nothing is used up, nothing fades" (159). The first produces a reading in which the play takes place in a "capacious, central public sphere, the realm of proper political order made possible through mind control, coercion, discipline, anxiety, and pardon"; the second, a reading in which it takes place in a "well-demarcated, marginal, private sphere, the realm of insight, pleasure, and isolation" (159). "It is this doubleness," Greenblatt asserts, "that Shakespeare's joint-stock company bequeathed to its cultural heirs. And the principal beneficiary in the end was not the theater but a different institution, the institution of literature" (160). Literature benefits because the second version of the mimetic economy allows Shakespeare's plays to have a new circulation within an economy in which the aesthetic, increasingly confined to a private realm of the imaginary, is bound in the book.

As a result, Greenblatt's final essay seems to fulfill the promise of his introduction. He shows how at the moment of production *The Tempest* was encoded with a doubleness that, on the one hand, involves circulation of social energy within Renaissance England, and, on the other, makes possible the play's recirculation within a culture with a different practice of the aesthetic, a culture in which Shakespeare became canonized as its greatest literary achievement. But, we might ask, is this second economy mimetic? It would seem closer to what Meyer Abrams taught generations of students to call an expressive theory of art rather than a mimetic one. To answer that question we need to go to an essay that directly or indirectly influenced Greenblatt's notion of a mimetic economy: Jacques Derrida's "Economimesis."

"Economimesis" examines Kant's theory of artistic autonomy, a theory often thought to break with mimesis. Derrida, however, links Kantian aesthetics to mimesis, not because the artist imitates things in nature, but because he imitates the act of God in creating nature. Mimesis for Kant is not "the reproduction of a product of nature by a product of art, . . . not the relation of two products but of two productions." In other words, Kantian mimesis does not imitate an already existing reality but brings something new into existence. By bringing something new into existence, the artist disrupts a bounded economy like that of the medieval era. As Derrida puts it, the Kantian artist in miming a divine action, asserts his freedom because he "submits to no exchange contract, his overabundance generously breaks the circular economy."[5]

Derrida's description of the Kantian artist matches the way in which various critics have read Prospero as a portrait of the artist Shakespeare in magical control over his imaginary creation. Indeed, whereas there is a long tradition of comparing God to an artist, the idea of the artist as God emerges with force in the Renaissance, only to receive its fullest articulation in the expressive theories of Romanticism. For instance, noting how the Greeks called the poet a maker, Puttenham goes on:

> Such as (by way of resemblance and reverently) we may say of God: who without any trauell to his divine imagination made all the world of nought, nor also by any patterne or mould, as the Platonicks with their Idees do phantastically suppose. Even so the very Poet makes and contriues out of his owene braine both the verse and matter of his poeme, and not by any foreine copie or example, as doth the translator, who therefore may well be sayd a versifier, but not a Poet.[6]

For Sidney imaginative works of poetry serve the divine function of lifting up the "mind from the dungeon of the body to the enjoying of his own essence."[7] The artistic world of the imagination frees us from bodily and worldly concerns.

For both Derrida and Greenblatt this sense of imaginative freedom has political consequences. In "Economimesis" Derrida demonstrates how the very positing of a separate world of the imaginative artist/god helps to legitimate the contractual political economy of capitalism from which he supposedly escapes. Greenblatt focusses on implications for the institution of literature. Having accounted for Shakespeare's power to recirculate through the new aesthetic economy of the book, Greenblatt wants to demonstrate the relationship of that economy to the economy at large. Unlike Shakespeare's Globe Theater, Greenblatt tells us, "the book is supremely portable. It may be readily detached from its immediate geographic and cultural origins, its original producers and consumers, and endlessly reproduced, circulated, exchanged, exported to other times and places" (160). Acknowledged as the "central literary achievement of English culture," Shakespeare's collected works, "served—and continue to serve—as a fetish of Western civilization, a fetish Caliban curiously anticipates" (161) when he urges the burning of Prospero's books.

In order to exemplify the "continued doubleness of Shakespeare in our culture: at once the embodiment of civilized recreation, freed from the anxiety of rule, and the instrument of empire" (161), Greenblatt ends his book with an anecdote about the power of books. The story, passed on to Greenblatt by Walter Benn Michaels, who discovered it while exploring the footnotes of William James, is told by the journalist H. M. Stanley.

Exploring central Africa, Stanley was confronted by natives who saw him writing in his notebook, which "contained a vast number of valuable notes; plans of falls, creeks, villages, sketches of localities, ethnological and philological details" (162). The natives fear that Stanley's writing will bring disaster to their land, and they insist that he burn the book. Not wanting to sacrifice his notes, which had so much of "general interest to the public" (162), Stanley rummages through his book box and comes upon a volume of Shakespeare, which was of the same size and had a cover similar to his notebook. Tricking the natives, he substitutes the Shakespeare, burning it, and saving the notebook that, as Greenblatt puts it, "proved invaluable in charting and organizing the Belgian Congo, perhaps the most vicious of all of Europe's African colonies" (162).

It is not clear whether Stanley's story is true or not. As Greenblatt notes, he could have made up the story. Its truth, however, is of little concern to him. "What matters is the role Shakespeare plays in it" (163). According to Greenblatt, the force of Stanley's narrative could have been achieved with only two books: Shakespeare and the Bible. "And had he professed to burn the latter to save his notebook, his readers would no doubt have been scandalized" (163). What Stanley's narrative becomes, then, is an allegory revealing Shakespeare's double role in our culture,

a role at once central and expendable—and, in some obscure way, not just expendable but exchangeable for what really matters: the writing that more directly serves power. For if at moments we can convince ourselves that Shakespeare *is* the discourse of power, we should remind ourselves that there are usually other discourses—here the notes and vocabulary and maps—that are instrumentally far more important. Yet if we try then to convince ourselves that Shakespeare is marginal and untainted by power, we have Stanley's story to remind us that without Shakespeare we wouldn't have the notes. Of course, this is just an accident—the accident of the books' resemblance—but then why was Stanley carrying the book in the first place (163)?

Greenblatt's reading of Stanley's story situates him in the current debate over the political status of canonized literature, here represented by Shakespeare. On the one hand, there is the extreme Foucauldian position, arguing that canonized literature is an instrument of power, power here used in the purely negative sense of domination. According to this argument the only way to remain "untainted by power" is to inhabit the margins. Thus hope for opposition lies with marginalized literature and discourse. On the other hand, there is the ideological critique of aesthetic culture itself, arguing that precisely because the realm of the aesthetic is marginalized it can do no work in the world. Neither of these accounts taken alone is satisfactory for Greenblatt, who refuses to accept simplistic either/or solutions.

One way to dispute the simplicity of such polar opposites would be to argue that neither one solution nor the other will do and to seek alternative, more complicated, solutions. Greenblatt, however, offers a different reading. Arguing against the notion that Shakespeare's plays are simply emblems of recreation, Greenblatt insists that we also see them as agents in the work of empire. Rather than dispute the simplicity of an either/or argument by rejecting both polar extremes, Greenblatt complicates it by concluding that Shakespeare's plays are both/and. They are *simultaneously* emblems of "recreation" *and* agents doing ideological work. If Shakespeare is not one, Greenblatt implies, he is the other. And since neither alone will do, he must be both.

In Greenblatt's hands Shakespeare's doubleness does not, however, lead to a New Critical balancing of paradoxical tensions. This is because the act of exchange in Stanley's story is not an even one. For Greenblatt, Stanley's story demonstrates that, although confined to a marginalized realm, the seemingly harmless emblem of recreation is capable of doing work in the service of the empire, if not directly, then through an act of exchange. The emblem of recreation can be absorbed by Greenblatt's model of circulation, but not vice versa. Shakespeare's doubleness itself gets recirculated within a mimetic economy in the service of empire, even if one more expansive than that described by those arguing for Shakespeare as simply the discourse of power.

Greenblatt's use of Stanley's story is fascinating, but it also points to problems with his account of how social energy, especially aesthetic manifestations of it, circulate within a mimetic economy. To be sure, in constructing a Shakespeare who is simultaneously marginalized and a discourse of power, he complicates the arguments of those who would argue for one or the other. Nonetheless, he continues to accept the oppositions that too often structure current debates about Shakespeare (indeed all canonical literature). That acceptance is, I will argue, related to his use of chiasmus, a figure allowing for an infinite amount of play, but play bounded by opposing two entities. Furthermore, the boundaries shaped by his particular chiasmatic formulation help to explain why his retention of a mimetic model is limited. But, first, another look at Greenblatt's use of Stanley's story: In analyzing the work of someone trying to connect literature and history, I find it appropriate to begin with Greenblatt's claim that it does not matter much whether Stanley's story is true or not.

· III ·

According to Greenblatt, whether Stanley's story is true or not, it reveals two things: (1) There are discourses other than Shakespeare—here the notebook—more important in the work of empire; (2) Shakespeare is, nonetheless, not completely marginal, because "without Shakespeare we wouldn't have the notes" (163). The first seems indisputable, but is the second? If Stanley's story is *not* true, Shakespeare was not, after all, sacrificed to save the notes. Indeed, even if the story is true, as Greenblatt admits, Shakespeare plays a role only because of an accident of external resemblance. He then counters by asking why Stanley was carrying Shakespeare in the first place. But if Stanley made up the story, we cannot be sure that he was. Furthermore, even if he was, Shakespeare was only one of a number of books that he was carrying. Would not these books be as complicit in the work of empire as Shakespeare? Their existence really does make Shakespeare's burning seem an accident of resemblance.

I stress the importance of whether Stanley's story is true or not in order to focus on precisely what Greenblatt means when he asserts that "*it* doesn't matter very much if the story 'really' happened" [my emphasis] (163). What is "it," then, that does matter? What matters for Greenblatt is the iconic value of Shakespeare. Indeed, that value is illustrated more forcefully if Stanley did fabricate his story, since it would indicate Stanley's awareness of how the idea of burning Shakespeare's works would affect his audience. In demystifying that iconic value, Greenblatt does important work, but he does not quite answer the problem he set out to answer. He began by trying to understand "the negotiations through which works of art obtain and amplify . . . powerful energy" (7). Stanley's story is proof that at a fairly recent moment of history they still manifested such power for a particular culture, but it gives us little insight as to why, other than to remind us, as if we needed reminding, that Shakespeare has become a cultural icon. Greenblatt links that iconic status to the development of a book culture. But why books of Shakespeare, not another author? To answer that question Greenblatt would need to do what switching to Stanley's story allows him not to do—stay focused on the reading of particular texts themselves. Ending by turning his attention to Shakespeare's iconic value, Greenblatt makes a mistake similar to the Africans' Stanley constructs in his story. Just as they presumably mistake a copy of Shakespeare for the notebook, so Greenblatt ends by mistaking the icon for the works themselves. To be sure, the boundaries between icon and works is not clear-cut. Nonetheless, boundaries do exist, unless, as someone like Stanley Fish seems to do, we eliminate them altogether. What too easily gets lost in the effacement of that boundary is the obligation to read the Shakespearean texts themselves.

For instance, Shakespeare's iconic value may make him a name to be included in E. D. Hirsch's vocabulary list for "cultural literacy." But just as Hirsch assures us that we can know Shakespeare's role in our culture without ever having read his works, so Greenblatt ends his book, not with a reading of Shakespeare, but a reading of an incident demonstrating what it means to read Shakespeare in our culture—or at least in turn-of-the-century culture. To move from readings or performances of Shakespeare's plays to Shakespeare as icon is to risk ignoring the most obvious lesson of Stanley's story. For the natives (at least according to Stanley) exchangeability is determined by physical resemblance. Members of a book culture, however, know better. It is not only the case, as Greenblatt emphasizes, that Stanley could replace a burnt edition with an identical copy. Once he returned to London or New York, he could restore his genial companion with a copy that had little outward resemblance to his original. We cannot, his story reminds us, tell a book by its cover.

Some of the problems with Greenblatt's shift from text to icon are illustrated by the conclusions that he draws from Stanley's comment that "during many weary hours of night," his "genial companion" had helped to relieve his "mind when oppressed by almost intolerable woes" (162). For Stanley, Greenblatt argues, Shakespeare's works do not produce salutary anxiety but relieve anxiety. Do they, however, necessarily relieve him from the "anxieties of rule" (198, n. 43)? Could not Stanley be speaking of anxieties other than those of rule? Furthermore, we know nothing of Stanley's specific response to *The Tempest*, which is the play that Greenblatt singles out to examine the circulation of salutary anxiety, using others to explore the circulation of different energies, such as charisma, sexual excitement, and religious power. Maybe Stanley, seeking relief from anxiety, completely avoided *The Tempest.* We cannot be sure. Finally, can Stanley's response speak for the way Shakespeare is read *today* with the reign of book culture coming to an end? As Gerald Graff wittily reminded us by entitling an essay, "Fear and Trembling at Yale,"[8] reading in certain circles today is more prone to create anxiety than relieve it.

For example, by recirculating various plays within a mimetic economy Greenblatt breathes new life into them and gives them the power once again to produce anxiety. Those experiencing the anxiety are not, however, rulers of colonial empires, but those rulers of the institution of literature, who would turn Shakespeare into a false cultural idol. For those intent on celebrating Shakespeare, Greenblatt's message is quite bleak. Restored to a mimetic economy this onetime pretender to virtue is in a no-win situation.

To circulate the plays in a mimetic economy of plentitude is to confine them to the realm of recreation. Shakespeare becomes no more than a genial companion. To circulate them in a mimetic economy of scarcity is to lodge them within the discourse of power. Shakespeare becomes an agent of empire. We can even have an exchange from one economy to the other in which he becomes an *indirect* agent in the work of empire. In all three cases, unless one favors existing power structures, Shakespeare loses. To rescue him from the marginalized realm of aesthetic recreation is to turn him into a tool of power. To deny his role in the discourse of power is to consign him to a marginalized role of pure recreation.

We do not have to defend Shakespeare as a cultural icon to note that Greenblatt's bleak scenario is related to the boundaries imposed by his chiasmatic, mimetic economy. Those boundaries are demarcated in the way he describes the theater's role in the circulation of social energy. The doubleness generated by that description corresponds to the doubleness he discovers in Shakespeare.

· IV ·

At times Greenblatt implies a very circumscribed role for the theater in the overall circulation of social energy. In this weak version the only important exchange takes place *within* the theater itself, between the play and its audience. "Through its representational means," he argues, "each play carries charges of social energy onto the stage; the stage in its turn revises that energy and returns it to the audience" (14). Nonetheless, intrigued by the fact that members of the audience return to the nontheatrical world, Greenblatt is tempted to adopt a strong version of his argument, in which exchange occurs not only between play and audience, but also between the theatrical and nontheatrical world. In this strong version, the theater's effect on the audience produces important "cultural work."

Both weak and strong versions counter the specter of passive mimesis that so haunts Greenblatt's work. In one case, the stage, in the other, the theater itself revise the energy circulated through it. But the two establish very different relations between the theater and culture-at-large. The weak version corresponds to Greenblatt's reading of Shakespeare as pure recreation. The circulation of aesthetic energy is quite literally circular, as it remains bounded by the aesthetic sphere of the theater itself. The second corresponds to Greenblatt's reading of Shakespeare as a discourse of power. Energy revised within the aesthetic sphere of the theater recirculates into the nontheatrical world that is transformed by it. What is missing in this account is what is most needed: an explanation of the relationship between the weak and strong versions. How *does* energy circulated within the theater then circulate within the society-at-large? Clearly, Stanley's story about the exchange of Shakespeare for a notebook is not an adequate explanation.

To be sure, in his introduction Greenblatt does give a general account of such a relationship. Admitting its vast complexity, he warns, "The mistake is to imagine that there is a single, fixed, mode of exchange; in reality, there are many modes, their character is determined historically, and they are continually renegotiated." Nonetheless, he does "note some of the more common types" (8). There is, for instance, the theater's appropriation of things in the public domain—most notably language. There is also exchange by purchase—often objects of high symbolic value such as costumes needed to stage a play—but also the labor of the playwright. Finally, there are various symbolic acquisitions, in which a social practice is transferred to the stage by means of representation.

This is a useful list. Nonetheless, although Greenblatt insists that theatrical representation involves an active "passing back and forth" (8) between the theatrical and nontheatrical world, all of these exchanges describe the theater representing or appropriating something from outside the theater. Such representations or appropriations may involve some reciprocal movement, but the balance of exchange is basically uneven, with the theater absorbing much more of the nontheatrical world than vice versa. Of the two mimetic economies Greenblatt claims are inscribed in *The Tempest*, this uneven exchange comes closer to—although it is not identical with—the one of plentitude, in which "things can be imitated, staged, reproduced without any loss or expense" (159). At pains to avoid such a singular reading, so close to the view of art he wants to challenge, Greenblatt insists upon recirculating theatrical energy in the mimetic economy of society-at-large by positing an equally strong reciprocal movement from the theatrical to the nontheatrical world. But, whereas he insists upon this movement, he offers no adequate account of how it occurs. Instead, he lets the rhetorical figure of chiasmus do his work for him. We need to look more closely at the chiasmatic formulation that Greenblatt uses to balance the exchange between the theatrical and nontheatrical worlds.

To recall, Greenblatt connects *The Tempest* with the world outside the theater by comparing its production of salutary anxiety with that produced by Latimer's sermon. Arguing that "if the practice Latimer exemplifies helps to empower theatrical representations, fictive representations have themselves helped to empower his practice" (147), Greenblatt delivers his chiasmatic summary: "This complex circulation between the social dimension of an aesthetic strategy and the aesthetic dimension of a social strategy is difficult to grasp because the strategy in question has an extraordinarily long and tangled history, one whose aesthetic roots go back at least as far as Aristotle's *Poetics*" (147).

To unwind what is implied by Greenblatt's chiasmatic coupling of the aesthetic and the social is to isolate many of the problems that I have with his attempt to circulate the aesthetic within a mimetic economy of society-at-large. Most important, in working so hard to have art escape the seemingly isolated realm of pure recreation, Greenblatt tends to overstate the role of art as one of the "creative agents in the fashioning and refashioning of historical experience" (*Representing* viii). To grant art such a powerful role is not, however, to grant it restorative powers. Instead, it is to turn it into a force of domination, an agent in the work of empire.

At first glance, Greenblatt's formulation might seem to do none of this. Indeed, his chiasmus seems designed to dethrone the aesthetic from the privileged position formalists granted it by reminding us that it is one social practice among many. Rather than leveling the aesthetic, however, Greenblatt's phrase can actually elevate it. This is because balancing the aesthetic with the social makes it too easy to grant the aesthetic a power equal to that of all other social practices combined. This privileging of art is not inevitable. Greenblatt, for instance, is careful to confine himself to *an* aesthetic strategy and *a* social strategy. Clearly there are social strategies that, from our present perspective, have an aesthetic dimension, and it is useful to analyze these particular cases of circulation. If confined to particular practices, Greenblatt's chiasmus is like ones so common today linking literature to a particular discipline, such as economics, psychology, or law. But, as we saw in the first chapter, new historicists have a tendency to employ such chiasmatic formulations as a form of synecdoche, allowing them to speak for relations between the entire field of social practices. Greenblatt's also suggests a total vision, although for a slightly different reason. Greenblatt's chiasmus appears to cover the entire field of social practices for the simple reason that he chooses the social as one of its poles. As a result, his chiasmus invites a strong reading in which aesthetic strategies circulate throughout society, helping to shape and fashion *all* social strategies. In such a reading Renaissance culture becomes a world bounded, on the one hand, by the social and, on the other, by the aesthetic. Like in a hall of mirrors, the two reflect one another, setting off an infinite circulation of energy, an energy produced by the play between identity and difference that the figure of chiasmus enacts. The energy produced is infinite, but it still takes place within set boundaries, one of which is the aesthetic.

It is by positing such a bounded, chiasmatic universe that Greenblatt can cite with approval Louis Montrose's claim that *A Midsummer Night's Dream* is "in a double sense a creation of Elizabethan culture: for it also creates the culture by which it is created, shapes the fantasies by which it is shaped, begets that by which it is begotten" (*Representing* viii, 56). To make such a claim about one play is certainly to articulate a less passive conception of mimesis, but it also suggests that Montrose himself might be caught in a dream, or if not in a dream, at least in the residue of an idealist tradition that grants art the power to shape reality. Walter Benjamin calls attention to the dangers of such chiasmatic balancing when he calls for a politicized aesthetics in order to *resist* fascism's aesthetization of politics.[9] Indeed, to grant Shakespeare's plays the power to create Elizabethan culture is to turn them into an instrument of the domination and containment embodied by that culture.

The bounded, chiasmatic world implied by the strong version of Greenblatt's argument also helps to explain how he falls prey to Walter Cohen's charge of arbitrary connectedness. Because the social and the aesthetic circulate through the entire network of practices, beliefs, and institutions comprising culture as a whole, analysis can begin anywhere and we can confidently assume that the starting point is connected somehow or other with plays produced in the period. To be sure, Greenblatt makes a concerted effort to respect the particularity of the various relationships between different works of art and Renaissance society's concrete practices, institutions, and beliefs. For instance, in his four essays he shows how a particular play has a closer relationship to some social practices than others. Nonetheless, such stress on particularity vanishes with the use of Stanley's story. Furthermore, to use "aesthetic" too generally is to risk having the aesthetic become the glue holding together a culture's network of practices. The passage I quoted earlier catches Greenblatt doing precisely this when he makes the commonplace error of confusing the aesthetic with the fictional.

It was, after all, Latimer's use of "fictive representations" that constituted the "aesthetic dimension" of his social practice. Without a doubt, many of us were trained to associate the aesthetic with imaginative fictions. But fictional representations, as such, do not necessarily originate in the realm of the aesthetic. For instance, in *An Apology for Poetry* Philip Sidney defends the fictions we encounter in poetry precisely because he knows that the law also uses fictions.

> And therefore, as in History looking for truth, they go away full fraught with falsehood, so in Poesy looking but for fiction, they shall use the narration but as an imaginative ground-plot of a profitable invention.
>
> But hereto is replied, that the poets give names to men they write of, which argueth a concert of an actual truth, and so, not being true, proves a falsehood. And doth the lawyer be then, when under the names of 'John a Stile' and 'John a Noakes' he puts his case?[10]

As Sidney knows, legal fictions do not have an aesthetic origin.

Part of Greenblatt's problem results from the slipperiness of the word "art." For literary critics it evokes the aesthetic. But it can also mean artificial or imitative, adroit or clever, and even crafty or deceitful. When Greenblatt argues in *Renaissance Self-Fashioning* that people's lives "are saturated with experience artfully shaped" (RSF 6), he does not necessarily mean that their lives have a connection to the realm of aesthetics. He merely claims that experience is not "free from interpretation" because "social actions are themselves always embedded in systems of public signification, always grasped, even by their makers, in acts of interpretation, while the words that constitute the works of literature that we discuss here are by their very nature the manifest assurance of a similar embeddedness" (RSF 5). There is a similarity between social actions and works of literature, but there is no necessary causal relationship. Indeed, the fact that people's lives "are saturated with experience artfully shaped" suggests that many social practices have a fictional component from the start. For Paul Ricoeur, one of the best contemporary spokesmen for mimesis, it is precisely the mediated nature of human activity that enables *poiesis*. Drawing, like Greenblatt, on the work of Clifford Geertz, Ricoeur puts it this way: "If human action can be recounted and poeticized . . . it is due to the fact that it is always articulated by signs, rules, and norms. To use a phrase from Clifford Geertz, human action is always symbolically mediated. An intentional activity of poetic representation can be grafted to these symbolic mediations because they already confer a basic readability on action."[11] Increasingly, however, when Greenblatt encounters "artfully shaped" behavior he grants it aesthetic origins. The mere presence of a fictional component in Latimer's sermon gives it an aesthetic dimension. But to identify the aesthetic with the fictional is to lapse into the formalism from which the new historicism hopes to escape, for it identifies the aesthetic with a particular kind of discourse, just as other formalists tried to identify it with a particular use of "literary" language.

Finally, as an old-fashioned philologist—or Raymond Williams—would remind us, the use of the term aesthetic to describe Renaissance practices is anachronistic. A tradition of poetics traces back to Aristotle, but only retrospectively a tradition of aesthetics, which despite its Greek sound was borrowed by the English from German and not used until the nineteenth century.[12] To identify fictional representations with the aesthetic is to posit the prior existence of a socially defined sphere that the new historicism, quite rightly, is at pains to show starting to take shape in the Renaissance. The same goes for literature. If one of the points of Greenblatt's essay is that the Renaissance marks a key moment in the establishment of the institution of literature, how can Latimer's tale be shaped by "literary convention?"[13] In other words, to find that fictional representations empower Latimer's social practice is not necessarily to identify an aesthetic or literary dimension. In fact it is probably safer to say that he illustrates how almost all social practices involve fictional constructs.

My point is not that works of art never influence social practice. To take one example, theatrical representation may at times heighten our awareness of the fictional component of a social practice. In addition, so-called cases of "life" imitating "art" are easy to find, and writers of novels seem especially fascinated with how people's lives are shaped by the reading of imaginative fictions. But despite examples of art helping to shape various social practices, it is as misguided to make exaggerated claims about its formative power as it is completely to deny it. Indeed, Greenblatt's metaphor of a register is useful here. A device used to measure an earthquake can do so because it is somehow connected to the thing it records. Nonetheless, it would be very hard to measure the effect of the register on the earthquake. One reason that works of art are often sensitive registers of cultural complexity is because they have the capacity to imitate so many social practices including their own. As Greenblatt notes, "everything" produced by a society can circulate into the theater. Thus it is much more likely that the theater will imitate the social practice of bearbaiting than bearbaiting will imitate the theater, even though it may appropriate certain theatrical elements.

If it is important to challenge Greenblatt's overexaggerated claims about the formative power of art, it is equally important to challenge the argument that its effects are confined to a realm of pure recreation. For instance, last chapter I disputed Jochen Schulte-Sasse's assertion that institutional demarcations are so firm that they "*never* permit our aesthetic norms of conduct to penetrate other realms of life"[14] (my emphasis). Greenblatt uses chiasmus to suggest the inevitable slippage from the aesthetic into the everyday world of experience artfully shaped. But that slippage cannot adequately be accounted for by a mimetic economy. To explore the limits of Greenblatt's mimetic economy in more depth we need to turn to a brief comparison between his version of a cultural poetics and Aristotle's *Poetics*.

Like Greenblatt, Aristotle stresses the dynamic nature of mimesis. There is, however, an important difference between Aristotelian mimesis and Greenblatt's mimesis. At stake is the critical relationship that a text's *energia* has to other social practices and discourses. We can start by examining Aristotle's comparison of poetry to another social practice with the capacity to imitate a multiplicity of social practices—the writing of history.

· V ·

For Aristotle mimesis helps to explain the difference between history and poetry. For him mimesis is not passive imitation but an activity intricately aligned with *poiesis*, or making. As Ricoeur puts it, "Far from producing a weakened image of preexisting things, mimesis brings about an augmentation of meaning in the field of action, which is its privileged field. It does not equate itself with something already given. Rather it produces what it imitates, if we continue to translate mimesis by imitation."[15] If Ricoeur's account of mimesis producing what it imitates sounds like Montrose's argument that a *Midsummer Night's Dream* "creates the culture by which it is created," there is an important difference.

Aristotle situates poetry between history and philosophy. If history deals with the concrete contingency of existing social practices and philosophy with universals, poetry offers concrete universals. When for Aristotle mimesis produces that which it imitates, he does not claim, as some new historicists do, that it shapes and fashions the contingent culture in which it takes shape. Instead, it helps bring into existence a concrete universal that is truer than the contingent world in which the poet lives. An understanding of the worldview that gave rise to mimesis can help explain this difference between new historical and Aristotelian mimesis.

Aristotle's stress on the universality of mimesis is appropriate to a worldview that assumed a closed cosmos in which all possible contents and forms of reality were complete. To be sure, in the Aristotelian cosmos, unlike the Platonic, universals take shape only as concrete particulars, which require the activity of mimesis to make them visible. Nonetheless, as we have seen, the Aristotelian belief in universality is at odds with a different way of constructing reality starting to arise with the Renaissance. With the Renaissance we get what Hans Blumenberg calls a sense of the "open" context that "removes the dubiousness from what is new."[16] The legitimacy granted to "new worlds" is temporal as well as spatial. Reality changes as time changes. In this worldview, without which the modern historical consciousness would be unthinkable, it is possible to conclude that the only reality available is the contingent history distrusted by Aristotle when he locates reality in concrete universals revealed through mimesis. Accepting this conclusion, but refusing to abandon a productive model of mimesis, Montrose and Greenblatt are tempted to claim that works of art simultaneously imitate and produce the contingent reality of history.

This claim is another example of Blumenberg's reoccupation thesis. In Blumenberg's terms Montrose and Greenblatt reoccupy the position in which mimesis claims to produce the reality that it imitates. By doing so within a worldview that denies the reality of universals, they grant mimesis an overextended role that results in exaggerated claims about its power to shape a contingent reality. We can see why by looking more closely at the role that *energia* plays in the Aristotelian tradition.

In an important book Kathy Eden has shown how the rhetorical figure of *energia* is closely related to the figure of *enargia*. Indeed, some classical rhetoricians even confuse the two. Puttenham, whose definition of *energia* Greenblatt quotes, is not one. Nonetheless, he treats the two together. For him *energia* is a figure of sense, whereas *enargia* is a figure of sound that satisfies and delights the ear.[17] For Aristotle, however, *enargia* is more than a figure of sound. In the *Poetics* it describes vividness of presentation and is essential for any poet hoping to move an audience. Indeed, in the *Rhetoric* Aristotle defines *energia* as a kind of movement that sets things "before the eyes, for the hearer should see the action as present."[18] As Eden points out, this need to represent a scene *enargically* in order to move an audience probably grew out of the Athenian court system. "Because in most legal cases demonstrative evidence was unavailable, testimony provided the most common form of proof. Without firsthand knowledge of the act in question and faced with the need to reconstruct the events, the jury had to rely on the detailed narration of litigants and their witnesses. Consequently, the narrator, whether witness or litigant, set out to reproduce the vividness of ocular proof through language."[19] Similarly, poets will most effectively move their audiences by first setting a scene to be represented before their own eyes, as if they were witnessing it firsthand.

This technique of showing rather than telling is one reason why Aristotle grants poetic fictions a greater chance to move an audience than historical accounts. Indeed, most of us have experienced the sensation of reading a work that transports us to the scene being represented, making us feel as if we were there. Within the Aristotelian world of mimesis, however, what the poetic fiction represents is not a historical actuality but a universal truth concretely embodied. It moves an audience because the evidence that it produces reveals the self-evidence of truth. To be sure, immersed in the contingency of historical reality the self-evidence of truth is often obscured. Thus it takes the act of mimesis to bring it vividly before our eyes. Operating within this tradition Joseph Conrad can claim that fiction is truer than history because it can reveal a glimpse of the truth we had forgotten to ask.[20]

For Aristotle, the power of mimesis concretely to embody higher laws aligns it with equity. Just as poetry is superior to both philosophy and history, so equity is superior to positive law because "it can move more freely between the generality of the law and the concrete case."[21] The similarities between the functions of poetic fictions and equity demonstrate the relationship that poetry has to human-made institutions within Aristotle's system. Rhetorical products of an insufficient human, not divine, reason, human institutions, like positive law, are themselves flawed. By revealing to us the self-evidence of cosmic laws, poetic mimesis resubordinates those historically constructed institutions to the rule of the *logos*, just as equity provides a remedy to the potential injustices of the legal system. In such a world, a work's *energia* creates a "stir to the mind" which upsets the *doxa*, or commonly held ideas, by pointing to the presence of truths whose origin is not human-made.[22] In the non-Aristotelian world of modernity, a work's *energia* does not disappear, but it takes on a different function.

Various modern thinkers who challenged the sovereignty of a cosmic *logos* tried to reoccupy the position it vacated with the sovereignty of human reason. One political consequence was the attempt to control the *doxa* by rationality. Thus, as Blumenberg notes, Thomas Hobbes objects to democracy because it relies on rhetoric to make decisions more "by a certain violence of mind" than by "right reason."[23] Discounting the existence of an inherent "right reason," cultural critics today are often attracted to a "critical reason" that will correct the false consciousness of a rhetorically-constructed *doxa* and inherent flaws in rhetorically-constructed institutions. Once we are forced to admit that "critical reason" itself is a rhetorical institution, however, we seem to be left with no critical ground on which to stand. To take one example, modern legal systems have virtually eliminated courts of equity that would remedy potential injustices committed by positive law. The only appeals that remain are legislative or judicial in the form of a higher, because later, form of rhetorical authority—a different court still regulated by the practices of positive law.

Paralleling the emasculation of equity has been a reluctance to appeal, as the New Critics did, to the transcendental authority of great works of literature to reveal a truth not even accessible to critical reason. Nonetheless, unlike equity, the institution of literature has not died out. Confined to Greenblatt's mimetic economy, however, literary works have lost their critical potential. They either do work complicit with the extension of power or remain confined to a marginalized realm of recreation. But as I suggested in the last chapter, the realm of recreation might be of more use to the new historicism than its emphasis on cultural work allows. Perhaps, in the admittedly circumscribed area of imaginative re-creation, literature can do some useful work. Politically concerned critics may worry because the political payoff of such work is not completely predictable. Plato's condemnation of artistic representation for subverting the social order may be as misguided as new historicist proofs that it supports it. Perhaps literary representation has a different function. This, at least, is the possibility I want to explore by turning to the recent work of Wolfgang Iser to challenge Derrida's and Greenblatt's characterization of literary re-creation as mimetic.

· VI ·

Greenblatt can call literary representation mimetic because the artist mimes, not things, but God's act of creation. What happens, however, if with Nietzsche we declare the death of God? What, then, is the artist miming? The answer, it seems, is nothing, neither a concrete universal, as in Aristotle, nor an act of God, as in Kant. Nonetheless, we are still left with an act of making, a human act that does not merely reflect something already existing in the world. We are left, in other words, with a situation similar to the one that Marx describes in *The Eighteenth Brumaire* in which it is after all human beings who make history. They do not, however, make it under conditions of their own choosing. Just as the making of history takes place within circumscribed historical conditions, so does *poiesis*. If Kant felt that the artist mimed God's freedom by creating *ex nihilo*, to deny the existence of a God to imitate is to restore *poiesis* to its historical circumstances, which is, as Greenblatt's work aptly demonstrates, to involve it in representational exchanges with existing discursive systems and social practices.

Certain poststructuralist polemics to the contrary, representation is necessary because, as Ricoeur puts it, what is produced "would never be understandable if it did not configurate what is already figured in human action."[24] But if Ricoeur evokes mimesis to defend representation against poststructuralist attacks, a more provocative move is Iser's that charts representation's nonmimetic aspect. Like Aristotelian mimesis, representation is an active reconfiguration of various social practices and discourses, not merely their passive imitation. Unlike traditional mimesis, however, that reconfiguration does not embody a universal truth. Furthermore, unlike Kantian mimesis, it has no divine act to imitate. It is an act of *poiesis* that breaks with its mimetic component.

To say that Iser offers a theory of representation that breaks with its mimetic component is to acknowledge that a mimetic component exists. Indeed, Iser's starting point is that "a piece of fiction devoid of any connection with known reality would be incomprehensible."[25] As a result, he is discontent with the binary opposition between fiction and reality and suggests the triadic configuration of the real, the fictional, and the imaginary. A literary text, as a special brand of the fictional, is a "'transitional object' between the real and the imaginary."[26] It is in its role as a transitional object that the literary text has its special function, which is to provoke the reader to cross boundaries of existing modes of constructing reality. This boundary crossing is induced by the interplay of various discursive systems that are selected and combined in the literary text. That a literary text involves the interplay of various discursive systems indicates that for Iser it is dialogical. In contrast to Bakhtin, however, Iser describes how this dialogical interplay can lead to a process of "coherent deformation" that undercuts the ability of any one of the systems to construct a stable consistency. As a result, we are forced to place our various ways of constructing reality in brackets. "Reality, then, may be reproduced in the fictional text, but it is there in order to be outstripped, as is indicated by its being bracketed. . . . The reality represented in the text is not meant to represent reality—it is a pointer to something which it is not although its function is to make that something conceivable" (217). The literary text is not so much characterized by its re-presentation of a world in its fullness as by its negativity, which keeps the various discursive systems appropriated by the text from uniting into a balanced organic harmony. Confronted by the deformation of these familiar ways of organizing the world, the reader is provoked "to extend beyond his habitual dispositions" (221).

In order to give a sense of how this process works, Iser turns to the example of an actor playing the role of Hamlet.

> He cannot identify himself totally with Hamlet, not least because even he does not know precisely who Hamlet might be. Thus he must always remain partly himself, which means that his body, his feelings, and his mind function as an analogue, enabling him to represent that which he is not; this duality makes it possible for him to offer a particular embodiment of that which Hamlet might be. In order to produce the determinate form of an unreal character, the actor must fade out of his own reality. Similarly with each of us as readers: to imagine what has been stimulated by the 'as-if' entails placing our faculties at the disposal of an unreality and bestowing on it a semblance of reality in proportion to a reducing of our own reality (221).

Iser's example from the theater is appropriate since in German an actor is a *Darsteller*, and the sense of representation that Iser wants to convey is best expressed through the German word *Darstellung* rather than the English "representation," which too easily implies a failed effort to re-present an already existing reality. In contrast, *Darstellung* gives the sense of a performance. It is a presentation, not re-presentation.[27] Furthermore, the performative act of the reader emphasizes that our reaction to the literary text has the quality of an event. "This event arises out of the crossing of boundaries and can no longer be equated with given frameworks, the surpassing of which qualifies the fictionalizing act" (222). The active participation of the reader or audience is, therefore, necessary to bring potential brave new worlds into existence, something stressed almost too obviously in *The Tempest* by Prospero's final address to the audience. This important exchange of energy between the play and its audience—an essential part of the theater's and book's mode of representation that disrupts any illusion of the self-contained autonomy of the play—is necessary because the play is not merely a register of existing social practices but an activity involving its audience in an imaginative transformation and refashioning of them.

At this point, it is well worth asking the pragmatic question: What is at stake in maintaining this distinction between representation and mimesis? After all, Greenblatt too stresses that a play is not the imitation of a social totality. Instead, elements are "crossed, torn apart, recombined, set against each other" (19). One way to answer that question is to look at the work of one of the most sophisticated defenders of mimesis, Luiz Costa Lima. Drawing on the work of Iser, Costa Lima offers a definition of mimesis that comes extremely close to my description of a nonmimetic notion of representation. "Mimesis," he argues, "contrary to its false translation, imitation, is not the production of similarity, but rather the production of difference. Difference, nevertheless, that is imposed on a horizon of expectations of similarity." Nonetheless, there is a difference with Iser. "Note as well, and even more carefully, that the communicational orientation does not necessarily lead to the recirculation of the concept of mimesis. Iser, its principal representative, or Jauss, its best known, do not recirculate it, nor would they agree that it is necessary to do so. To Iser it would seem necessary to deal with the fictional nature of the text for the aesthetic experience to take place. To us, however, it seems necessary to distinguish between the mimetic process—whose realm of action does not begin or end in the poetic or artistic production, since man is socialized on the basis of the mimetization of common behaviors and values—and the fictional result."[28]

Like Greenblatt, Costa Lima seems to risk conflating the fictional and the aesthetic. But that conflation is less important than another aspect of his argument. Also like Greenblatt, Costa Lima has a notion of mimesis that accounts for difference as well as resemblance. Furthermore, both

Greenblatt and Costa Lima are intent on recirculating the concept of mimesis out of the realm of the aesthetic into the realm of the social. Indeed, a problem with Iser for socially concerned critics seems to be that he offers no guarantee that the imaginative transformations made possible by aesthetic experience will circulate out of the theater in such a way as to alter social practices at large. When Costa Lima argues that the mimetic realm of action does not begin or end in the aesthetic he seems to provide for a circulation of the aesthetic without falling prey to Greenblatt's error of attributing aesthetic *origins* to social practices. Nonetheless, the limits of mimesis for the new historicism are indicated by Costa Lima's claim that "man is socialized on the basis of the mimetization of common behaviors and values."

To a large extent this is true. But to understand socialization solely in terms of mimesis is to lock us into the world described by Stanley Fish. As we saw in chapter 4, Fish argues that there is never a break with existing practices, only a mimetic extension of them.[29] To the objection that his model rules out the possibility of change, Fish argues that, on the contrary, it produces perpetual change. Costa Lima's definition of mimesis as the production of difference "based on a horizon of expectations of similarity" helps to explain why. Existing practices are mimed, but in the very act of re-presenting them difference is produced. Given a world in which socialization occurs through the mimesis of existing practices, behaviors, and values, social change is inevitable. The problem with this account of change is that, despite its stress on difference, it still implies a sense of temporal continuity. Indeed, in a world in which change has come to be expected, an account of the world that makes change inevitable is, paradoxically, one that confirms the status quo. It is at this point that Iser's distinction between representation and mimesis can become useful for the new historicism, because a nonmimetic mode of representation can disrupt the flow of the mimetic economy.

The irreality that the reality represented in the text points to and helps to make conceivable does not result, as in a mimetic economy, from the *expansion* of existing discursive boundaries. Instead, it results from the *crossing* of boundaries induced by the interplay of the variety of discursive systems selected and recombined in the text. Rather than an extension of any one particular discursive system, it is, as it were, a new language that resists translation into any of those that helped bring it into existence. This resistance to translation is the literary text's strength and weakness.

It is its weakness because, by resisting translation, it seems incapable of circulation. Indeed, the effect that Iser describes is clearly a potential effect. More often than not readers establish coherence precisely by extending the discursive system they are most familiar with into their own master narrative, thereby translating the text into an existing discursive system. For Iser, such readings inevitably exclude elements of the text's repertoire. Nonetheless, they do have the advantage of immediate circulation in the social economy of mimesis. In fact, given Iser's description of the act of representation, any attempt to create coherence would seem to move us away from aesthetic experience into the realm of historically determined readings that limit the play of the text and are thus prone to further deformation. Iser, then, would seem to locate aesthetic experience in what Greenblatt calls the "freedom of the imagination and hence in liberation from the constraints of the body" (159). Aesthetic experience for him seems to be a realm of "pure plentitude" (159), free from the constraints of history. But it is a bizarre sort of plentitude that depends upon a lack or negativity.

Rather than implying a freedom from the constraints of history, Iser's model confronts us with our finiteness as historical subjects who are forced to make sense of the text as world on the basis of insufficient evidence. This sense of the historical subject is one Iser shares with Blumenberg, who links it to the question of rhetoric. A brief detour to Blumenberg's speculations about rhetoric can clarify why aesthetic experience for Iser is not an experience of plentitude.

In a seminal essay entitled, "An Anthropological Approach to the Contemporary Significance of Rhetoric," Blumenberg develops Arnold Gehlen's notion that a human being is a *Mangelwesen* (creature of deficiencies). Adopting the language of the metaphysical tradition, Blumenberg argues that,

> man does not belong to this cosmos (if in fact it exists); and this is not because of a transcendent "surplus" that he possesses but because of an immanent deficiency, a deficiency of pre-given, prepared structures to fit into and of regulatory processes for a connected system that would deserve to be called a "cosmos" and within which something could be called part of the cosmos. In the language of modern biological anthropology, too, man is a creature who has fallen back out of the ordered arrangements that nature has accomplished, and for whom actions have to take the place of the automatic controls that he lacks or correct those that have acquired an erratic inaccuracy. Action compensates for the "indeterminateness" of the creature man, and rhetoric is the effort to produce the accords that have to take the place of the "substantial" base of regulatory processes in order to make action possible (433).

Human beings, then, are condemned to a "rhetorical situation," the prerequisites of which are "being compelled to act" while "lacking definitive evidence" (441). Recognition of this situation is especially acute in contemporary Western society, which faces the failure of previous efforts to find a ground for moral action in self-evident natural truths or an absolute foundation of rationality. Humanity's historicity is defined by this rhetorical situation. Double-edged subjects of history, human beings occupy a position at the moment in which the past is transmitted to the future; that is, the moment of now. Whereas that moment has the appearance of continuity with that which came before and that which comes after, it is, as Blumenberg puts it, a position of "reoccupation," a moment of translation or *Übersetzung* (a setting over).

So long as the transmission of history is a rhetorical transaction, history cannot be fit into a human-made *logos*, for, as Blumenberg puts it, "the axiom of all rhetoric is the principle of insufficient reason" (447). At the same time, to call the transmission of history rhetorical is not necessarily to claim that rhetoric makes history. Those who have recently done so recognize, with Blumenberg, the insufficiency of human reason but absolve human beings of responsibility for their historical acts by positing as a motor of history "an instrument that [humanity] invented" (453), just as earlier generations explained historical change in terms of fate, providence, or teleological progress. Even so, the rhetorical nature of humankind's historical situation cautions us that any making of history is not freely chosen. After all, rhetoric itself is historically constructed, as is the subject of history. The relationship between self and history that this rhetorical situation implies becomes clearer if we compare it to the one implied by Costa Lima's mimetic model.

As Costa Lima admits, his sense of mimesis posits a *"common infralogical mark in mankind."* Such a common mark need not be a fixed substance. Instead, for Costa Lima it is more like a common structure that accounts for the production of difference. Nonetheless, what is not questioned is the constancy of the mark itself, just as Ricoeur continues to champion mimesis because it makes evident basic structures of temporality. Costa Lima's common mark turns the position occupied by historical subjects into a structural rather than a rhetorical one. It makes humanity at home in the cosmos, but at a high cost, the cost of fitting human nature and the course of history into "pre-given, prepared structures." In other words, it fits both into a very complicated, but still closed, cosmos of the sort that gave rise to mimesis, defined by Aristotle in such a way as to combat Plato's distrust of rhetoric by subsuming it and human action under the *logos*. For Costa Lima the transmission of history is basically unproblematic and continuous. Indeed, hand in hand with his positing of a "common infralogical mark in mankind" is an "unverifiable" bet "that what history has presented up until now serves as a proof that it cannot assume a radically different shape."[30]

In contrast, when the position occupied by the historical subject is a rhetorical one the mimetic economy does not flow automatically from one point to the next. Similarly, Iser's model makes the transmission of history problematic. As a result, it indicates the wisdom of making a different, if not directly opposed, bet, one described by Blumenberg as modernity's wager that human beings, the subjects of history, can also make history. Such a bet may be lost, but without it humanity relinquishes the possibility it might have to remake and refashion the social world which it inhabits. To understand the limited, but not completely irrelevant, role that literary history can play in such activities, I want to look at differences implied by Iser's and Greenblatt's models for reading literary works from the past. Before turning to that comparison, I should provide a brief summary of previous attempts to use mimesis to solve this central, but most perplexing problem facing all attempting to combine the disciplines of history and literature.

· VII ·

What is the relationship of present audiences to past works? Any serious historical criticism needs to confront this question because to assume that reality changes with the passage of time is to posit the radical otherness of the past. Past epochs may be, in Ranke's phrase, "immediate before God,"[31] but they have worldviews and logics different from those of the present. How, then, can a reader, locked within a present perspective and separated from the past by an irreversible temporal distance, understand a work that has taken shape in a culture that no longer exists? The question is especially complicated for new historicists who, on the one hand, retain a mimetic model and, on the other, deny the existence of universal truths that Aristotelian mimesis claimed to reveal. But new historicists are clearly not the only critics to retain a mimetic model. If it really causes such difficulty for present audiences' ability to relate to works from the past, how has mimesis proved so durable?

One reason is that although the worldview of the open context arose to challenge the ancient and medieval view of a closed cosmos, it by no means completely replaced it. Many people continue to believe in the constancy of the human condition. For them concrete circumstances might change, but the universal truth revealed by mimesis speaks to us as vividly today as in the past.

Even for those disputing this point of view, it can help correct overenthusiastic new historicists who are prone to declare that radical breaks in the human condition occur every twenty-five years. Can the modern bourgeois subject really have been constituted in the Renaissance, the eighteenth century, and the nineteenth century? The danger of declaring too much change is that we blind ourselves to those moments of important change, of legitimate newness.

In part this danger grows out of the institutional practice of period specialization. If my argument about the nonsynchronicity of the synchronic is true, tensions present in the Renaissance between competing ideologies may still be present, in altered form, in the eighteenth, nineteenth, and even twentieth centuries. In each of these periods the modern bourgeois subject is, indeed, emerging, but those who confine themselves to synchronic analysis might mistakenly conclude that the emergence is occurring for the first time in the period under study.

The opposite mistake comes from those who recognize the persistence of particular conflicts and tensions over long periods of time and conclude that they were "always already" there. Thus certain deconstructionists assume the sameness of difference instead of providing a history of its concrete differences. This leads some to posit a constancy in the human condition, even if that constancy is a permanent instability. For instance, J. Hillis Miller has argued that humankind's "situation in relation to language" or "the human condition generally" will not be affected by a "change in the material base or in the class structure."[32] Rigorous texts, past or present, are the ones that speak to humankind's inevitable "situation in relation to language."

But it is not only a continued belief in the constancy of the human condition that helps to account for the durability of mimesis. If the historicist assumption that reality changes over time disrupted the closed cosmos of the ancients, history could still be enclosed within a teleological, Aristotelian narrative of beginning, middle, and end. Different from one another, various epochs are, nonetheless, stages in the working out of a totality within history. This sense of historical totality along with a faith in mimesis to reveal the totality of an era unite critics as different as Auerbach and Lukács. For instance, Lukács celebrates realistic art that makes possible the "objective knowing of the totality of a historical situation and the laws of history underlying it."[33] Similarly, Auerbach ends *Mimesis* asserting that whereas "it is still a long way to a common life of mankind on earth," it is the literary representation of "an economic and cultural leveling process"[34] that makes this goal visible. Insofar as the great works of realism give the most accurate representation of stages in the unfolding of such teleological visions, their ability to speak to the present is assured.[35]

Nonetheless, as effective as this model proved for Lukács and Auerbach, it proves untenable for the new historicism, which questions the notion of totality. For instance, Greenblatt begins his book by acknowledging his desire to speak with the dead. His original attempt was flawed, he admits, because he mistakenly believed in a "total artist" and a "totalizing society" (2). In abandoning those totalizing notions, he hopes to find a way of fulfilling his desire. Indeed, he ends his introduction declaring,

"I had dreamed of speaking with the dead, and even now I do not abandon this dream. But the mistake was to imagine that I would hear a single voice, the voice of the other. If I wanted to hear one, I had to hear the many voices of the dead. And if I wanted to hear the voice of the other, I had to hear my own voice" (20). In between, he presents his theory of a mimetic circulation of social energy that presumably explains how Shakespeare's plays enable this mingling of many voices, including those of past and present. It is time to compare Greenblatt's account of diachronic negotiations between past and present with the one implied by Iser's textual model.

Opposing the formalism in which he was trained, Greenblatt insists that "the attempt to locate the power of art in a permanently novel, untranslatable formal perfection will always end in a blind alley" (4). Its power results only through acts of translation. Shakespeare's plays sustain their power when future readers/audiences transform and refashion the "social energy initially encoded" (6) in them. This does not mean that the "aesthetic power" of the plays is a "direct transmission from Shakespeare's time to our own" (6). Instead, the contemporary existence of its energy "depends upon an irregular chain of historical transactions that lead back to the late sixteenth and early seventeenth centuries" (6). Those transactions have produced a continuous refiguring of the plays. "But those refigurations do not cancel history, locking us into a perpetual present; on the contrary, they are signs of the inescapability of a historical process, a structured negotiation and exchange, already evident in the initial moments of empowerment" (6).

Greenblatt's insistence that present refigurations do not cancel history registers his annoyance with those who claim to be interested in the past and yet retreat to a naive presentism that refuses to engage its otherness. Nonetheless, his insistence reveals problems with his account of how past and present voices mingle to keep a work alive in its moment of reception. One problem has to do with what Greenblatt posits for present readers to translate. What we translate, Greenblatt asserts, are "textual traces that have survived from the Renaissance" (6). These traces should not in themselves be equated with the text's *energia*. But because we cannot experience it directly, they are our only record of it. Thus, from the start, Greenblatt confronts the reader/audience with the suggestion of a lost presence demanding translation. The way in which we approach that lost presence brings us to a second problem. This problem has to do with Greenblatt's sense of tradition. Not a direct encounter with the text, our reception of it is mediated by its entire history of reception. In having the encounter between past text and present reader mediated by this tradition, Greenblatt risks locking us into a sense of temporal continuity that rules out a notion of breaks within history. To be sure, he speaks of refigurations, but they produce a continuous, if "irregular *chain*" that is part of an inescapable "historical *process*" (my emphasis). If we turn to Iser's model, we find the potential for a very different relationship between present readers and past texts, one leaving open the possibility of discontinuities within the inescapable historical process constituted by Greenblatt's irregular chain.

Both Iser's and Greenblatt's models position readers according to the "structured negotiation and exchange" generated by a text's moment of production. But they imply very different positionings for readers trying to negotiate the exchange between past and present. If Greenblatt's model places readers in an indirect relationship to the historical otherness of a past text, Iser's allows for a much more direct encounter. The readers' indirect relationship in Greenblatt's model follows from their efforts to preserve the historical otherness of the text by positing an originary moment of its *energia*. That originary moment generates a history of reception that projects itself linearly in a diachronic relationship of mimesis. For Greenblatt, on the one hand, a text renews its power when readers extend the "irregular chain of historical transactions" that constitute the history of its reception. On the other, that chain is generated by renewed efforts of each generation of readers to restore the lost presence suggested by the textual traces that manifest its energy. As a result, Greenblatt's account of how a text renews its power is similar to one presented by Gadamer, in which tradition is preserved through a continuous "fusion" of past and present horizons.[36] By abandoning the mimetic model in which a text is constituted by traces suggesting the existence of a lost presence to be re-presented, Iser lets us see how the fusion of present readers and past texts has the potential to disrupt the chain of temporal continuity, however irregular it may be.

Greenblatt offers a model in which we are left with textual traces that invite us to decode in a transformed manner what was originally encoded. In contrast, Iser, while not denying the existence of the text, insists that it does not come to us encoded with an original meaning. Instead, from the start the text's "structured negotiation and exchange" make the reader a necessary component in the construction of the world of the text. The history of a text's reception is not one of renewed efforts to re-present an original presence suggested at the moment of production, but renewed efforts, sparked by the text's negativity, to bring into existence a world that has no prior existence. According to his model, these acts of world-making are not so much reconstructive as constructive.

Iser's model has caused critics to accuse him of being less historical than his colleague at Constance, Hans Robert Jauss, whose reception aesthetics adhere much more closely to Gadamer's notion of tradition.[37] Indeed, his model plays havoc with the historical method proposed by someone like E. D. Hirsch, who insists upon the distinction between the stability of a text's original meaning and its changing significance brought about by attempts to reconstruct that meaning in new historical circumstances.[38] In contrast, for Iser the original moment of production does not provide us with a stable meaning to be reconstructed. This is not because he abandons the historical otherness of the text. The text indeed registers social discourses from the past. But it registers and structures them in such a way as to make possible the readers' imaginative transformations and re-fashionings of them. Given his efforts to challenge the notion that text and context have a single, stable meaning, Greenblatt would seem to agree with Iser's description. Nonetheless, by retaining a mimetic model, he positions present readers as the last link of a chain constituting the history of a text's reception that has as its goal the reconstruction of a lost originary moment. Iser allows us to break loose from that chain by having readers "reoccupy" a position structured by a text and its discursive systems from the past, a position from which we transmit the text into the present.

To be sure, in reoccupying that position we do not become a subject of the past. We cannot, as Greenblatt reminds us, merely eliminate the historical distance between us and the Renaissance and, as an older historicism advocated, empathetically relive a past era. But it is precisely this inability that makes Iser's model useful for the new historicism. Unless we are professionally trained literary critics, who have traced the entire history of a play's reception, our encounter with it is probably not mediated by the irregular chain of transactions posited by Greenblatt. Instead, re-figuring the text by circulating our present ways of seeing within the negotiations and exchanges structured by a work produced in the past, we have the possibility of creating constellations between the present and a moment in the past. Such constellations, Benjamin insists, can blast "open the continuum of history."[39] How they can do so is clarified by a closer look at Greenblatt's claim that our refigurations of a text "do not cancel history, locking us into a perpetual present" (6).

As we have seen, in refusing to "cancel history" Greenblatt combats a presentism that would deny a text's historical otherness. He is certainly correct to insist that our present ways of constructing the world result from a complex network of historical transactions. For new historians not necessarily content with the direction history has taken, however, one task is to imagine different ways of constructing it. Indeed, this is a challenge that Benjamin poses to historians in his "Theses." And when he does, he speaks of the need to "cancel" history. By cancel Benjamin does not mean to forget or deny. Instead, "cancel" is used to translate the German "aufheben," which means simultaneously to preserve, to elevate, and to cancel. Thus he urges a method that will blast "a specific life out of the era or a specific work out of the lifework. As a result of this method the lifework is preserved in this work and at the same time cancelled."[40] It is precisely such cancellations that enable the construction of a historical plot challenging those who tell the story of the past as a continuous series of present moments lodged within an inescapable historical process. There are at least two ways in which readers reoccupying a historical position structured by texts from the past can participate in these acts of historical construction.

First of all, as I stressed at the end of the last chapter, such a reoccupation allows readers to recognize that the direction history has taken is not inevitable but contingent. History may have happened one way, but with historical hindsight we can see that different actions and ways of constructing the world could have set it on a different path. This sense of past alternatives can work dialectically to produce a second response, one exposing the limits of the present point of view that enables our historical hindsight. Condemned to a present moment in which we cannot seek alternatives in a transcendental world elsewhere or utopian visions in a nonexistent future, we can negotiate an exchange with texts from the past that can give us a sense of the otherness of our own point of view, thus provoking us to grope for alternative ways of world-making. The text might provoke such groping, but it provides no sure foundation to guide the direction which it should take. Nonetheless, the groping itself calls attention to our position in the muddled middle of a present that is a moment of historical *translation*, not one of mere *transition* within an inevitable historical process.

· VIII ·

To make such sweeping generalizations produces in me a certain amount of anxiety (salutary, no doubt), if for no other reason than the logical consequence of my description of a potential response to reading past texts is that it is not an inevitable response. To describe the way in which we transmit a text from the past into the present as a rhetorical transaction is to admit that the mode of transmission is contestable. What my description does, in other words, is argue for a possible way of reading, a way that a strictly mimetic model closes off. It does not, however, deny the historical actuality of other ways of reading.

There continue to be those, like Don Quixote, Madame Bovary, and Tom Sawyer, who mistake a literary fiction for historical actuality. Indeed, the textual *energia* so necessary to provoke the response that I describe invites readers to feel *as if* they are being transported to a world of vivid reality. Thus Benjamin himself retains an essentially mimetic model of the literary text, one that emphasizes a work of art's ability to represent the totality of an era. In describing works by Flaubert, for instance, he quotes Ranke. "Witiko and Salambo (sic) represent their epochs as self-enclosed, 'immediate before God.' Just as the novels explode the temporal continuum, historiography ought to be able to follow suit."[41] I have argued that such an explosion is possible precisely because the text's *energia* does not re-present a world but enables an act of world building. Nonetheless, that act would not be provoked without a vivid reproduction of aspects of the real. One of the unintended benefits of Greenblatt's appeal to *energia* to combat formalism is that a historical understanding of the figure's function reminds us of the importance of work like Auerbach's or Ian Watt's intent on examining the techniques by which a formal realism can create the illusion of reality.

Hypersensitive to the illusory quality of that experience, recent critics have emphasized that any act of re-presentation produces and reproduces a structure of internal difference. The gaps inherent in any act of representation are, on the one hand, opportunities to unmask ideology—it is in such gaps that efforts to achieve ideological closure are exposed—and, on the other, an essential element in the ideological makeup of the text—as a re-presentation the text is always a mis-representation. The very moment of recognition depends upon a misrecognition.

Iser's model, as I use it, does not free literature from ideology, but it does relocate its relationship to it.[42] In this model both the moments of production and reception are ideological. The moment of production, because the selection of discourses making up the text's repertoire is not neutral but a way of constructing a subject-position for the reader. The moment of reception, because readers seeking consistency construct modes of closure, and even new ways of constructing the world do not transcend ideology. Nonetheless, there remains that moment of now in which the act of reception becomes an act of production. That moment can provoke us to assume a role in which we are forced to imagine alternative ways of constructing and aligning existing institutional practices.

For instance, without a doubt, the discourse of colonialism is an important part of *The Tempest*'s textual repertoire. This is one reason that it has taken on almost canonical status for new historicists. But, as Greenblatt's argument about the play's doubleness confirms, it is not the only discourse at work. For Greenblatt, the play generates two readings, seemingly at odds with one another, much like the gestalt figure of the rabbit/duck. Recognizing that alone neither one reading nor the other does the play justice, he finds consistency in his both/and interpretation. I would argue, however, that there is more than a doubleness at work. In his reading of the play as the place of power, Greenblatt calls it the "place in which all individual discourses are organized by the half-invisible ruler" (158). But that act of organization, as the play makes clear, is an imaginary act.

Interacting with one another, the play's multiplicity (not doubleness) of discourses threatens efforts of its half-visible ruler/reader to impose a hierarchical order. Both resisting and inviting acts of organization, the interplay of these numerous discourses can make possible not only the recognition of the play's discourse of colonialism (a recognition requiring little imagination) but also its realignment, as it and the play's other discursive systems mingle with the various discursive systems brought to bear on the play by a new ruler/reader.

Greenblatt's reading is itself proof of the links between the imagnination and questions of power. It is a *powerful* reading precisely because it accomplishes an imaginative realignment of the play's various discourses. To be sure, in retrospect we can link his reading to the irregular chain that seems merely mimetically to extend the history of the play's reception. But before it was produced the precise nature of his imaginative act of organization could not have been predicted. If it could have been, it would have lost its power. The actual political power of such imaginative realignments should not, however, be exaggerated. First of all, there is no concrete mechanism for their actualization. Second, even if there were, their lack of predictability would make their political effects uncertain. Nonetheless, in a world in which critical reason has undermined its own foundation along with that of various other ways of criticizing existing institutions, the importance of an institutional space inviting imaginative realignments of existing discursive systems should not be completely dismissed.

That importance is linked to what Blumenberg calls our rhetorical situation. Existing institutions have traditionally been questioned by appeals to higher laws, self-evident truths, critical reason, or inherent human rights. All of these, however, lose their foundational status when defined rhetorically. As Blumenberg puts it in terms of efforts to define human nature, "What remains as the subject matter of anthropology is a 'human nature' that has never been 'nature' and never will be. . . . Man comprehends himself only by way of what he is not. It is not only his situation that is potentially metaphorical; his constitution already is" (456). Lacking "fixed biological dispositions" that would make them feel at home in the world, human beings survive "by not dealing with their reality directly. The human relation to reality is indirect, circumstantial, delayed, selective, and above all 'metaphorical'" (439). Lacking the immediacy of self-evidence, a rhetorical situation undercuts efforts to ground criticism of existing institutions. On the contrary, it gives rise to institutions, for it is institutions, metaphorically not foundationally based, that serve as humanity's indirect means of dealing with reality. Any challenge to institutions that appeals to the real or natural is limited because that appeal can be shown to be as rhetorical as that which it challenges. It seems to follow, then, that "as soon as what was considered to be 'real' no longer exists, the substitutions themselves become 'the real'" (444).

Someone like Stanley Fish would have one crucial disagreement with this formulation. He would eliminate the quotation marks. Since we have no access to a reality beyond institutions and rhetoric, institutions and rhetoric become the real. Thus, whereas we can always expose the conventional in the natural, Fish ends by naturalizing convention. For Fish, institutions are not, as Marx would have it, humankind's second nature; they are its nature.[43]

Given such an argument, I have tried to define a role that the institution of literature can play for those more and more aware of humankind's rhetorical situation. Literature, I have argued, can be a rhetorical means to question the adequacy of present constructions of rhetoric. If it is harder to think of the literary text as presenting a utopian vision, it does not follow that it merely re-presents (even with a difference) existing constructions of reality. Instead, according to Iser, it establishes a field of coherent deformation creating conditions that can provoke the imagination to bring forth a different construction of reality. If not a vision of utopian perfection, that different way of constructing reality still retains the capacity to challenge the particular rhetorical constructions of existing public opinion or the *doxa*.

In the Aristotelian tradition, poetry's mimetic function allows it to provide correctives to truths derived from public opinion. The *energia* of an act of mimesis places before the audience's eyes a vivid representation of self-evident truths grounded in a cosmic realm governing human actions. In this tradition, mimesis does not create a stir to the mind through persuasion but through revelation. By *dis-covering* the self-evidence of a truth obscured by historically-constructed ways of seeing the world, mimesis allows the audience to see reality anew. No amount of persuasion can force an audience to see poetic truth. Its self-evidence is either experienced or it is not. This is why New Critics argued that the truth of a poem could not be paraphrased. Translated into ordinary language, poetic truths are paradoxical; quite literally beyond the *doxa*.

For new historicists the New Critical emphasis on paradox leads to an ahistorical account of the literary. To be sure, because it defies the logic of rhetorical debate within the marketplace, the paradoxical nature of poetic truth caused many New Critics to associate it with a religious order, just as Aristotle associated it with a cosmic realm. Paradox, after all, is a favorite trope of religion. Like God, literature's paradoxes seem to be both of this world and above it, making the experience of its truth akin to the experience of God.

No longer believing in a higher realm of self-evident truth but retaining a mimetic model, new historicists have anxiously fit literature's paradoxes back into existing historical constructions of the *doxa*. But in doing so, they deny it the capacity to challenge public opinion. Instead, circulating within and helping to generate a mimetic economy bounded by the *doxa*, it becomes an agent of mimetic socialization. There is, however, a way of linking literature to history that does not deny its ability to generate paradoxes.

Rather than confine literature to a mimetic economy that fits its paradoxes into the *doxa* or a particular historical "logic," we can relate its paradoxical nature to contradictions produced by conflicting deployments of rhetoric within particular societies. To relate its paradoxes to those contradictions is not, however, to establish a relationship of identity. Literary works do not merely reflect or register existing discursive systems. They select various ones, reshaping them for play within their textual fields. Such refashionings may attempt to harmonize the conflicts generated by the various discursive systems at play within the text, but any such effort is doomed to failure. Literature's paradoxes result from that failure. Literary texts generate paradoxes, not because they successfully represent a world of plentitude above history, but because they are constituted by a lack, a space of negativity allowing readers to participate in their discursive play. Such participation does not create a stir to readers' minds by allowing us to recover or re-present the text's original meaning. Instead, by mingling past and present "voices," it can force us to confront what Iser once called the embarrassing predicament of the failure of our understanding.[44]

There are only historical ways of knowing, and yet they are always limited. If the paradoxical experience of the text points to a reality that it is not, that reality is not one outside of history that can be re-presented. Instead it is one demanding historical construction. The text's critical potential does not result from its ability to reveal a foundation of self-evident truth or even, as Althusser would have, the ideology that produces it. Instead, if we can speak of a critical capacity at all, it results from readers being provoked to bring into existence evidence not made available by existing standards of reasonableness.

Even so, taking place within an institutional space marked out for the imagination, literature's critical capacity is clearly limited and quite different from appeals to critical reason. Like appeals to the critical capacity of mimesis, appeals to critical reason depend upon a logic of unmasking. Mimesis provides a critical foundation because it can unmask the inadequacies of historically constructed truths in order to reveal the self-evident truth that they obscure. Similarly, critical reason works to unmask the rhetorical constructions of existing historical institutions in an attempt to locate a foundation in rationality. In contrast, the critical capacity of the literary is not founded on a *logos* that provides the starting point for an activity of unmasking. Instead, generated by a lack, it confronts us with the insufficiency of existing historical constructions, including the one constituting critical reason. Thus the literary can question even the limits of criticism itself. And it is at this point that the institutionally demarcated space of the literary can become a potential strength.

As Blumenberg points out, it is sometimes rational not to demand too much rationality. To demand a rational foundation for all of our institutions would leave us with no institutions at all. "Where an institution exists," Blumenberg argues, "the question of its rational foundation is not, of itself, continually urgent, and the burden of proof always lies on the person who objects to the arrangement that it carries with it." But if it is in our self-interest not to destroy all existing institutions in an effort to achieve an impossible grounding in rationality, it is also in our interest critically to scrutinize those institutions. "If we can speak of a development of human culture taking place over the millenniums, in doing so we imply that the conditions of selection no longer reach and have an effect on man as a physical system to the extent that he has learned to subject his artifacts and instruments, instead of himself, to the process of adaptation. The world we live in is a less Darwinistic world the more theory and technology *are* (objectively transposed) Darwinistic worlds. It is to these, rather than their producer, that the 'survival of the fittest' applies."[45]

It follows that we should even be cautious about dismissing the institutionally constructed activities of critical reason merely because they lack the foundation of rationality that they claim. In such a situation, one function of literature as a critical institution results precisely from its status as play. Realignments and refashionings of institutional structures can be imagined, but without the inevitable costs involved in their historical realization. Instead, the literary provides a space in which possible costs can be played out. If imaginative refashionings provoked by the literary are to have a practical payoff, they will have to be circulated in the marketplace of ideas. Nevertheless, how much it pays for us to retain an institutional space like the literary is suggested by the likelihood that it would take a literary text to provoke us to imagine what it would be like for human cultures to exist without it. Literature as an institution is not immune to the critical scrutiny brought to bear on other institutions. Many critics today claim that as an institution it no longer serves a useful function. In countering such claims, I am not arguing that its function is an unchanging one. To be sure, because of similarities between its present function and the function that Aristotle granted poetry, there is an appearance of continuity within Western history. But there are crucial historical differences. The "literary" may reoccupy the position Aristotle granted poetry, but his mimetic model is no longer adequate to describe its role in a historically contingent world.

As Renaissance new historicists remind us, literature was institutional-ized as part of the larger sphere of the aesthetic during the rise of moder-nity. Contributing to and resulting from the breakup of a closed world turning back on itself in resemblance, it is a realm in which modernity's emphasis on human self-assertion and the possibility of the new can be played out. Boswell, for instance, records Samuel Johnson defining the aesthetic as "everything that enlarges the sphere of human powers."[46] A work like The Tempest poignantly dramatizes how the modern impulse to create brave new worlds carries with it major risks. The very effort to enlarge the sphere of human powers can be linked with the Western drive toward imperialistic control of the world. A question facing the new his-toricism is whether, given those links, it should abandon the attempt to create new worlds. To do so, I have argued, would not be to provide an alternative world, but to abandon us to the structures of domination that already exist.

My description of literature as a rhetorical means to question present constructions of rhetoric is in large part a response to the structures of domination prevalent within societies ruled by representative forms of democratic government. In governments of the people, by the people, and for the people, rhetoric reigns supreme, as ideally rule by law is gen-erated by the free exchange of ideas in the marketplace. The ideal of full representation is, however, never achieved; no particular set of laws rep-resents the interests of the entire society. Forced to confront the failure of representative governments to be truly representative, we also seem un-able to conceive of a more just mode of governing. Wrestling with this dilemma within the United States, Reinhold Niebuhr spoke of the "irony of American history" and Carlos Bulosan the "paradox of America."[47] In representative democracies, a form of rhetoric that explores the limits of rhetorical representation continues to have an important role to play.

In a short book Blumenberg traces the image of shipwrecks observed from Lucretius through European literature up to the Vienna Circle's Otto Neurath, who compared the modern epistemological dilemma with the task seafarers faced in rebuilding their ship at sea. Over the years the distance between gazer and wreckage has narrowed, so that by the twenti-eth century the spectator has no secure point from which to contemplate the disaster. Thrust onto the wreckage at sea with no haven to retreat to, the gazer senses the urgency to rebuild the ship but has to wonder where the foundation and material can be found for a successful reconstruction. Blumenberg's answer is a question: Probably from earlier shipwrecks?[48]

The new historicism's very label implies its commitment to a tradition that has tried to use history to bring about the new. Committed to goals of emancipation, but forced to admit that the acts of production designed to fulfill those goals cannot be controlled by a critical reason guaranteeing their political value in advance, new historicists find themselves in an uncomfortable position. As Brecht remarked to Benjamin, chiding among others Lukács, "Production makes them uncomfortable. You never know where you are with production; production is the unforeseeable."[49]

An important part of my argument has been to stress the need for the new historicism to accept the risks of the unforeseeable. The use of the literary in our histories can, I have argued, add the sense of the unforeseeable, because histories of literature are not merely histories of the way things were. They do not only try to recover things as they were and ask, "Why?" They can also provoke us to ask, "Why not?" That in *Back to Methuselah* George Bernard Shaw put that question in the mouth of the serpent in the Garden of Eden gives a sense of why it is a risky one to ask. That the country in which Robert Kennedy popularized it has given rise to prophecies of the end of history is a measure of the need to keep it alive. A new historicism in literary studies can contribute to that effort. In this book I have tried to suggest ways of doing so.

Notes

Preface

1. Allan Bloom, *The Closing of the American Mind* (New York: Simon and Schuster, 1987), p. 29. Fred Matthews calls attention to the centrality of Bloom's attack on historicism in "The Attack on 'Historicism': Allan Bloom's Indictment of Contemporary American Historical Scholarship," *The American Historical Review* 95 (1990), 429–47. For an example of the political assumptions underlying Bloom's worship of the Founders see Thomas L. Pangle, *The Spirit of Modern Republicanism: The Moral Vision of the American Founders and the Philosophy of Locke* (Chicago: University of Chicago Press, 1988). Of the many responses to Bloom one of the best is Martha Nussbaum, "Undemocratic Virtues," *New York Review of Books* 34 (November 5, 1987), 20–26.

2. See Edward Pechter, "The New Historicism and Its Discontents: Politicizing Renaissance Drama," *PMLA* 102 (1987), 292–303.

3. Catherine Gallagher, "Marxism and the New Historicism," in *The New Historicism*, ed. H. Aram Veeser (New York: Routledge, 1989), p. 47. I agree with the main thrust of Gallagher's argument: that cultural or critical "practices are seldom *intrinsically* either liberatory or oppressive, that they seldom contain their politics as an essence but rather occupy particular historical situations from which they enter into various exchanges, or negotiations, with practices designated 'political'" (p. 37). But I do have disagreements with the narrative she presents about the rise of the new historicism. Admitting that the story is more complicated, she focusses on the new historicism's roots in the New Left and the "spread" of "feminist self-consciousness" among "activists" (p. 42), which "was not the end of politics for many of us, but it was the end of a naive faith in the transparency of our own political consciousness" (p. 43). One difference between the new historicism and its marxist critics, Gallagher implies, is such a "naive faith." Not only do I have trouble with Gallagher's use of the first person plural for this particular narrative, I also have problems with her developmental narrative of the new historicism's superior move from political innocence to experience. The problems with her narrative are highlighted when we compare her admission that much of what she attributes to the new historicism comes from people like "Lukács, Adorno, Althusser, indeed Marx himself" (p. 47) with her description of the political criticism, especially its "left formalism" (p. 39), from which the new historicism supposedly distanced itself. "The Marxist criticism that circulated most widely in those years [the 1960's]," Gallagher tells us, "tended to be the work of Western Marxists, especially Lukács [a Western Marxist?] and members of the Frankfurt school" (p. 39). So the same marxists who share with the new historicists a distrust of a naive "left formalism" were also responsible for it. Perhaps the political naivete that Gallagher remembers, one that believes that a "system of power" could be "*easily* vulnerable to its own contradictions" (p. 42, my emphasis), had less to do with marxism, one strain of which has always emphasized the need for revolution-

ary struggle, and more to do with a political innocence that some 1960s radicals in the United States brought to their adolescent engagements with marxism. Perhaps what Gallagher presents is a fairly typical American narrative about the loss of innocence. Perhaps the political naivete that she speaks to has more to do with its links to a native American tradition than she would allow. At least this is what my narrative in chapter 4 implies.

4. Stephen Greenblatt, "Towards a Poetics of Culture," in *The New Historicism*, p. 2. For another account of the relationship between marxism and the new historicism, see Anne Mack and J. J. Rome, "Marxism, Romanticism, and Postmodernism: An American Case History," *South Atlantic Quarterly* 88 (1989), 605–32.

5. Frederick Crews, "Whose American Renaissance?" *New York Review of Books* 35 (October 27, 1988), 68–69. Ihab Hassan, "Fictions of Power: A Note on Ideological Discourse in the Humanities," *American Literary History* 1 (1989), 131–42. Richard Poirier, "American Manscapes," *London Review of Books* 11 (October 12, 1989), 18–22. For a response to Crews see Donald E. Pease, "New Americanists: Revisionist Interventions into the Canon," *boundary 2* 17 (1990), 1–37.

6. Francis Fukuyama, "The End of History?" *National Interest* 16 (1989), 4.

7. Allan Bloom, "Response," *National Interest* 16 (1989), 19.

8. Poirier, "Manscapes," 19.

9. Richard Poirier, "Hum 6, or Reading before Theory," *Raritan* 9 (1990), 29. Poirier claims to be part of an American tradition of reading running from Emerson through William James and Frost, an alternative to the Modernist one running through T. S. Eliot. But his argument that we can find current critics in Emerson is extremely close to Eliot's notion of tradition. Moreover, one important work that he fails to include in his tradition is Pound's *ABC of Reading*. To do so would complicate the politics of his apolitical claims. As early as *A World Elsewhere: The Place of Style in American Literature* (New York: Oxford University Press, 1966), Poirier wrote, "Emerson in many respects *is* American literature" (p. 69). See also *The Renewal of Literature: Emersonian Reflections* (New York: Random House, 1987). In addition to Poirier, Stanley Cavell has played an important role in using Emerson to export American exceptionalism. See *This New Yet Unapproachable America: Essays after Emerson after Wittgenstein* (Chicago: University of Chicago Press, 1988) and *Conditions Handsome and Unhandsome: The Constitution of Emersonian Perfectionism, The Carus Lectures, 1988* (Chicago: University of Chicago Press, 1990). In a very different way Harold Bloom has also appealed to Emerson to contain the import of Continental theory, referring to him as "Mr. America," *New York Review of Books* (November 22, 1984), 19–24. I am indebted to Rob Wilson for criticism of the quasi-religious nature of the Emersonian revival. See "Literary Vocation as Occupational Idealism: The Example of Emerson's 'American Scholar,'" *Cultural Critique* 15 (Spring 1990), 83–114. The effort to make one figure or one text represent the essence of American literature or the "American ideology," whether it be Emerson or *The Scarlet Letter*, is one thing that I hope to dispute.

10. Steven B. Smith, "Ideology and Interpretation: The Case of Althusser," *Poetics Today* 10 (1989), 484.

11. Perhaps a better chance for leftist intellectuals in this country to effect polit-

ical reform is in Eastern Europe. Recently, for instance, ten Critical Legal Studies scholars were invited to Czechoslovakia and Poland. See Peter Gabel, "Left Meets East," *Tikkun* 5 (May/June 1990), 22–23, 93–95.

12. Walter Benn Michaels, *The Gold Standard and the Logic of Naturalism* (Berkeley: University of California Press, 1987).

13. "Hum 6," 30.

14. Poirier, "Hum 6," 30, 23. If Poirier looks nostalgically at Harvard's Humanities 6 and how literature was taught at all-male Amherst College, the last entry in my acknowledgments points to another way to teach first-year humanities courses. The Humanities Core Course at the University of California, Irvine, also stresses the importance of close reading of texts, but for 1989 to 1991, it selected texts that confronted students in a diverse culture not only with words but also issues that are central to how the culture will define itself for the next generation. The course did not offer clear-cut answers to those issues. Indeed, its rigorous reading pointed to the difficulty of finding simple answers. Nonetheless, at the same time that texts raised complicated questions, students also learned the reading and rhetorical skills that they need to wrestle with those questions. Courses on cultural diversity do not rule out the need for rigorous reading; they demand it.

15. John Barth, "The Literature of Exhaustion," *The Atlantic* 220 (1967), 29–34.

16. Morris Ernst, "Preface" to James Joyce's *Ulysses* (New York: Random House, 1934, reset and corrected 1961), v, vi.

17. *Ulysses*, p.vi.

18. *The United States v. One Book Entitled "Ulysses" by James Joyce: Documents and Commentary—A 50-Year Retrospective*, eds. Michael Moscato and Leslie LeBlanc (Frederick, Maryland: University Publications of America, 1984), p. 264.

19. One of the first to point out the new historicism's need to confront the problem of representativeness was Jean E. Howard, "The New Historicism in Renaissance Studies," *English Literary Renaissance* 16 (1986), 13–43, especially 37–39. Robert Weimann has consistently raised the question of representation and representativeness.

20. By July 1990, faced with problems of capitalistic marketing and distribution, another group of protestors in Leipzig added a new variation. Displaying signs, "There is no people without farmers," they registered the move toward a pluralistic society in which a people is "united" by competing interest groups.

Chapter 1

1. Roy Harvey Pearce, *Historicism Once More* (Princeton: Princeton University Press, 1969); Wesley Morris, *Toward a New Historicism* (Princeton: Princeton University Press, 1972); and Stephen Greenblatt, "Introduction" to "The Forms of Power and the Power of Forms in the Renaissance," *Genre* 13 (1982), 1–6.

2. Herbert Schaedelbach, *Geschichts philosophie nach Hegel: Die Problem des Historismus* (Freiburg/Munich: Karl Aller, 1974).

3. Herbert Lindenberger, "Toward a New History in Literary Studies," *Profession 84*, (1984), 22, n. 4. See Lindenberger's collection, *History in Literature: On Value, Genre, Institutions* (New York: Columbia University Press, 1990).

4. Stephen Greenblatt, "Towards a Poetics of Culture," in *The New Historicism*, ed. H. Aram Veeser (New York: Routledge, 1989), p. 1.

5. Fredric Jameson, "Marxism and Historicism," *New Literary History* 11 (1979), 43.

6. *The New Historicism*, pp. 1–76.

7. Stephen Greenblatt, *Shakespearean Negotiations* (Berkeley: University of California Press, 1988), p. 19.

8. A major casualty of my narrative framework is Jerome McGann and his important work. See *The Romantic Ideology* (Chicago: University of Chicago Press, 1983); *A Critique of Modern Textual Criticism* (Chicago: University of Chicago Press, 1983); *The Beauty of Inflections* (Oxford: Clarendon Press, 1985); and *Social Values and Poetic Acts* (Cambridge: Harvard University Press, 1988). See also *Historical Studies and Literary Criticism*, ed. Jerome J. McGann (Madison: University of Wisconsin Press, 1985). For an excellent short summary of McGann's work see Michael Fischer, "Review," *Blakean Illustrated Quarterly* 23 (1989), 32–39.

9. Michael Warner, "Literary Studies and the History of the Book," *The Book* 12 (1987), 5.

10. Louis Montrose, "The Poetics and Politics of Culture," in *The New Historicism*, p. 20. Montrose used the phrase in an earlier version of this essay, "Renaissance Literary Studies and the Subject of History," *English Literary Renaissance* 16 (1986), 8.

11. Leo Spitzer, *Linguistics and Literary History* (Princeton: Princeton University Press, 1948), p. 32, n. 8. Foucault's translation appears as Leo Spitzer, "Art du Language et Linguistique" in *Etudes de Style* (Paris: Gallimard, 1970), pp. 45–78.

12. Clifford Geertz, *Local Knowledge* (New York: Basic Books, 1983). For a criticism of the new historicist reliance on local knowledge see Vincent P. Pecora, "The Limits of Local Knowledge" in *The New Historicism*, pp. 243–76.

13. Leo Spitzer, "American Advertising Explained as Popular Art," *Essays on English and American Literature* (Princeton: Princeton University Press, 1962), p. 249, n. 3. The essay first appeared in Leo Spitzer, *A Method of Interpreting Literature* (Northampton: Smith College, 1949), pp. 102–49.

14. Spitzer, *Linguistics*, p. 10.

15. *PMLA* 102 (1987), 1028.

16. H. Aram Veeser, "Introduction," *The New Historicism*, p. xi.

17. Herman Melville, *Billy Budd, Sailor*, eds. Harrison Hayford and Merton M. Sealts, Jr. (Chicago: University of Chicago Press, 1962), p. 62.

18. For two very different examples see Stephen L. Collins, "Where's the History in the New Literary Historicism? The Case of the English Renaissance," *Annals of Scholarship* 6 (1989), 231–47 and Christopher P. Wilson, "Containing Multitudes: Realism, Historicism, American Studies," *American Quarterly* 41 (1989), 466–95.

19. A pioneer in this field is, of course, Hayden White, especially his *Metahistory* (Baltimore: Johns Hopkins University Press, 1973). The work of Dominick LaCapra has been equally influential. See, especially, *History and Criticism* (Ith-

aca: Cornell University Press, 1985). In what follows I will discuss White's work only briefly and virtually ignore LaCapra's. Like McGann, they become casualties of my narrative framework, but for different reasons. As I will explain later, my focus is on literary critics moving to history, not vice versa. Nonetheless, I should note that in a recent essay White has some provocative new things to say about historical writing and synecdoche. See "'Figuring the nature of the times deceased': Literary Theory and Historical Writing," in *The Future of Literary Theory*, ed. Ralph Cohen (New York: Routledge, 1989), pp. 38–39 and 414, fn. 32. In this essay White promises to move beyond contradictions that plagued his essays collected in *The Content of the Form* (Baltimore: Johns Hopkins University Press, 1987). These contradictions resulted from his not working out tensions between his previous semiotic assumptions and those resulting from an engagement with Paul Ricoeur's phenomenological hermeneutics. On these tensions see my review "Narrative Questions," *Novel* 22 (1989), 247–49. I still, however, have problems with White's style. Like Warner, he has a tendency to simplify by establishing identities. For instance, in an important rejoinder to those seeking a pure logic of historical writing, White responds, "The 'logic' of historical discourse is 'rhetoric'" (p. 412, fn. 17). This formulation risks turning rhetoric itself into a foundation, as White's insistence on four *basic* rhetorical figures reveals. I would prefer seeing historical discourse resulting from an attempted alliance (but also tensions among) logic, rhetoric, and grammar.

20. I cite just a few examples. Thomas Bender, "Wholes and Parts: The Need for Synthesis in American History," *Journal of American History* 73 (1986), 120–36 and "The New History—Then and Now," *Reviews in American History* 12 (1984), 612–22. Herbert G. Gutman, "The Missing Synthesis: Whatever Happened to History?" *Nation*, (November 21, 1981), 521, 553–54. The renewed call to narrative has been widespread. See, for instance, Lawrence Stone's "The Revival of Narrative: Reflections on a New Old History," *Past and Present* 5 (1979), 3–24 and Bernard Bailyn, "The Challenge of Modern Historiography," *American Historical Review* 87 (1982), 1–24. The most challenging treatment of historical writing and narrative is Paul Ricoeur, *Time and Narrative*, trans. Kathleen McLaughlin and David Palmer (Chicago: University of Chicago Press, 1984). See also David Carr, *Time, Narrative, and History* (Bloomington: Indiana University Press, 1986). Some feminist historians are also concerned about the limits of social history. See Jean Wallach Scott, *Gender and the Politics of History* (New York: Columbia University Press, 1988). Some marxists are too. See, for instance, Eugene Genovese, "The Political Crisis of Social History: A Marxian Perspective," *Journal of Social History* 10 (1976), 205–20.

21. For a debate about the new cultural history see the forum entitled "The Old History and the New," *American Historical Review* 94 (1989), 654–98. Especially interesting is Gertrude Himmelfarb's "Some Reflections on the New History," 661–70. In a recent book Himmelfarb attacked the new social history. See *The New History and the Old* (Cambridge: Harvard University Press, 1987). Confronted with the new cultural history, however, she seems to prefer the social historians. Although I disagree with much that Himmelfarb has to say, I do not want simplistically to dismiss her. See, for instance, her excellent response to

Fukuyama's "End of History" thesis in *National Interest* 16 (1989), 24–26. For a sampling of work by cultural historians see *The New Cultural History*, ed. Lynn Hunt (Berkeley: University of California Press, 1989).

22. Jean-Christophe Agnew, "The Consuming Vision of Henry James," in *The Culture of Consumption*, eds. Richard Wightman Fox and T. J. Jackson Lears (New York: Pantheon, 1983), p. 69. For a general argument for the return of literature in historical studies see David Harlan, "Intellectual History and the Return of Literature," *American Historical Review* 94 (1989), 581–609.

23. Clifford Geertz, "Thick Description: Toward an Interpretive Theory of Culture," *The Interpretations of Culture* (New York: Basic Books, 1973), pp. 3–30.

24. Jean-Christophe Agnew, "History and Anthropology," *The Yale Journal of Criticism* 3 (1990), 29–50.

25. "Preface" to *Essays*, p. vii.

26. Spitzer, *Linguistics*, p. 23.

27. Brook Thomas, *Cross-examinations of Law and Literature* (New York: Cambridge University Press, 1987).

28. Erich Auerbach, "Philology and *Weltliteratur*," trans. Marie and Edward Said, *Centennial Review* 13 (1969).

29. James Baldwin, "Everybody's Protest Novel," *Partisan Review* 16 (1949), 578–85.

30. Auerbach, 16.

31. David Lowenthal, *The Past Is a Foreign Country* (New York: Cambridge University Press, 1985).

32. Jean Baudrillard, *America*, trans. Chris Turner (London: Verso P., 1988). See also Jean-Philippe Mathy, "Out of History: French Readings of Postmodern America," *American Literary History* 2 (1990), 267–98. Greenblatt distances his cultural poetics from poststructuralism as well as marxism, a distancing that also acknowledges a debt. See "Poetics of Culture."

33. Howard Horwitz, "'I Can't Remember': Skepticism, Synthetic Histories, Critical Action," *South Atlantic Quarterly* 87 (1988), 800. Others whose argument depends upon assuming that revisionist historians are arguing for necessary causality are Stanley Fish, Walter Benn Michaels, and Steven Knapp. As I will argue in chapter 4, they betray their pragmatic past by forgetting that more than they realize we live in what Charles S. Peirce called a "world of chance." More often than not, the argument that they oppose is conducted in terms of probability, not absolutes. I deal with Fish and Michaels in depth. Knapp presents his position in "Collective Memory and the Actual Past," *Representations* 26 (1989), 123–49. His argument takes off by asserting that revisionist histories implicitly assume that the "truth about the collective past has a *necessary or intrinsic* relevance to ethical and political action in the present," (124) (my emphasis). Paradoxically, it is *necessary* for Knapp to make that assumption to construct his argument. Horwitz turns me into one of those arguing for a necessary causality. See my brief response to him in "Bringing about Critical Awareness Through History in General Education Literature Courses" in *Reorientations*, eds. Bruce Henricksen and Thais E. Morgan (Urbana: University of Illinois Press, 1990), p. 245 (fn. 5).

34. See Fredric Jameson, "Historicity is neither a representation of the past nor a representation of the future (although its various forms *use* such representations):

it can first and foremost be defined as a perception of the present as history: that is, as a relationship to the present which somehow defamiliarizes it and allows us that distance from immediacy which *we* call historical." "Nostalgia for the Present," *South Altantic Quarterly* 88 (1989), 523.

35. Quoted in Peter Novick, *That Noble Dream: The "Objectivity Question" and the American Historical Profession* (New York: Cambridge University Press, 1988), p. 366.

36. Leonard Tennenhouse, *Power on Display: The Politics of Shakespeare's Genres* (New York: Methuen, 1986).

37. Fredric Jameson, "Criticism in History," in *The Weapons of Criticism*, ed. Norman Rudich (Palo Alto: Ramparts Press, 1976), p. 46.

38. Greenblatt writes that "the rapidity of the shift between modernism and postmodern charted in Jameson's shift [in his mode of criticism] is, to say the least, startling" and complains that "Jameson himself does not directly account for the sudden reversal in his thinking; he suggests rather that it is not his thinking that has changed but capitalism itself" ("Poetics of Culture" p. 13, n.4). But Greenblatt does not note the change in political climate in which Jameson is writing. Nor does he always note the shifts in his own work from totalizing narratives to ones militantly opposed to such totalization. Instead, such shifts are accomplished through subtle revisions in essays between stages of publication. Greenblatt's strategy of revising in order to imply a continuity to his argument is in stark contrast to Jameson's effort to announce historical breaks. It is one way of showing how their different senses of history get embodied in their styles.

39. For occasional complications of my generalizations and for peripheral skirmishes with some figures not properly treated the reader is advised to scrutinize the footnotes with care.

40. A different, but equally sophisticated, example of what Sacvan Bercovitch calls "ideological mimesis" is Bercovitch's *The Office of 'The Scarlet Letter'* (Baltimore: Johns Hopkins University Press, 1991). See also Mary Poovey's "literature reproduces the system that makes it what it is." *Uneven Developments: The Ideological Work of Gender in Mid-Victorian England* (Chicago: University of Chicago Press, 1988), p. 123.

41. Greenblatt, *Shakespearean Negotiations*, p. 6.

Chapter 2

1. See the various essays collected in *The New Historicism*, ed. H. Aram Veeser (New York: Routledge, 1989). Some of the most hostile responses are Edward Pechter, "The New Historicism and Its Discontents: Politicizing Renaissance Drama," *PMLA* 102 (1987), 292–303; Marguerite Waller, "Academic Tootsie: The Denial of Difference and the Difference It Makes," *Diacritics* 17 (1987), 2–20; and Howard Felperin, "Making it 'Neo': The New Historicism and Renaissance Literature," *Textual Practice* 1 (1987), 262–77.

2. Louis Montrose, "Renaissance Literary Studies and the Subject of History," *English Literary Renaissance* 16 (1986), 7.

3. Jean E. Howard, "Historicism in Renaissance Studies," *English Literary Renaissance* 16 (1986), 13–43.

4. See Albrecht Wellmer, *Zur Dialektik von Moderne und Postmoderne* (Frankfurt a.M.: Suhrkamp, 1985); Wolfgang Welsch, *Unsere Postmoderne Moderne* (Weinheim: vclt, Acta Humaniora, 1987); and F. R. Ankersmit, "Historiography and Postmodernism," *History and Theory* 28 (1989), 137–53.

5. Cathy N. Davidson, *Revolution and the Word* (New York: Oxford University Press, 1986), p. vii.

6. Jane Tompkins, *Sensational Designs: The Cultural Work of American Fiction* (New York: Oxford University Press, 1985), p. xiii. (Further references will appear parenthetically in the text.)

7. Turning against her masterful use of polemics in *Sensational Designs*, Tompkins has recently urged us to experiment with new ways of writing critical essays, ones that would renounce the "violence" implied by attacks on other critics. She concludes by citing Amy, played by Grace Kelly in *High Noon*, "I don't care who's right or who's wrong. There has to be some better way to live!" What she does not mention is the final act of violence that Amy brings herself to commit in order to keep alive the possibility of a better world for her and her lover. See "Fighting Words: Unlearning to Write the Critical Essay," *The Georgia Review* 42 (1988), 585–90. Tompkins' colleague Marianna Torgovnick also advocates a new form of critical writing, one that communicates with an audience by exposing herself in her writing, "Experimental Critical Writing," *Profession 90*, 25–27. I remain skeptical about critics' desires to grant their lives representative status.

8. Timothy Brennan, "India, Nationalism, and Other Failures," *South Atlantic Quarterly* 87 (1988), 131–46. For an intelligent critique of the nationalistic appeal in the Irish situation see David Lloyd, *Nationalism and Minor Literature: James Clarence Mangan and the Emergence of Cultural Nationalism* (Berkeley: University of California Press, 1987).

9. There are far too many important examples to list. One collection that speaks directly to the concerns that I raise is *Nation and Narration*, ed. Homi K. Bhabba (New York: Routledge, 1990). In ethnic criticism, the work of Cornel West is exemplary, even if I disagree with him on the uses of pragmatism. See, for instance, "Demystifying the New Black Conservatism," *Praxis International* 7 (1987), 143–51. See also R. Radhakrishnan, "Ethnic Identity and Post-Structuralist Difference," *Cultural Critique* 6 (1987), 199–220. For a less theoretical, but provocative piece, see Kenneth W. Warren, "Delimiting America: The Legacy of DuBois," *American Literary History* 1 (1989), 172–89. In the field of gender studies the journal *Genders* is devoted to exploring the tensions I describe. See also *Feminism/Postmodernism*, ed. Linda J. Nicholson (New York: Routledge, 1990). From a different perspective Lee Edwards criticizes Sandra M. Gilbert and Susan Gubar for accepting the existing framework of Norton Anthologies in their *The Norton Anthology of Literature by Women: The Tradition in English* in *Women's Review of Books* 3 (June 1986), 16–17. The difficulties involved in this mode of criticism are highlighted in the title of an excellent recent book: Mary Poovey, *Uneven Developments: The Ideological Work of Gender in Mid-Victorian England* (Chicago: University of Chicago Press, 1988). The notion of "uneven development" can also be put to repressive uses. See my "Preserving and Keeping Order by Killing Time in *Heart of Darkness*," in *Heart of Darkness*, ed. Ross Murfin (New York: St. Martin's Press, 1989), pp. 237–55. Finally, even the fairly common practice today

of referring to a first and second generation of feminists, with the first employing the sort of narratives of progressive emergence that I describe and the second more sophisticated narratives of interrelatedness, implies its own narrative of the emergence of a more enlightened mode of analysis. For a stimulating engagement between feminism and the new historicism, see Judith Newton, "History as Usual? Feminism and 'The New Historicism,'" *Cultural Critique* 9 (Spring 1988), 87–122. In contrast, Gillian Brown and Lynn Wardley have successfully combined feminist and new historical (proper) analysis.

10. See, for instance, Rhonda Cobham-Sander, "Misgendering the Nation: African Nationalist Fictions and Nuruddin Farah's *Maps*," (forthcoming). A case can also be made for considering James Joyce, who has been so important for poststructuralists, a colonial writer. If the category postcolonial were stretched to the breaking point, all writing of the United States could be considered postcolonial.

11. Jean-Francois Lyotard, *The Postmodern Condition: A Report on Knowledge*, trans. Geoff Bennington and Brian Massumi (Minneapolis: University of Minnesota Press, 1984). Another example of poststructuralist or postmodern attitudes toward narrative is Roland Barthes. One difference between Barthes, the structuralist and the poststructuralist, is his move from structurally analyzing narrative to an increasing distrust of narrative as an ideological imposition upon reality. Although he resists the label "postmodern," Jacques Derrida also expresses his suspicion of narrative. See "The Law of Genre," *Critical Inquiry* 7 (1980), 55–82.

12. Hans Blumenberg, "The Concept of Reality and the Possibility of the Novel," *New Perspectives in German Literary Criticism*, eds. Richard E. Amacher and Victor Lange (Princeton: Princeton University Press, 1979), p. 33.

13. Quoted in Reinhart Koselleck, *Futures Past*, trans. Keith Tribe (Cambridge: MIT Press, 1985), p. 250.

14. Leopold von Ranke, *Geschichten der romanischen und germanischen Volker von 1494 bis 1514*, 2nd ed. (Leipzig: Dunkeru. Humblot, 1874), p. vii.

15. For Benjamin see his "Theses on the Philosophy of History" in *Illuminations*, trans. Harry Zohn (New York: Schocken, 1969). For the relationship of *Historismus* to the philosophy of history see, among others, Herbert Schaedelbach, *Geschichts philosophie nach Hegel: Die Problem des Historismus* (Freiburg/Munich: Karl Aller, 1974); Hans-Georg Gadamer, *Truth and Method* (New York: Crossroad, 1982), pp. 173–234, 460–90; and Hans Robert Jauss, "History of Art and Pragmatic History" in *Toward an Aesthetic of Reception*, trans. Timothy Bahti (Minneapolis: University of Minnesota Press, 1982), pp. 46–75.

16. Quoted in Georg G. Iggers, *The German Conception of History: The National Tradition of Historical Thought from Herder to the Present* (Middletown: Wesleyan University Press, 1968), p. 175.

17. Paul de Man, "Criticism and Crisis," in *Blindness and Insight*, 2nd ed., revised (Minneapolis: University of Minnesota Press, 1983), pp. 15, 16.

18. Wendy Steiner, "Collage or Miracle: Historicism in a Deconstructed World," in *Reconstructing American Literary History*, ed. Sacvan Bercovitch (Cambridge: Harvard University Press, 1985). Note also that J. Hillis Miller's turn to deconstruction followed an engagement with what he saw as the dead end of historicism. In 1963 Miller wrote, "Historicism does not mean merely an aware-

ness of the contradictory diversity of cultures and attitudes. The ancient world had that. The modern historical sense means rather the loss of faith in the possibility of ever discovering the right and true culture, the right and true philosophy or religion." *The Disappearance of God* (Cambridge: Harvard University Press, 1963), p. 10.

19. David Hackett Fischer, *Historians' Fallacies* (New York: Harper and Row, 1970), p. 156.

20. Werner Sollors, "A Critique of Pure Pluralism," in *Reconstructing American Literary History*, pp. 3, 19.

21. Stephen Greenblatt, "Introduction" to "The Forms of Power and the Power of Forms in the Renaissance," *Genre* 15 (1982), 5.

22. Montrose, 12.

23. Walter Cohen, "Political Criticism of Shakespeare" in *Shakespeare Reproduced: The Text in History and Ideology*, ed. Jean E. Howard and Marion F. O'Connor (London: Methuen, 1987), p. 34.

24. Stephen Greenblatt, "Filthy Rites," *Daedalus* 111 (1982), 8, 9.

25. Howard and O'Connor, p. 12.

26. Cohen, pp. 33–34.

27. Stephen Greenblatt, "Marginal Notes," *Village Voice Literary Supplement* (October 1988), 155.

28. Joseph Litvak, "Back to the Future: A Review-Article on the New Historicism, Deconstruction, and Nineteenth-Century Fiction," *Texas Studies in Literature and Language* 30 (1988), 127. The phrase is one of Litvak's section titles.

29. Leo Spitzer, *Linguistics and Literary History: Essays in Stylistics* (Princeton, Princeton University Press, 1948), pp. 24, 23, 24.

30. Erich Auerbach, *Mimesis: The Representation of Reality in Western Literature*, trans. Willard P. Trask (Princeton, Princeton University Press, 1953), p. 552.

31. Spitzer, p. 24.

32. Auerbach, p. 552.

33. Alan Liu, "The Power of Formalism: The New Historicism," *English Literary History* 56 (1989), 770, n. 92. Liu's provocative and entertaining essay stresses new historicism proper's formalism by examining its spatial metaphors. In contrast, I concentrate on its modes of temporality. But our two projects complement one another, since one of my arguments is that new historicists, like Greenblatt and Michaels, too often spatialize time. Liu's essay appeared too late for me fully to take it into account. For another charge that the new historicism proper remains formalistic, see Carolyn Porter, "Are We Being Historical Yet?" *South Atlantic Quarterly* 87 (1988), 743–86.

34. Cohen, p. 35.

35. "Introduction," *Representing the Renaissance*, ed. Stephen Greenblatt (Berkeley: University of California Press, 1988), p. xiii.

36. Among many see Mark Poster, *Foucault, Marxism, and History* (New York: Basil Blackwell, 1985) (especially chapter 5); Gilles Deleuze, *Foucault*, trans. Seán Hand (Minneapolis: University of Minnesota Press, 1988); Paul Bové, *Intellectuals in Power* (New York: Columbia University Press, 1986) and his foreword to Deleuze's *Foucault*, "The Problematics of Style," pp. v–xxxv.

37. Greenblatt, "Forms of Power," 6.

38. Cohen, p. 35.

39. Bové, "The Problematics of Style," p. xxxv.

40. Bové, *Intellectuals in Power*, p. 310.

41. An example of Bové's pleading for other critics to play fair is his criticism of Charles Taylor's reading of Foucault. Taylor's reading, Bové argues, "follows the path taken recently by powerful thinkers such as Habermas and Nancy Fraser in trying to oblige Foucault to answer questions about issues raised within the very system of discourse that, as Foucault himself put it once, come from the very 'mind set' he was trying to critique" (p. ix). Bové seems to imply that because Foucault has criticized their "mind set" Taylor and others should recognize the validity of his critique. But a Foucauldian critique does not necessarily mean that a particular mind set will disappear. On the contrary, if, as Bové argues, such a mind set is necessary for success, it is very likely that it will be around for awhile. Foucault is said to have taught us that the will to power is productive, not merely repressive. But the effectiveness of Bové's brand of Foucauldian politics seems to depend upon a utopian moment when people will will not to will.

In fact, Bové, despite his attacks on the "regime of truth" (p. xv), seems to maintain at least part of the mind set he deplores when he demands that Taylor demonstrate more "critical sympathy" in order to "begin his critique by trying to 'understand' Foucault in his own terms" (p. xvii). Apparently Bové has discovered a "truth" in Foucault that Taylor has missed. Bové may be right about Taylor's misreading, but only because he has read Foucault more accurately. (References from "The Problematics of Style.")

42. I acknowledge here a debt to a seminar paper by Steve Cohen.

43. William Spanos, "Interview," *Critical Texts* 3 (1985), 22.

44. The need of "minority theories" to rethink modernism is the point of Nancy Hartsack's, "Rethinking Modernism: Minority vs. Majority Theories," *Cultural Critique* 7 (Fall 1987), 187–206. See also Sabina Louibond, "Feminism and Postmodernism," *New Left Review* 178 (1989), 5–28.

45. E. P. Thompson, *The Making of the English Working Class* (New York: Pantheon Books, 1963).

Chapter 3

1. *'Race,' Writing and Difference*, ed. Henry Louis Gates, Jr. (Chicago: University of Chicago Press, 1987), p. 104. (Future references will appear parenthetically in the text.) For a fascinating account of the etymology of "race," one intended to refute Hitler's biological racism, see Leo Spitzer, "Race," in *Essays in Historical Semantics* (New York: Russell and Russell, 1948), pp. 147–69.

2. Hans Blumenberg, *Work on Myth*, trans. Robert Wallace (Cambridge: MIT Press, 1985), p. 19.

3. Quoted in *The Thin Disguise: "Plessy v. Ferguson,"* ed. Otto H. Olsen (New York: Humanities Press, 1967), p. 117.

4. Ernst Bloch, "Nonsynchronism and Dialectics," *New German Critique* 11 (1977), 22–38.

5. See Reinhart Koselleck, *Futures Past*, trans. Keith Tribe (Cambridge: MIT

Press, 1985), pp. 246–59. See also chapter 2, fn. 9 for a brief discussion of "uneven development."

6. William Spanos, "Interview," *Critical Texts* 3 (1985), 22.

7. Stephen Greenblatt, "Filthy Rites," *Daedalus* III (1982), 8–9. In a recent article Boris Groys argued that Bakhtin's use of Nietzschean structures of Dionysian carnival and Apollonian order helped to justify the carnivalesque massacres of Stalinism in the name of order. This argument seems historically inaccurate. Nonetheless, it does remind us that the carnivalesque is not inherently liberating. "Grausamer Karneval," *Frankfurter Allgemeine Zeitung*, (June 21, 1989), p. N.3.

8. Sacvan Bercovitch, *The American Jeremiad* (Madison: University of Wisconsin Press, 1979).

9. An early work by a member of *Representations'* editorial board does directly confront the problem of pluralism. Michael Paul Rogin, *The Intellectuals and McCarthy: The Radical Spector* (Cambridge: MIT Press, 1967).

10. Erich Auerbach, "Philology and *Weltliteratur*," trans. Edward and Marie Said, *Centennial Review* 13 (1969), 7. One of the most interesting recent interpretations of Auerbach is Paul Bové's in *Intellectuals in Power: A Genealogy of Critical Humanism* (New York: Columbia University Press, 1986). After devoting two chapters to Auerbach, Bové argues that in exhausting humanistic possibilities he points in the direction of Said and Foucault by indicating "at least two necessities for contemporary scholarship: to write discontinuous history as engaged history of the present and to bring the skills of rational, scholarly inquiry to bear on the present social and political conditions out of which all cultural and intellectual discourse emerges" (p. 208). I agree that Auerbach indicates these two needs so important for a new historicism. I would counter, however, that in doing so he does not illustrate the exhaustion of humanism, but its potential viability—as in the work of Said himself. For further differences with Bové and his discipleship to a certain version of Foucault, see chapter 2, n. 40.

11. Ernst Robert Curtius, *European Literature and the Latin Middle Ages*, trans. Willard P. Trask (New York: Pantheon, 1953), p. x.

12. Erich Auerbach, *Literary Language and Its Public in Late Latin Antiquity and in the Middle Ages*, trans. Ralph Mannheim (New York: Pantheon, 1965), p. 22.

13. Auerbach, "*Weltliteratur*," 17.

14. Erich Auerbach, *Mimesis: The Representation of Reality in Western Literature*, trans. Willard P. Trask (Princeton: Princeton University Press, 1953), p. 552.

15. Geoffrey Gorer, *The American People* (New York: Norton, 1948, rev. 1964), p. 223.

16. Auerbach, "*Weltliteratur*," 16.

17. Raymond Williams, *The Country and the City* (New York: Oxford University Press, 1973).

18. Jean E. Howard, "The New Historicism in Renaissance Studies," *English Literary Renaissance* 16 (1986), 13–43.

19. René Wellek, "Auerbach's Special Realism," *Kenyon Review* 16 (1954), 305.

20. Albert J. von Frank, "Review," *Nineteenth-Century Literature* 43 (1989), 530.

21. Taylor Branch, *Parting the Waters: America in the King Years 1954–63* (New York: Simon and Schuster, 1988), pp. xii, xii, xi.

22. Stephen Greenblatt, *Renaissance Self-Fashioning* (Chicago: University of Chicago Press, 1980), p. 227–28; Edward W. Said, *Orientalism* (New York: Random House, 1978); and Tzetan Todorov, *The Conquest of America: The Question of the Other*, trans. Richard Howard (New York: Harper and Row, 1984).

23. Jacques Derrida, "Structure, Sign, and Play in the Discourse of the Human Sciences," in *Writing and Difference*, trans. Alan Bass (Chicago: University of Chicago Press, 1982), pp. 292–93.

24. Hans Blumenberg, *The Legitimacy of the Modern Age*, trans. Robert Wallace (Cambridge: MIT Press, 1983), p. 48. (Future references will appear parenthetically in the text.)

25. Hans Blumenberg, "An Anthropological Approach to the Contemporary Significance of Rhetoric," in *After Philosophy*, eds. Kenneth Baynes, James Bohman, and Thomas McCarthy (Cambridge: MIT Press, 1988), pp. 451–52.

26. Blumenberg, "Rhetoric," p. 452.

27. Herbert Hrachovec, "Learning Not to Learn from History," *Raritan* 4 (1984), 113. This distinction should distance Blumenberg somewhat from the debate between Jürgen Habermas and Jean-Francois Lyotard about modernism and postmodernism, although the English title of his book might lead some to think that it is an intervention into that debate. But Blumenberg's book, the first version of which appeared in 1966, does not directly confront the postmodernists' argument. Furthermore, some confusion can arise from translation. "Modern age" is the English for the German "Neuzeit." Of course, "Neuzeit" is a modern concept. Blumenberg's position in this debate would be complex. On the one hand, as I note, he has much in common with poststructuralism's criticism of what it considers to be modernity. On the other, he might agree with Habermas in seeing the impulse toward modernity as an incomplete project, not one that has been completely discredited. Although there are similarities between Habermas's and Blumenberg's positions, Blumenberg clearly distances himself from the sort of ideological critique that Habermas conducts. This distancing has led Richard Rorty to call Blumenberg a liberal. But then Rorty tries to turn most philosophers whom he admires into liberals. "Against Belatedness," *London Review of Books*, (June 16–July 6, 1983), 3–5 and "The Historiography of Philosophy: Four Genres," in *Philosophy in History*, eds. Richard Rorty, J. B. Scheewind, and Quentin Skinner (New York: Cambridge University Press, 1984), pp. 49–75. Hrachovec does a good job of explaining why Rorty is wrong. I should also add one more connection between Blumenberg and thinkers influenced by the Frankfurt school, even if it is an indirect one. One of the best qualifications of both Habermas's and Theodor Adorno's positions is Albrecht Wellmer's *Zur Dialektik von Moderne und Postmoderne* (Frankfurt a.M.: Suhrkamp, 1985). As a corrective to Adorno's aesthetic Wellmer cites the work of Gabriele Schwab. Schwab's work, in turn, is indebted to Blumenberg through the intermediary of Wolfgang Iser.

28. One reservation that I have with Blumenberg is his seeming assent in *Work on Myth* to a "Darwinism" of cultural products that implies that those myths that survive are ones that have demonstrated their usefulness to humankind. His argument that humankind advances when it is able to "subject his artifacts and instru-

ments, instead of himself, to the process of adaptation" (p. 165) is extremely provocative. But it can also lead to an understanding of myth as a history of the victors.

29. Here I take issue with Martin Jay's interpretation of Blumenberg. See his
"Review Essay," *History and Theory* 24 (1985), 183–96.

30. Blumenberg, *Work on Myth*, p. 163.

31. Jacques Derrida, "How to Avoid Speaking: Denials," in *Languages of the
Unsayable*, eds. Sanford Budick and Wolfgang Iser (New York: Columbia University Press, 1989), pp. 3–70.

32. Paul de Man, "Semiology and Rhetoric," in *Allegories of Reading* (New
Haven: Yale University Press, 1979), pp. 3, 19.

33. Nancy Fraser, "Foucault's Body Language: A Post-Humanist Political Rhetoric?" *Salmagundi* 61 (1983), 59.

34. Michel Foucault, "Nietzsche, Genealogy, History," in *Language, Counter-
Memory, Practice*, trans. Donald F. Bouchard and Sherry Simon (Ithaca: Cornell
University Press, 1977), p. 163.

Chapter 4

1. George Santayana, "Dewey's Naturalistic Metaphysics," in *Obiter Scripta*
(New York: Scribner's, 1936), pp. 237–38. Louis O. Mink's dissertation, "Knowledge of the Past," confirms the argument, developed in this chapter, that pragmatism faces special problems when confronted with historical knowledge. See "Editor's Introduction" to Louis O. Mink, *Historical Understanding*, eds. Brian Fay,
Eugene O. Golob, and Richard Vann (Ithaca: Cornell University Press, 1987), pp.
4, 9.

2. Jane Tompkins, "'Indians': Textualism, Morality, and the Problem of History," *Critical Inquiry* 13 (1986), 118. For the argument as first formulated see
Steven Knapp and Walter Benn Michaels, "Against Theory," *Critical Inquiry* 8
(1982), 723–42. Since then a book has been devoted to the debate, Knapp and
Michaels have added a sequel to their argument, and various others have expanded upon or refined the argument. Obviously, the "Against Theory" position
has not stopped the practice of theory as Knapp and Michaels call for but led to a
proliferation of theoretical debates. This irony is not lost on Stanley Fish who
merely classifies theory as one more practice that will be extended like any other
practice. Fish in turn has made a practice of repeating his argument again and
again. See *Doing What Comes Naturally* (Durham: Duke University Press, 1989).
For a more developed response to Fish than I can offer here see my "Stanley Fish
and the Uses of Baseball: The Return of the Natural," *Yale Journal of Law and the
Humanities* 2 (1990), 59–88.

3. Frank Lentricchia, *Ariel and the Police* (Madison: University of Wisconsin
Press, 1988) and Cornel West, *The American Evasion of Philosophy: A Genealogy
of Pragmatism* (Madison: University of Wisconsin Press, 1989).

4. For a historian's appeal to "pragmatic truth" as a middle ground between
objectivity and relativism see James T. Kloppenberg's review of Peter Novick's
*That Noble Dream: The "Objectivity Question" and the American Historical Pro-
fession* (New York: Cambridge University Press, 1988): "Objectivity and Historicism: A Century of American Historical Writing," *The American Historical Review*

94 (1989), 1011–30. Kloppenberg claims that the best American histories of this century have been the product of a "pragmatic hermeneutics" that offers "useful" but "tentative" knowledge. Kloppenberg offers a reasonable and measured appeal to escape the constraining and simplistic opposition of objectivity and relativism. His problem comes, however, in fitting poststructuralism into the very opposition that he would escape. The poststructuralist challenge to historians is not, as is commonly assumed, an attack on objectivity by declaring all texts indeterminant. Instead, it is a questioning of the sense of temporal continuity at the heart of pragmatism as well as traditional historicism and hermeneutics. Kloppenberg's own pragmatic hermeneutics is a perfect example of the persistence of that sense of continuity and an inability of most historians to imagine an alternative to it without raising the specter of relativism.

5. Cushing Strout, *The Pragmatic Revolt in American History: Carl Becker and Charles Beard* (Ithaca: Cornell University Press, 1958). I focus on the new historicism's debt to pragmatism in terms of historiography. Another way to trace that debt would be through Clifford Geertz to the social science school of "symbolic interaction" and its debt to John Dewey and George Herbert Mead. See, for instance, *Symbolic Interaction and Cultural Studies*, eds. Howard S. Becker and Michael M. McCall (Chicago: University of Chicago Press, 1990). In a letter Stephen Greenblatt acknowledged to me his early debt to Mead. For a different effort to locate the new historicism in a context of the United States that does not link it to pragmatism see Don E. Wayne, "Power, Politics, and the Shakespearean Text: Recent Criticism in England and the United States," in *Shakespeare Reproduced: The Text in History and Ideology*, eds. Jean E. Howard and Marion F. O'Connor (New York: Methuen, 1987), pp. 47–67.

6. Walter Cohen, "Political Criticism of Shakespeare," in *Shakespeare Reproduced*, p. 21. For Montrose's argument see, "Renaissance Literary Studies and the Subject of History," *English Literary Renaissance* 16 (1986), 7.

7. Van Wyck Brooks, "On Creating a Usable Past," *The Dial* 64 (1918), 337–41.

8. See Myra Jehlen, *American Incarnation: The Individual, the Nation and the Continent* (Cambridge: Harvard University Press, 1986).

9. See Novick, *That Noble*, pp. 87–88.

10. William James, "Pragmatism's Conception of Truth," *Essays in Pragmatism* (New York: Hafner, 1968), p. 172. (Future references will appear parenthetically in the text.)

11. John Dewey, "The Historical Background of Corporate Legal Personality," *Yale Law Journal* 35 (1926), 660–61.

12. Oliver Wendell Holmes, Jr., Southern Pacific R. R. Co. v. Jensen 244 US 205 at 222 (1917), dissenting.

13. Oliver Wendell Holmes, Jr., "Law in Science and Science in Law," *Harvard Law Review* 12 (1898–99), 443. (Future references appear parenthetically in the text.) For Holmes's most famous account of the law see *The Common Law*, ed. Mark DeWolfe Howe (Cambridge: Harvard University Press [Belknap Press], 1963). *The Common Law* first appeared in 1881.

14. Oliver Wendell Holmes, Jr., Abrams v. United States 250 US 616 at 630 (1919), dissenting.

15. I should make clear what I am *not* arguing. By linking the pragmatic defini-

tion of truth with an implied mode of political governance, I am not arguing that what I call pragmatic progressivism constitutes the entire tradition of liberal democratic thought within the United States, not even its progressive wing. That tradition is extremely complicated and has included various attacks on pragmatic notions. Although many of those doing the attacking have more pragmatic assumptions than they would admit, it is not my purpose to provide a history of political thought within the United States. Instead, I am focusing on a particular tradition that helps to explain the rise of a new historicism in this country. Although I too am indebted to that tradition, I am interested in ascertaining its limits. One argument that I will not make against it, however, is the one linking the pragmatic definition of truth to totalitarianism. This argument was popular as fascism rose, and it contributed to pragmatism's decline in favor during and immediately after World War II. I do not want to deny the theoretical possibility that, transplanted into a very different cultural and historical situation, the pragmatic definition of truth could serve a variety of purposes. But to compare Holmes to Hitler as some did is completely to ignore the concrete historical situations in which both operated. (See Ben Palmer, "Hobbes, Holmes and Hitler," *American Bar Association* 31 (1945), 569. My interest is in those features in pragmatic thought that contribute to its present revival—and limits.

16. Oliver Wendell Holmes, Jr., Lochner v. New York 198 US 45 at 76 (1905), dissenting.

17. Robert W. Gordon, "Legal Thought and Legal Practice in the Age of American Enterprise, 1870–1920," in *Professions and Professional Ideologies in America*, ed. Gerald L. Geison (Chapel Hill: University of North Carolina Press, 1983), p. 96.

18. Thomas Haskell, *The Emergence of Professional Social Science* (Urbana: University of Illinois Press, 1977), pp. 67–68.

19. John Dewey, "Logical Method and the Law," *Cornell Law Quarterly* 10 (1924), 24.

20. James Harvey Robinson, *The New History: Essays Illustrating the Modern Historical Outlook* (New York: Macmillan, 1912), pp. 22, 23. (Future references will appear parenthetically in the text.) On Robinson see Luther V. Hendricks, *James Harvey Robinson: Teacher of History* (New York: Columbia University Press, 1946); John Braeman, "What is the Good of History? The Case of James Harvey Robinson," *Amerikastudien* 30 (1985), 75–89; Morton White, *Social Thought in America: The Revolt Against Formalism* (Boston: Beacon, 1957); John Higham, *History: The Development of Historical Studies in the United States* (Princeton: Princeton University Press, 1965); Novick; Clarence Walworth Alvord, "The New History," *The Nation* 94 (1912), 457–59; Carl Becker, "The New History," *The Dial* 13 (1912), 19–22; Lewis Mumford, "The New History," *The New Republic* 50 (1927), 338–39; Thomas Bender, "The New History—Then and Now," *Reviews in American History* 12 (1984), 612–22. For a comparison with the *Annales* group of France see Ernst Breisach, "Two New Histories: An Exploratory Comparison," *At the Nexus of Philosophy and History*, ed. Bernard P. Dauenhauer (Athens: University of Georgia Press, 1987), pp. 138–56.

21. Charles A. Beard and Mary R. Beard, *The Rise of American Civilization* (New York: Macmillan, 1927), v. 1, p. 443.

22. John Dewey, *Logic: The Theory of Inquiry* (New York: Holt, 1938), pp. 238–39.

23. Quoted in Novick, pp. 130, 131.

24. Karl Heussi, *Die Krisis des Historismus* (Tübingen: Mohr, 1932).

25. Charles A. Beard, "Written History as an Act of Faith," *American Historical Review* 39 (1934), 219–29; and Carl Becker "Every Man His Own Historian" in *Everyman His Own Historian: Essays on History and Politics* (New York: F. S. Crofts, 1935), pp. 233–55.

26. Charles A. Beard, *The Discussion of Human Affairs* (New York: Macmillan, 1936), p. 79. Similarly, Perry Miller quotes Holmes, "History has to be rewritten because history is the selection of those threads of causes or antecedents that we are interested in." *Jonathan Edwards* (New York: William Sloane, 1949), p. 310.

27. Henry Adams, *The Education of Henry Adams* (Boston: Houghton Mifflin, 1973), p. 410.

28. Robinson may well have been influenced by a letter that Adams circulated to history professors in 1909. For a copy of the letter see Adams, pp. 515–18.

29. Charles A. Beard, *An Economic Interpretation of the Constitution of the United States* (New York: Macmillan, 1913), p. 4.

30. Nicholas St. John Green, "Proximate and Remote Cause," *American Law Review* 4 (1870), 201. See Morton J. Horwitz, "The Doctrine of Objective Causation," in *The Politics of Law*, ed. David Kairys (New York: Pantheon Books, 1982), pp. 201–13.

31. Quoted in Novick, pp. 387–88.

32. Beard and Beard, v. 1, p. 738.

33. Meinecke quoted in Georg G. Iggers, *The German Conception of History: The National Tradition of Historical Thought from Herden to the Present* (Middletown: Wesleyan University Press, 1968), p. 175.

34. René Wellek, "Van Wyck Brooks and a National Literature," *American Prefaces* 7 (1942), 306.

35. David Hackett Fischer, *Historians' Fallacies* (New York: Harper and Row, 1970), p. 156.

36. David W. Noble, *The End of American History* (Minneapolis: University of Minnesota Press, 1985).

37. Sacvan Bercovitch, *The American Jeremiad* (Madison: University of Wisconsin Press, 1979).

38. Quoted in Novick, p. 89.

39. Quoted in Strout, p. 84.

40. Carl Becker, "Some Aspects of the Influence of Social Problems and Ideas upon the Study and Writing of History," *American Journal of Sociology* 18 (1912–13), 642.

41. Charles S. Peirce quoted in *Classical American Philosophers*, ed. Max H. Fisch (Englewood Cliffs: Prentice-Hall, 1951), p. 26.

42. Stanley Fish, "Change," *South Atlantic Quarterly* 86 (1987), 424, 433, 432.

43. Walter Benjamin, *Gesammelte Schriften*, 5 vols., eds. Rolf Tiedemann and Herman Schweppenhäuser (Frankfurt a. M.: Suhrkamp, 1972), I, pp. 2, 667.

44. Fish, "Change," 423–44. The advantage of the metaphor of extension is that it combats the notion that we can have *complete* breaks with the past. So long as we

emphasize the tensions contained in extension, it can be a useful metaphor to retain. For more on this point see my, "The Uses of Baseball."

45. Leopold von Ranke, *Über die Epochen der neueren Geschichte* (Leipzig: Dunker Humblot, 1888) pp. 7, 8.

46. Stanley Fish, "Commentary: The Young and the Restless," in *The New Historicism*, ed. H. Aram Veeser (New York: Routledge, 1989), p. 313.

47. For an example, consider Howard Horwitz's claim that "critical historicism does not (because no one can) employ a new cognitive method." Horwitz cannot prove his parenthetical claim by an appeal to history, since the very contingency of history that elsewhere he evokes implies that at some time in the future new cognitive methods might be possible. Instead, he tries to prove it by an appeal to logic, a logic that denies possibilities within history. Quoted in "'I Can't Remember': Skepticism, Synthetic Histories, Critical Action," *South Atlantic Quarterly* 87 (1988), 800.

48. Steven Mailloux, *Rhetorical Power* (Ithaca: Cornell University Press, 1989), p. 169, n. 28.

49. In his 1912 review Carl Becker raised a crucial problem for those who believe in progress. "A profound faith in progress we have; a world of light talk about it,—that we have also; but the truth is we never know what form progress will take until after the event" ("The New History," 21).

50. Van Wyck Brooks, "Our Awakeners," *Seven Arts* 2 (1917), 235–48. Although granting pragmatists a "vein of poetry" ("golden" in James, "silver" in Dewey), Brooks concluded that in making them "students of the existing fact" their training ultimately rendered the vein "too thin" to qualify them as our awakeners. See also fn. 69 in this chapter.

51. See Stephen Fuller, "Playing Without a Full Deck: Scientific Realism and the Cognitive Limits of Legal Theory," *Yale Law Journal* 97 (1988), 549–80.

52. Paul de Man, "Lyric and Modernity," in *Blindness and Insight*, 2nd ed., revised (Minneapolis: University of Minnesota Press, 1983), p. 183.

53. Paul de Man, "Literary History and Literary Modernity," in *Blindness and Insight*, p. 151.

54. For a criticism of Robinson on similar points see David Gross, "'The New History': A Note of Reappraisal," *History and Theory* 13 (1974), 53–58.

55. Michel Foucault, "Nietzsche, Genealogy, History," in *Language, Counter-Memory, Practice*, trans. Donald F. Bouchard and Sherry Simon (Ithaca: Cornell University Press, 1977), p. 144.

56. Jacques Derrida, "Sending: On Representation," *Social Research* 49 (1982), 325. Also see Andrew Parker, "Futures for Marxism: An Appreciation of Althusser," *Diacritics* 15 (1985), 57–72.

57. William Dean Howells, *A Hazard of New Fortunes* (1890 repr., Bloomington: Indiana University Press, 1976), p. 437.

58. Even the argument that Fish most likes to refute—the one that theoretical inquiry leads to "changes in assumptions, institutions, and practice"—does not claim that theory guarantees such change. It merely claims that the *probability* of such change is higher with theoretical inquiry than without it. Since Fish himself admits that "change, in the form of the reconsideration of received opinion, would be prompted by a suggestion that came from a source assumed in advance to be,

if not authoritative, at least weighty," it seems to follow from his own argument that theory could be recognized as such a source and thus more likely to produce such change than other socially constructed sources. Quotations from "Change," 437, 429.

59. Peirce, in *Classical American Philosophers*, p. 37.

60. George Santayana, "Dewey's Naturalistic Metaphysics," pp. 237–38. Santayana once complained that Royce insisted that he write a dissertation on Lotze rather than Hegel. But his criticism of Dewey's pragmatism is clearly indebted to Lotze.

61. Walter Benjamin, "Theses on the Philosophy of History" in *Illuminations*, trans. Harry Zohn (New York: Schocken, 1969), p. 262. (Future references will appear parenthetically in the text.)

62. Hermann Lotze, *Mikrokosmus: Ideen zur Naturgeschichte und Geschichte der Menschheit* (Leipzig: Meiner, 1909), p. 50. I am strongly indebted to H. D. Kittsteiner, "Walter Benjamin's Historicism," *New German Critique* 39 (1986), 179–215.

63. Lotze, p. 51.

64. Benjamin, *Gesammelte Schriften*, v. 5, p. 573.

65. E. P. Thompson, *The Poverty of Theory and Other Essays* (New York: Monthly Review Press, 1978), p. 42.

66. Kittsteiner, 187–88. For a poignant example of how the editor of one popular reconstructionist anthology remains lodged within the progressive sense of history, consider Paul Lauter's justification for excluding selections by pro-slavery antebellum Southern writers. "The victors, it is said, write history; perhaps, too, they establish the terms on which culture continues." As Lauter should know, the victors on questions of race have not always been on his side. *The Heath Anthology of American Literature*, v. 1, ed. Paul Lauter (Lexington, Mass.: D.C. Heath and Co., 1990), p. 1194.

67. Karl Marx and Friedrich Engels, *Werke* (Berlin: Dietz, 1957–72), v. 8, pp. 115–17.

68. Terry Eagleton, "History, Narrative, and Marxism," in *Reading Narrative*, ed. James Phelan (Columbus: Ohio State University Press, 1989), p. 279. For another attempt to articulate a Benjaminian narrative that also contrasts Benjamin to the future-oriented sense of history embodied both in pragmatism and Marx's beginning of *The Eighteenth Brumaire* see David Luban, "Difference Made Legal: The Court and Dr. King," *Michigan Law Review* 87 (1989), 2152–2224, esp. 2218–24.

69. In *Rhetorical Power* Mailloux makes a typical neopragmatic move when, conducting a reception study, he argues that "the distinction between the literary and extraliterary *completely* breaks down" (p. 118, my emphasis). Giles Gunn agrees with me that neopragmatists reduce the possibilities of art. For instance: "Rorty is compelled to reduce severely the heuristic value of art and particularly the novel to a largely diagnostic function." Gunn argues that Dewey and James did not share this fault. I partially agree but still maintain that pragmatic assumptions limited even their ability to wrestle with the complexities of art's social function. "Rorty's *Novum Organum*," *Raritan* 10 (1990), 80–103, quotation from 103. See fn. 50 in this chapter.

70. Horwitz, "I Can't Remember," 798.

71. Fish, "Commentary," p. 313. To cite just one example of a historian who would dispute Fish's and Horwitz's assumption that the practice of history has always been concerned with determining what happened, Becker, in his review of Robinson notes that "it was about the middle of the eighteenth century that the 'Philosophers' announced a 'new history,' a history which was to tell the average man, not what actually happened, but what he ought to think about what had happened, and especially what might happen," "The New History," 19.

72. Fish, "Commentary," p. 312.

Chapter 5

1. *The Gold Standard and the Logic of Naturalism* (Berkeley: University of California Press, 1987). Future references will appear parenthetically in the text.

2. Stephen Greenblatt, "Introduction" to "The Forms of Power and the Power of Forms in the Renaissance," *Genre* 15 (1982), 5.

3. "*Walden's* False Bottoms," *Glyph* 1 (1977), 132–50.

4. "The Interpreter's Self: Peirce on the Cartesian 'Subject,'" *Georgia Review* 31 (1977), 383–402. (Future references will appear parenthetically in the text.)

5. Stanley E. Fish, "With Compliments of the Author: Reflections on Austin and Derrida," *Critical Inquiry* 8 (1982), 693–721.

6. See Jacques Derrida's comment, "If the word 'history' did not in and of itself convey the motif of a final repression of difference, one could say that only differences can be 'historical' from the outset and in each of their aspects." *Margins of Philosophy*, trans. Alan Bass (Chicago: University of Chicago Press, 1982), p. 11.

7. Jacques Derrida, *Writing and Difference*, trans. Alan Bass (Chicago: University of Chicago Press, 1978), pp. 292–93.

8. Jonathan Arac also notices affinities between the "Yale critics" and the jeremiad. *Critical Genealogies* (New York: Columbia University Press, 1987), p. 32.

9. Ernst Bloch, "Nonsynchronism and the Obligation to Its Dialectics," *New German Critique* 11 (1977), 22–38.

10. See Jean B. Quandt, *From the Small Town to the Great Community* (New Brunswick: Rutgers University Press, 1970) and Robert H. Wiebe, *The Search for Order* (New York: Hill and Wang, 1967).

11. E. P. Thompson, *The Poverty of Theory and Other Essays* (New York: Monthly Review Press, 1978).

12. Louis Althusser, "A Letter on Art in Reply to André Daspre," "*Lenin and Philosophy*" and Other Essays, trans. Ben Brewster (London: New Left Press, 1971), p. 222.

13. Greenblatt, "Introduction," 6.

14. Michaels's titles tend to suggest larger claims than the essays themselves make. The most obvious example is "Against Theory," which he wrote with Steven Knapp. Confronted by such a provocative title, the reader finds theory defined very narrowly in the essay. Perhaps this false advertising helps to explain the "intensity of rejection" (244, n. 31) with which that essay was greeted. *Against Theory*, ed. W. J. T. Mitchell (Chicago: University of Chicago Press, 1985). See

also his narrow definition of politics in "Is There a Politics of Interpretation?" *Critical Inquiry* 9 (1982), 248–58.

15. Arac, p. 207.

16. Paul de Man, *Blindness and Insight*, 2nd ed. (Minneapolis: University of Minnesota Press, 1983), p. 18.

17. Walter Benjamin, "On Some Motifs in Baudelaire," in *Illuminations*, ed. Hannah Arendt (New York: Schocken Books, 1969), p. 174.

18. I am fully aware that in referring to a work of literature's material existence I make myself vulnerable to deconstruction, since the material existence of a work of literature—writing—is already inhabited by a structure of internal difference. But I invite such deconstruction, because when pursued rigorously it must pay careful attention to the specific marks of writing that make up a particular work, a specific materiality that makes each work and the potential effects of each work different. Thus I welcome radically empirical—and historical—deconstructive readings. See, for instance, Derrida's comments in n. 6 earlier. I should also make it clear that, in relating a work's use-value to its material existence, I am not lapsing into "a certain literary formalism" that "becomes in its most desperate moments indistinguishable from goldbug materialism" (p. 174). I am merely reminding us that we cannot forget the importance of a text's specific materiality.

19. In a footnote that did not appear in the original "The Phenomenology of Contract," Michaels admits that "the law of contract was already being displaced" (136, n. 20). Of course, even though the law of contract was displaced from its dominance it was not completely replaced. John Dewey shows an understanding of how complex any historical discussion of a concept must be when he discusses the "chameleon-like change" of the notion of personality in Western culture, "This change, moreover, has never effected complete replacement of an earlier by a later idea. Almost all concepts have persisted side by side in a confused intermixture." "The Historical Background of Corporate Legal Personality," *Yale Law Journal* 35 (1926), 658.

To complicate the "logic" of naturalism even more, we can refer to an essay by Michaels's student, Howard Horwitz. Horwitz considers "corporate practice and literary or philosophical practice as isomorphic cultural formations demanding the same analysis." The identity that he establishes is between "Emerson's logic of the transcendental self and the logic of the trust." That identity finds literary expression in Dreiser, Howells, and Cather. So, it appears, the *real* account of selfhood for the period is not homologous with the autonomous individual of laissez-faire capitalism nor the corporate self of corporate capitalism, but the transcendental self of the trust, which is best understood as "an Emersonian decapitation of the corporation. As the body for Emerson is the transmitter of sensuous representations, the primary form in which the self is represented to consciousness, so the corporation, judicially designated a 'legal person,' is the institutional form representing the fluid and often intangible capital composing it. . . . The trust simultaneously perfects and annihilates the corporation." Similarly, the student is able to use the trust form to perfect and annihilate the teacher's argument about the corporate self. Can the period's literature simultaneously have homologous structures with three such different notions of the self? Can we really link the trust to Emerson when it is a legal form with beginnings in English common law of the Middle

Ages? See "The Standard Oil Trust as Emersonian Hero," *Raritan* 6 (1987), 99, 117, 109.

20. Frequently I quote Michaels quoting a source. I indicate both page numbers. Royce's works that I cite parenthetically are: *The Feud at Oakfield Creek* (1887 repr., Upper Saddle River, New Jersey: Gregg Press, 1970) and *California* (Boston: Houghton Mifflin Co., 1986), and *The Philosophy of Loyalty* (New York: Macmillan Co., 1908). I also cite parenthetically Machen's "Corporate Personality," *Harvard Law Review* 24 (1911), 253–67 and 347–65. Michaels's "Corporate Fiction" first appeared in *Reconstructing American Literary History*, ed. Sacvan Bercovitch (Cambridge, Mass.: Harvard University Press, 1986), pp. 189–219.

21. John Clendenning, *The Life and Thought of Josiah Royce* (Madison: University of Wisconsin Press, 1985), p. 159. See also Mae Fisher Purcell, *History of Contra Costa County* (Berkeley: Gillick Press, 1940), pp. 127–201. On Royce and Mussel Slough see Irving McKee, "Notable Memorials to Mussel Slough," *Pacific Historical Review* 12 (1948), 19–27.

22. Leo Spitzer, *Linguistics and Literary History* (Princeton: Princeton University Press, 1948), p. 33 n. 8. and Dewey, "Corporate Legal Personality." Michaels's use of verbal echoes to stitch his argument together persists. The argument of a recent essay depends upon exploiting a similarity between social "class," as in the working class, and "classy." "*An American Tragedy*, or the Promise of the American Way of Life," *Representations* 25 (1989), 71–98.

23. Dartmouth College v. Woodward, 17 U.S. (4 Wheat.) 518, 636 (1819). My discussion of corporate legal history is indebted to Morton Horwitz's tireless research. See especially "*Santa Clara* Revisited: The Development of Corporate Theory," *West Virginia Law Review* 88 (1985), 173–224. I do, however, try to distinguish between real and natural entity theories, which he uses interchangeably. For me natural entity theory is a subset of real entity theory.

24. San Mateo v. Southern Pacific Railroad, 13 F. 743–44 (1882).

25. Royce's association of corporations with robber baron-like individualism lets us see *The Feud at Oakfield Creek* as a feud between misplaced loyalty to groups exemplified by Alf and misdirected individualism exemplified by Alonzo. The former for Royce represented labor unions; the latter, corporations. Royce's sense of the destructiveness of such a feud was heightened, no doubt, by the Haymarket Riots. For him both sides needed to direct loyalty to the higher order of the state.

26. Hale v. Henkel 201 U.S. 43 (1906). Machen does not cite this case, but he clearly knew about it.

27. Michaels quotes this passage so as to leave out Machen's reference to the Roman Catholic Church.

28. A "spatial" reading of Norris is certainly useful, since, as many have noted, his training as a painter seems to have influenced his narrative mode of presenting "framed" scenes. My criticism of Michaels is similar to that which David Wyatt levels against Richard Chase. "Although Chase sensibly observes that [Norris's] 'scenes are more successful in telling us about the characters than are Norris's theoretical devices,' he goes on to illustrate this claim in the style of a New Critic, and so treats Norris's scenes as simultaneously arrayed in space rather than as unfolding in a significant sequence. He pays more heed to the content . . . than to the syntax of Norris's fictional strategies, and so overlooks the fact that in *The*

Octopus, meaning also emerges through devices of repetition, pacing, and juxtaposition." *The Fall into Eden* (Cambridge: Cambridge University Press, 1986), p. 114.

29. See especially Hans Blumenberg, "The Concept of Reality and the Possibility of the Novel," in *New Perspectives in German Literary Criticism*, eds. Richard E. Amacher and Victor Lange (Princeton: Princeton University Press, 1979), pp. 29–48. Blumenberg argues that the novel has taken "as its theme its own possibility, not as a fiction of reality, but as a *fiction of the reality of realities*" (p. 48). As a work like *Tristram Shandy* indicates, "By demonstrating the impossibility of the novel, a novel becomes possible" (p. 43).

Chapter 6

1. James Harvey Robinson, *The New History: Essays Illustrating the Modern Historical Outlook* (New York: Macmillian Co., 1912), p. 51.

2. Hans Blumenberg, "The Concept of Reality and the Possibility of the Novel," *New Perspectives in German Literary Criticism*, eds. Richard E. Amacher and Victor Lange (Princeton: Princeton University Press, 1979), p. 32–33.

3. Cushing Strout, "Carl Becker and the Haunting of American History," *Reviews in American History* 15 (1987), 338–43.

4. John Higham, "The Schism in American Scholarship," in *Writing American History* (Bloomington: Indiana University Press, 1970), pp. 3–24.

5. Cleanth Brooks, "Criticism, History, and Critical Relativism," in *The Well Wrought Urn* (New York: Harcourt, Brace, and World, 1947), p. 235.

6. Lee Benson, *Toward the Scientific Study of History* (Philadelphia: Lippincott, 1972), p. 96.

7. Linda Orr, "The Revenge of Literature: A History of History," *New Literary History* 18 (1986), 1–23.

8. Cathy Davidson, *Revolution and the Word* (New York: Oxford University Press, 1986), p. vii.

9. Hayden White, *The Tropics of Discourse* (Baltimore: Johns Hopkins University Press, 1978), p. 98.

10. The preface to a document entitled "Propositions in Historiography" circulated in draft to history professors in order to prepare for Bulletin 54 of the Social Science Research Council, *Theory and Practice in Historical Study: A Report of the Committee on Historiography* (New York, 1946) asserted, "Advances in science, thus resting upon accepted propositions, are made by devising hypotheses or fictions for further appraisal, exploration, testing, correction, and generalization." Charles A. Beard was largely responsible for such language and the reminder of the fictional component to science. Quoted in Peter Novick, *That Noble Dream: The "Objectivity Question" and the American Historical Profession* (New York: Cambridge University Press, 1988), p. 388.

11. Hayden White, *The Content in the Form* (Baltimore: Johns Hopkins University Press, 1988). For a lucid response to White see David Carr, *Time, Narrative, and History* (Bloomington: Indiana University Press, 1986).

12. Luiz Costa Lima, "Erich Auerbach: History and Metahistory," *New Literary History* 19 (1988), 470–71.

13. Walter Benn Michaels, *The Gold Standard and the Logic of Naturalism* (Berkeley: University of California Press, 1987) p. 27.

14. Stephen Greenblatt, *Renaissance Self-Fashioning* (Chicago: University of Chicago Press, 1980), p. 5.

15. Stephen Greenblatt, "Introduction" in "The Forms of Power and the Power of Forms in the Renaissance," *Genre* 15 (1982), 6.

16. Greenblatt, *Self-Fashioning*, p. 6. By evoking the metaphor of literature as a register, Greenblatt, unwittingly I suspect, aligns himself with Ezra Pound who wrote, "Specifically we are considering the development of language as a means of registration." *ABC of Reading* (New York: New Directions, 1960), p. 56.

17. Jane Tompkins, *Sensational Designs: The Cultural Work of American Fiction* (New York: Oxford University Press, 1985) and Philip Fisher, *Hard Facts* (New York: Oxford University Press, 1986).

18. Lee Benson, p. 96.

19. Northrop Frye, *The Anatomy of Criticism* (Princeton: Princeton University Press, 1957), pp. 244–45.

20. Stanley Fish, "How Ordinary Is Ordinary Language?" (originally published in 1973 in *New Literary History*), *Is There a Text in This Class?* (Cambridge: Harvard University Press, 1980), pp. 108–9.

21. It is important to remember that Frye does not maintain a naive, essentialist view of art. "The question of whether a thing 'is' a work of art or not is one which cannot be settled by appealing to something in the nature of the thing itself. It is convention, social acceptance, and the work of criticism in the broadest sense that determines where it belongs" (*Anatomy* p. 345).

22. One exploration into the function of literature is a German collection of essays edited by Dieter Henrich and Wolfgang Iser, *Funktionen des Fiktiven* (Munich: Wilhelm Fink Verlag, 1983).

23. Although he is more interested in the temporality of literature than in its changing social function, Paul de Man makes a similar point in his essay "Literary History and Literary Modernity": "If literature rested at ease within its own self-definition, it could be studied according to methods that are scientific rather than historical. We are obliged to confine ourselves to history when this is no longer the case, when the entity puts its own ontological status into question." *Blindness and Insight*, 2nd ed. (Minneapolis: University of Minnesota Press, 1983), p. 164.

24. Jonathan Culler makes a similar point in *The Pursuit of Signs* (Ithaca: Cornell University Press, 1981), p. 35.

25. Terry Eagleton, *Literary Theory: An Introduction* (Minneapolis: University of Minnesota Press, 1983), p. 199. For an attack on the entire field of aesthetics as an ideologically corrupt realm see, among many, Tony Bennett, "Really Useless 'Knowledge'—A Political Critique of Aesthetics," *Literature and History* 13 (1987), 38–57. More recently, Eagleton has reconsidered his position, arguing that, despite its ideological baggage, the aesthetic offers a limited realm of freedom. See *The Ideology of the Aesthetic* (Cambridge, Mass.: Basil Blackwell, 1990). Indeed, there seems to be a trend in ideological criticism toward a reconsideration of the aesthetic. For instance, Michael Sprinker began a recent study prepared to expose the limitations of aesthetic ideology and switched his position midstream.

See *Imaginary Relations: Aesthetics and Ideology* in *The Theory of Historical Materialism* (New York: Verso, 1987).

26. See my *James Joyce's "Ulysses": A Book of Many Happy Returns* (Baton Rouge: Louisiana State University Press, 1982). For more thorough arguments see John Paul Riquelme, *Oscillating Perspectives* (Baltimore: Johns Hopkins University Press, 1983) and Fritz Senn, *Joyce's Dislocutions* (Baltimore: Johns Hopkins University Press, 1984).

27. Immanuel Kant, *Analytic of the Beautiful*, trans. Walter Cerf (Indianapolis: Bobbs-Merrill, 1963), p. 32.

28. See Owen M. Fiss, "Objectivity and Interpretation," *Stanford Law Review* 34 (1982), 762–63.

29. Jochen Schulte-Sasse, "Afterword," Luiz Costa Lima, *Control of the Imaginary*, trans. Ronald W. Sousa (Minneapolis: University of Minnesota Press, 1988), p. 225.

30. Raymond Williams, *Politics and Letters* (London: New Left Books, 1979), p. 252.

31. Steven Knapp and Walter Benn Michaels, "Against Theory," *Critical Inquiry* 8:4 (Summer 1982), 723–42.

32. Fredric Jameson, *The Political Unconscious* (Ithaca: Cornell University Press, 1981).

33. Walter Benjamin, "Literaturgeschichte und Literaturwissenschaft" [Literary History and Literary Science], in *Gesammelte Schriften*, 5 vols., eds. Rolf Tiedemann and Hermann Schweppenhäuser (Frankfurt a. M.: Suhrkamp Verlag, 1972), 3:283–90. My translations of Benjamin's prose are indebted to an unpublished translation of the essay done by Joan Keck Campbell and Nina Zimnik. Since my work on the essay, Delphine Bechtel has published a translation, "Literary History and Literary Scholarship," *Critical Texts* 7 (1990), 3–9.

34. Walter Benjamin, "Theses on the Philosophy of History," in *Illuminations*, trans. Harry Zohn (New York: Schocken, 1969), p. 256.

35. See Paul de Man, "The Return to Philology," in *The Resistance to Theory* (Minneapolis: University of Minnesota Press, 1986), pp. 21–26. De Man acknowledges his debt to Benjamin. He is misleading, however, when he takes one sentence of Benjamin in "Task of the Translator" as the basis for arguing that Benjamin "dismisses any notion of poetry as being oriented, in any sense toward an audience or reader" (p. 77). For a suggestion of Benjamin's influence on Jauss and *Rezeptionsästhetik* see n. 36 to this chapter.

36. Terry Eagleton, *Walter Benjamin or Towards Revolutionary Criticism* (London: Verso, 1981), p. 49, n. 94. The end of the essay is also translated (more correctly) in Hans Robert Jauss, "Literary History as a Challenge to Literary Theory" in *Toward an Aesthetic of Reception*, trans. Timothy Bahti (Minneapolis: University of Minnesota Press, 1982), p. 196, n. 68.

37. Northrop Frye, *Fables of Identity* (New York: Harcourt, Brace, & World, 1963), p. 53.

38. Wolfgang Iser, "Feigning in Fiction," in *Identity of the Literary Text*, eds. Mario J. Valdés and Owen Miller (Toronto: University of Toronto Press, 1985), pp. 204–28; "Representation: A Performative Act," in *The Aims of Representation*, ed.

Murray Krieger (New York: Columbia University Press, 1987), pp. 217–32; and "Fictionalizing Acts," *Amerikastudien* 31:1 (1986), 5–15. Although Iser does not make the connection, *Darstellung* is also a crucial concept for Marx. Althusser, for instance, argues that it is the key to understanding the marxist theory of value. These points are discussed in Sprinker's *Imaginary Relations*, p. 289. On *Darstellung* in Hegel see Andrzej Warminski, "Pre-positional By-play," *Glyph* 3 (1978), 105–6.

Chapter 7

1. William James, "Pragmatism's Conception of Truth," *Essays in Pragmatism* (New York: Hafner, 1968), p. 167.

2. Stephen Greenblatt, *Shakespearean Negotiations: The Circulation of Social Energy in Renaissance England* (Berkeley: University of California Press, 1988), p. 19. Future pages will appear parenthetically in the text, as will references to his *Renaissance Self-Fashioning: From More to Shakespeare* (Chicago: University of Chicago Press, 1980) and *Representing the English Renaissance* (Berkeley: University of California Press, 1988) which he edited.

3. Walter Cohen, "Political Criticism of Shakespeare," in *Shakespeare Reproduced: The Text in History and Ideology*, eds. Jean E. Howard and Marion F. O'Connor (New York: Methuen, 1987), p. 34.

4. Stephen Greenblatt, "Introduction," to "The Forms of Power and the Power of Forms in the Renaissance," *Genre* 15 (1982), 6.

5. Jacques Derrida, "Economimesis," *Diacritics* 11 (1981), 9, 11. Elsewhere Greenblatt acknowledges his debt to Derrida for the notion of "circulation." "Capitalist Culture and the Circulatory System," in *The Aims of Representation*, ed. Murray Krieger (New York: Columbia University Press, 1987), p. 266.

6. George Puttenham, *The Arte of English Poesie*, in *English Literary Criticism: The Renaissance*, ed. O. B. Hardison (New York: Oxford University Press, 1963), p. 148. On the artist as God see Ernst Robert Curtius, *European Literature and the Latin Middle Ages*, trans. Willard R. Trask (New York: Pantheon, 1953), pp. 544–46 and Thomas M. Green, *The Light in Troy: Imitation and Discovery in Renaissance Poetry* (New Haven: Yale University Press, 1982), pp. 73–76.

7. Sir Philip Sidney, *An Apology for Poetry*, ed. Geoffrey Shepherd (London: Manchester University Press, 1965), p. 104.

8. Gerald Graff, "Fear and Trembling at Yale," *The American Scholar* 46 (1977), 467–78.

9. Walter Benjamin, "The Work of Art in the Age of Mechanical Reproduction," in *Illuminations*, trans. Harry Zohn (New York: Schocken Books, 1969), p. 242. The bounded world generated by Montrose's chiasmus is similar to the one assumed by Paul de Man when he argues that all efforts toward modernity are "swallowed up and reintegrated into a regressive historical process." Paul de Man, "Literary History and Literary Modernity," in *Blindness and Insight*, 2nd ed., revised (Minneapolis: University of Minnesota Press, 1983), p. 151.

10. Sidney, p. 124.

11. Paul Ricoeur, "Mimesis and Representation," *Annals of Scholarship* 2 (1981), 19.

12. Raymond Williams, *Keywords: A Vocabulary of Culture and Society* (New York: Oxford University Press, 1976), pp. 27–28.

13. As Montrose argues, "Literature" is "an historical formulation that had barely begun to emerge at the turn of the seventeenth century." "Renaissance Literary Studies and the Subject of History," *English Literary Renaissance* 16 (1986), 12.

14. Jochen Schulte-Sasse, "Afterward," Luiz Costa Lima, *Control of the Imaginary*, trans. Ronald W. Sousa (Minneapolis: University of Minnesota Press, 1988), p. 225.

15. Ricoeur, 16.

16. Hans Blumenberg, "The Concept of Reality and the Possibility of the Novel," in *New Perspectives in German Literary Criticism*, eds. Richard E. Amacher and Victor Lange (Princeton: Princeton University Press, 1979), 33n.

17. Puttenham, p. 175. See Rosemond Tuve's discussion in *Elizabethan and Metaphysical Imagery* (Chicago: University of Chicago Press, 1947), p. 29. Although Greenblatt seems unaware of it, his turn to the figure of *energia* brings the poststructuralist response to structuralism full circle. Saussure's synchronic analysis of language as system reacted against a nineteenth-century concept of language best articulated by Wilhelm von Humboldt's famous "*Sie selbst* [language] *ist Kein Werk (Ergon), sondern eine Thätigkeit (Energia)*." *Schriften zur Sprachphilosophie* (Stuttgart: J. G. Cotta'sche, 1963), p. 418.

18. Kathy Eden, *Poetic and Legal Fiction in the Aristotelian Tradition* (Princeton: Princeton University Press, 1986), p. 71.

19. Eden, p. 72.

20. Joseph Conrad, Preface to *The Nigger of the 'Narcissus,'* in *Great Short Works of Joseph Conrad* (New York: Harper and Row, 1966), p. 59.

21. Eden, p. 48.

22. See Stephen Fuller, "Playing Without a Full Deck: Scientific Realism and the Cognitive Limits of Legal Theory," *Yale Law Journal* 97 (1988), 549–80.

23. Hans Blumenberg, "An Anthropological Approach to the Contemporary Significance of Rhetoric," in *After Philosophy: End or Transformation?* eds. Kenneth Baynes, James Bohman, and Thomas McCarthy (Cambridge: MIT University Press, 1988), p. 452. (Future references to this essay will appear parenthetically in the text.)

24. Ricoeur, 20.

25. Wolfgang Iser, "Fictionalizing Acts," *Amerikastudien* 31 (1986), 5.

26. Wolfgang Iser, "Feigning in Fiction," in *Identity of the Literary Text*, eds. Mario J. Valdes and Owen Miller (Toronto: Toronto University Press, 1985), p. 209. (Future references to this essay will appear parenthetically in the text.)

27. For *Darstellung* in the marxist tradition, see chapter 6, fn. 38.

28. Luiz Costa Lima, "Mimesis, A Proscribed Concept," *Eutopias* 2 (1986), 253.

29. I discuss Fish's mimetic extension of practice in "Stanley Fish and the Uses of Baseball," *Yale Journal of Law and the Humanities* 2 (1990), 59–88.

30. Luiz Costa Lima, "Erich Auerbach: History and Metahistory," *New Literary History* 19 (1988), 495. Although I disagree with Schulte-Sasse's extreme use of "never," he provides an interesting criticism of the limits of Costa Lima's mimetic model. See fn. 14.

31. Leopold von Ranke, *Uber die Epochen der neueren Geschichte* (Leipzig: Dunker Humblot, 1888), p. 7.

32. J. Hillis Miller, "Theory and Practice: Response to Vincent Leitch," *Critical Inquiry* 6 (1980), 612.

33. Quoted in Hans Ulrich Gumbrecht, "History of Literature—Fragment of a Vanished Totality," *New Literary History* 16 (1985), 470.

34. Erich Auerbach, *Mimesis: The Representation of Reality in Western Literature*, trans. Willard R. Trask (Princeton: Princeton University Press, 1953), p. 552.

35. For spirited recent defenses of mimesis see Barbara Foley, *Telling the Truth: The Theory and Practice of Documentary Fiction* (Ithaca: Cornell University Press, 1986). (Foley argues for a materialist view in which the social contract between author and reader continually evolves.); Christopher Prendergast, *The Order of Mimesis* (Cambridge: Cambridge University Press, 1986); and Robert Weimann's work in general, especially the final chapter of *Structure and Society in Literary History* (Baltimore: Johns Hopkins University Press, 1984). See also Sacvan Bercovitch's provocative notion of "ideological" mimesis noted in chapter 1, fn. 40. For a brief argument that Louis Althusser also posits a mimetic relation between literature and ideology see chapter 5. Once again, I fully agree that literary texts have a mimetic component. There is truth in the common formulation that they help to produce and reproduce a society's ideology. My point, however, is that they can do more.

36. Hans-Georg Gadamer, *Truth and Method* (New York: Crossroad, 1982).

37. See especially Hans Robert Jauss, *Toward an Aesthetic of Reception*, trans. Timothy Bahti (Minneapolis: University of Minnesota Press, 1982).

38. E. D. Hirsch, Jr., *Validity in Interpretation* (New Haven: Yale University Press, 1967).

39. Walter Benjamin, "Theses on the Philosophy of History," in *Illuminations*, p. 262.

40. Benjamin, p. 263.

41. Walter Benjamin, *Gesammelte Schriften*, 6 vols. (Frankfurt a.M.: Suhrkamp, 1972), I, p. 1244.

42. A word of caution about my uses of Iser: In a forthcoming book, he will offer an extensive theoretical account of his theory of play. My use of him to counter Greenblatt's model does not mean that I agree with all of the details of his theory. Indeed, he may not completely agree with the ways that I appropriate his general model for historical criticism. He might especially dispute my account of play's relation to ideology.

43. See Stanley Fish, *Doing What Comes Naturally* (Durham: Duke University Press, 1989).

44. Wolfgang Iser, "Indeterminacy and the Reader's Response in Prose Fiction," in *Aspects of Narrative*, ed. J. Hillis Miller (New York: Columbia University Press, 1971), 1–45.

45. Hans Blumenberg, *Work on Myth*, trans. Robert M. Wallace (Cambridge: MIT University Press, 1985), pp. 166, 165.

46. Quoted in Blumenberg, "The Concept of Reality," p. 48.

47. Reinhold Niebuhr, *The Irony of American History* (New York: Scribner's:

1952); Carlos Bulosan, *America Is in the Heart: A Personal History* (Seattle University of Washington Press, 1973).

48. Hans Blumenberg, *Schiffbruch mit Zuschauer* (Frankfurt a. M.: Suhrkamp, 1979).

49. Benjamin, VI, 537.

Index

Abrams, Meyer, 186
Adams, Henry, 92–93, 235n.28
Adorno, Theodor, 219n.3, 231n.27
affirmative action, 54, 61, 108
"Against Theory," 22, 78–80, 97–103, 115–16, 132, 172, 232n.2, 238n. 14
Agnew, Jean-Christophe, 11–12
Agnew, Spiro, 29
Althusser, Louis, xi, 127–28, 215, 219n.3, 244n.38, 246n.35
American exceptionalism, vii–viii, x–xi, xvi, 16, 81–83, 91–92, 94–97, 103, 122, 126
Arac, Jonathan, 129, 238n.8
arbitrary connectedness, 40, 42–47, 92, 97, 151, 179, 194
Aristotle, xv, 12, 23, 104–5, 153, 156, 177, 182, 196, 197, 200, 205, 206, 207, 214, 216; *The Poetics*, 153, 182, 184, 193, 197–99; *The Rhetoric*, 198
Auerbach, Erich, 8, 13–16, 22, 43–45, 62–66, 157, 207; *Mimesis*, 13, 64–65, 207, 212, 230n.10; "Philology and *Weltliteratur*," 13–15, 62–64

Baker, Houston A., 55–58, 65
Bakhtin, Mikhail, 37, 41, 59–60, 65, 68, 95, 148, 201, 230n.7
Baldwin, James, 14
Balzac, Honoré de, 67, 127
Barth, John, xiv
Barthes, Roland, xi, 26, 227n.11
Baudelaire, Charles, 128–29
Baudrillard, Jean, 16
Beard, Charles, viii, 15, 90–94, 96–97, 103, 154, 241n.10; *The Development of Modern Europe* (with James Harvey Robinson), 93; *Economic Interpretation of the Constitution of the United States*, 93; *The Rise of American Civilization* (with Mary Beard), 11, 94; "Written History as an Act of Faith," 92, 94
Beard, Mary, 90, 154; *The Rise of American Civilization* (with Charles Beard), 11, 94
Becker, Carl, viii, 15, 91, 97, 154, 236n. 49, 237n. 71; "Every Man His Own Historian," 92

Benjamin, Walter, 17, 20, 22, 68, 82, 101, 109–15, 128–31, 173–78, 194, 210–12, 218, 237n.68; "Die Passagen-Arbeit," 111; "Literaturgeschichte und Literaturwissenschaft," 173–77, 243n.33; "Task of the Translator," 243n.35; "Theses on the Philosophy of History," 109–14, 174–76, 210
Bennett, William, vii, x
Benson, Lee, 155, 157, 160–61, 163
Bercovitch, Sacvan, 60, 96, 124, 225n.40, 246n.35, *The American Jeremiad*, 60, 96, 124
Bloch, Ernst, 58, 126; and nonsynchronism, 58–59, 126, 207, 226n.9, 229–30n.5, 239n.19
Bloom, Allan, vii, viii, x–xii, 14, 219n.1
Blumenberg, Hans, 17, 22, 32, 53, 69–75, 105, 109, 153, 197–99, 216–17, 231n.27, 231–32n.28, 241n.29; "An Anthropological Approach to the Contemporary Significance of Rhetoric," 204–6, 213–14; *The Legitimacy of the Modern Age*, 69; *Work on Myth*, 69
Boorstin, Daniel, 95
Boswell, James, 217
Bové, Paul, 47, 229n.41, 230n.10
Branch, Taylor; *Parting of the Waters*, 66
Brecht, Bertold, 68, 177, 218
Brooks, Cleanth, 154
Brooks, Van Wyck, xiii, 14, 18, 95, 104, 115, 236n.50; *America's Coming of Age*, 14
Brown, Gillian, 227n.9
Buck, Pearl, 63–64
Bulosan, Carlos, 217
Burke, Kenneth, xi
Bush, George, vii
Button v. Hoffmann, 140, 142–43, 147

Cather, Willa, 239n.19
Cavell, Stanley, 220n.9
Cervantes, Miguel de, *Don Quixote*, 211
Chase, Richard, 240n.28
chiasmus, 7, 9, 10, 12, 13, 23, 84, 89, 97, 98, 160, 183–85, 189, 191, 193–96, 244n.9
civil rights movement, 66, 95